Inquiry, Literacy, and Learning in the Middle Grades

Inquiry, Literacy, and Learning in the Middle Grades

by

Lauren Freedman,
Western Michigan University

and

Holly Johnson,
Texas Tech University

Christopher-Gordon Publishers, Inc.
Norwood, Massachusetts

Copyright Acknowledgments

Every effort has been made to contact copyright holders for permission to reproduce borrowed material where necessary. We apologize for any oversights and would be happy to rectify them in future printings.

Nine Information Literacy Standards. From *Information Power: Building Partnerships for Learning*, by American Association of School Librarians and Association for Educational Communications and Technology. Copyright © 1998 by the American Library Association and Association for Educational Communications and Technology. Reprinted by permission of the American Library Association.

p. 101 from Buehl, Doug. (2001). *Clasroom Strategies for Interactive Learning, Second Edition*. Newark, DE: International Reading Association. Reprinted with permission of Doug Buehl and the International Reading Association. All rights reserved.

CALVIN AND HOBBES cartoon Copyright © 1995 Watterson. Reprinted with permission of UNIVERSAL PRESS SYNDICATE. All rights reserved.

Christopher~Gordon Publishers, Inc.
Bridging Theory and Practice

1502 Providence Highway, Suite #12
Norwood, Massachusetts 02062

800-934-8322
781-762-5577

Printed in the United State of America
10 9 8 7 6 5 4 3 2 1   07 06 05 04

ISBN: 1-929024-75-4
Library of Congress Catalogue Number: 2004100009

Dedications

For Brenda Dinius with fond memories of those early inquiry journeys.
For Katie Lawrence and Meghan Luckett with love and gratitude.

. . . lf

For middle school students like Ian and Kait, who continue
to ask questions and inquire about the world.

. . . haj

Acknowledgments

We want to thank Kathy Short for her unwavering confidence in the worth of our project; Karen Thomas, and Robin Abbott for their continuous and generous encouragement; Kate Liston and Sue Canavan for their support and guidance.

We want to express our gratitude to the teachers of West Texas and West Michigan who have allowed us to work in their middle school classrooms. During these times, they took the challenge to trust their students and move beyond the standards. Our appreciation also goes to the middle school literacy coaches in Battle Creek who have worked so hard to support their teachers' use of inquiry and multiple materials.

Table of Contents

Foreword

—Kathy G. Short

Inquiry is one of those catch phrases frequently thrown into educational conversations in a vague, general manner. Typically, inquiry is taken to mean that students are engaging in some type of research, but everything else about the nature of that research, including who poses the problem and how that problem is defined and investigated, lacks a shared understanding among educators. In fact, educators often are coming from different theoretical perspectives and their beliefs and practices may be in opposition even though they are using the same language.

Lauren Freedman and Holly Johnson are not content with talking about inquiry in a vague or general manner. They thoughtfully reflect on the theoretical beliefs and scholarly fields of study that provide the foundation for their understandings of inquiry. They are explicit about their theory, but also go beyond that theory to describe how those beliefs are being put into practice in middle school classrooms. Their book is not about how teachers *should* do inquiry but reflects their actual experiences working in their own and other teachers' classrooms to think about belief and practice within the complexity of life in real schools.

Lauren and Holly avoid the current trend of prescribing a set of exact procedures for instruction. They recognize that inquiry is, first and foremost, a philosophy, a perspective that cuts across the school day and all areas of the curriculum. In fact, one could argue that inquiry is a philosophy of life, of living and being in the world. Inquiry is the act of going beyond and so lies at the boundary between knowing and not knowing. Inquiry arises out of and goes beyond present understandings as learners search for tensions that are worth investigating.

Young children are a constant demonstration of inquiry as a natural way to approach learning. They simply immerse themselves into life and out of that living comes an interest or issue that intrigues them. They pursue that focus, gathering experiences and information until that focus develops into a specific question that they can wonder about and investigate. Those investigations lead to new understandings, but more importantly, they lead to more complex questions that keep the inquiry process in a never-ending cycle of learning. Inquiry, then, is not a spe-

cific instructional approach found only in schools, but the way in which both children and adults continuously learn outside of school contexts. Inquiry is life work,
not school work.

At the heart of inquiry as a critical perspective on life is Paulo Freire's (1970)
notion that learners need to be both problem-posers and problem-solvers if they
are to be in control of their own learning. Most approaches to inquiry focus on
problem-solving, emphasizing the strategies that learners need to be able to use in
order to engage in systematic research of a specific question or topic. What is often
overlooked is the origin of the problem that students are investigating—frequently
those problems are established by the teacher or the textbook, not by students.
And even when students are encouraged to ask questions, they ask questions about
a problem that has already been determined. When students investigate a problem
that does not matter to them, their research often remains half-hearted—they gather
information on a topic to get the assignment done, but invest little of themselves.

Freire (1970) argues that students must learn to search out questions and question answers, not merely answer questions. Students do need to be able to reason
through a question or issue in order to develop possible solutions, but they also
need strategies for identifying what is significant to think about in the first place.
In a mass media world characterized by an overwhelming amount of available
information, the ability to critically sort out what might be significant to pursue,
what really matters, is increasingly essential for life, not just school. The topics of
study may already be determined in schools, but inquiry provides the space for
students to collaboratively negotiate problems and issues that are significant to
them within those mandated topics.

Inquiry also avoids the common dichotomy between process and content—
inquirers need content in order to inquire thoughtfully as problem-posers and
problem-solvers. A common misperception is that inquiry means asking students
at the beginning of a unit of study what they want to know and using those questions to frame their investigations. As Lauren and Holly point out, inquiry begins
through connections to students' own experiences and immersing them in a topic
to expand their understandings and knowledge. The search for a problem worth
investigating is based on a solid knowledge of that topic—students can't think
critically about something they know nothing about. Inquiry involves providing
learners with multiple materials and the time they need not only to build a knowledge base of facts and concepts, but to also go beyond those facts to ask bigger
questions and to search for tensions that are worth spending time investigating.
Facts do matter, but they aren't enough. Inquiry places the learning of information
within broader conceptual frameworks and provides a critical perspective from
which to view and make use of that information. That knowledge base leads to a
compelling sense of uncertainty as learners engage in making sense of and
problematizing their current understandings and perspectives.

Throughout this book, Lauren and Holly continuously demonstrate that curriculum involves putting these beliefs about inquiry into practice in classrooms

and that there is no one set of procedures for how this might be done. Instead they use an inquiry cycle as a curricular framework for thinking about curriculum with teachers and students. A curricular framework is based in theoretical beliefs and shows the visual relationships between those beliefs in order to provide the bigger picture of teaching and learning that undergird a curriculum. By planning engagements within that framework, teachers can more strongly ground their teaching in their beliefs and make theory-based predictions about their teaching and student learning. Because inquiry is based in valuing students as problem-posers, an inquiry cycle provides space for students' voices in collaboration and negotiation with teachers and school mandates.

An inquiry cycle also provides space for teachers' voices. The cycle creates a frame of theoretically-based principles and instructional strategies, but there is no one organizational structure or set of methods that must be followed. Inquiry never looks the same from classroom to classroom. Lauren and Holly continuously demonstrate the ways in which their cycle supports teachers and students in multiple interpretations of inquiry through examples from a range of classrooms and through teachers' own accounts of their teaching.

Often books about curriculum either stay too general by only providing theoretical principles and general descriptions of classrooms or too specific by listing exact steps and lessons. The specific books tend to present simple answers to what *must* be done in the classroom and don't address the complexity of classroom life or provide space for teachers' and students' voices in the curriculum process. The general books are frustrating to teachers who walk away wondering, "but what does it look like in the classroom?" The assumption is often that this comment means that teachers want to be told exactly what to do. What teachers really want is a vision of what might be possible in their classrooms. Lauren and Holly provide that vision for readers of this book through descriptions of classroom scenes, dialogue, teacher thinking, and student work along with theory. They invite readers into classrooms and into a vision of curriculum as a process of teachers and students inquiring together about issues that really matter in their lives and worlds. They understand that we don't inquire to eliminate alternatives, but to find more functional possibilities, create diversity, and broaden our thinking.

Kathy G. Short
University of Arizona

Freire, P. (1970). *Pedagogy of the oppressed.* New York: Continuum.

Introduction

To get us started, Mrs. Fremont told us to skim through the books wolf example
and magazines about the environment. I really got interested in this
one article that told about wolves and how the ranchers and farmers
were killing them because they were killing their cattle. And, how
they are becoming endangered. I want to know more about how we
can protect the wolves and also protect the cattle.

—*Marian, Seventh Grader*

Marian and three of her classmates sit at one of the six tables in the room. In the center of each table is a large, blue plastic container filled with a variety of print materials including books, newspapers, magazines, pamphlets, and brochures. As the students browse the materials, they discuss where they might begin their new exploration, on environmental concepts. Around the room computers, reference books, and students' work from previous investigations such as newsletters, posters, timelines, models, webs, and charts, invite the students to engage in a broad exploration into the reciprocal relationship that exists between the environment and the human beings living within it. Mrs. Fremont explains that they will delve *envir.* into the ways human beings have a responsibility to be both participants within *participate* the environment and conservators of the environment. She shares that they will be *conserve* studying how humans use their ingenuity to understand, to respond to, and to plan for the ramifications of this reciprocal relationship in both positive and negative ways. The students' browsing helps them to visualize and to connect with this broad exploration into environmental issues.

As the students quickly connect with the notion that they live daily in a reciprocal relationship with the environment, they realize that environmental issues affect everyone. They aren't quite sure, though, what the specific impact of this relationship is, how to study it, and how to work toward the changes in human behavior necessary to prevent the negative impact and to increase the positive. As the students engage in their broad exploration and continue to browse, read, talk, and think, they generate ideas and questions. They also begin to recognize each other as resources for pertinent information and experiences about environmental issues. They build their desire to know, to understand, and to apply what they

generate ideas & questions
recognize each other as resources

are learning as they pursue these environmental issues. As they read, write, and think, the students also develop, broaden, and strengthen the literacy strategies they use to accomplish the goals they have set for themselves. It is in this way that the literacy strategies they employ within an inquiry framework will enhance deeper learning of the disciplines.

Let's look in on Mrs. Fremont's seventh grade classroom again. The students are studying environmental issues that go far beyond the scope and sequence of any science textbook. The textbook publisher assumes the material included will provide a knowledge base on environmental issues that is appropriate for seventh graders around the country. While the concepts included may be important ones to acquire and understand, the textbook can cover them only superficially due to the space limitations inherent in the format. This limitation is further compounded when the textbook material serves as the entire curriculum supplanting the standards and benchmarks developed by educators at both the state and district levels. Fortunately, this is not the case in Mrs. Fremont's classroom.

In addition to curricular limitations, the textbook also contains instructional flaws that run counter to what many educators call "best practices" (Zemelman, Daniels, & Hyde, 1998) as it directs the students to memorize specific vocabulary and to answer specific questions when they finish reading each section. Each of the major concepts such as region, ecosystem, climate, culture, and human interaction may be labeled, defined, and described. Yet, the opportunities for students to wonder and to question, to develop curiosity and to make connections with previous learning and experience are sorely missing. With a text set of multiple materials (see the list below), students will entertain the required aspects of the environment as they explore facets of the environment that intrigue them.

Abbreviated Set of Multiple Materials on the Environment

Cole, J. (1996). *Wet all over: A book about the water cycle.* New York: Scholastic Inc.

Dobson, C., & Beck, G. (1999). *Watersheds: A practical handbook for healthy water.* Buffalo, NY: Firefly Books.

Duncan, B. (1996). *Explore the wild: A nature search-and-find book.* New York: HarperCollins.

Gallant, R. (1995). *Sand on the move.* New York: Grolier.

Graham, A., & Graham, F. (1981). *A changing desert.* Sierra Club Books.

Harrison, C., & Greensmith, A. (1993). *Birds of the world.* New York: Dorling Kindersley.

Hesse, K. (1997). *Out of the dust.* New York: Scholastic.

Kaplan, E. (1996). *Biomes of the world: Temperate forest.* Tarrytown, NY: Benchmark Books.

Llamas, A. (1996). *The vegetation of rivers, lakes, and swamps.* New York: Chelsea House Publishers.

Moore, P. (1987). *The encyclopedia of animal ecology.* New York: Facts On File Publications.

Parker, J. (1999). *Saving our world: Rainforests.* Brookfield, CT: Copper Beech Books.

Paulsen, G. (1987). *Hatchet.* New York: Puffin Books.

Rootes, D. (1995). *The arctic.* Minneapolis, MN: Lerner Publications.

Warburton, L. (1990). *Lucent overview series our endangered planet: Rainforests.* San Diego: Lucent Books.

Within and across the multiple materials in Mrs. Fremont's classroom, her students are also likely to find contradictions. Within an inquiry framework, evaluating resources promotes critical thinking and additional exploration. Although textbooks claim accuracy, they do contain errors and are rarely current after the first year of an adoption. Through the use of multiple materials, students learn to identify and evaluate the sources of their information. They learn who the experts are in a given field of study, as the materials they are using are written by authors who have a vested interest in their subjects unlike the relatively anonymous authors of textbooks.

Our Inquiry Framework

We have adapted the Inquiry Cycle as created and described by Short, Harste, and Burke (1996) for use within middle level classrooms. Although the intent of the cycle is not changed, we have made adaptations that are in keeping with the middle school model and lend themselves to teams of teachers working collaboratively. The framework as we present it can be adapted for full integration of the content area disciplines or it can be used within a single content classroom.

The Inquiry Cycle (see model on the right) requires that teachers maintain a global view of curricular mandates (school, district, and state). They plan their classroom curriculum and instruction around the interests and prior knowledge of each particular

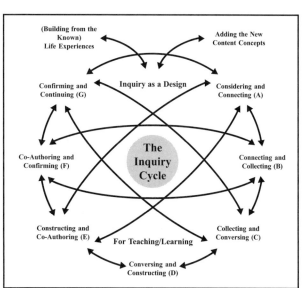

The Inquiry Cycle

(Building from the Known) Life Experiences — Adding the New Content Concepts

Confirming and Continuing (G) — Inquiry as a Design — Considering and Connecting (A)

Co-Authoring and Confirming (F) — Connecting and Collecting (B)

The Inquiry Cycle

Constructing and Co-Authoring (E) — For Teaching/Learning — Collecting and Conversing (C)

Conversing and Constructing (D)

group of learners. Embedding the mandates as they fit by either broadening the inquiry or suggesting additional questions and problems within the inquiry investigations, the teacher addresses the requirements and concerns of all the stakeholders.

Chapter Overviews

As the chapters in this book describe and illustrate, inquiry is a fluid, learning-centered framework that provides ways of mediating learning, bridging the space between the learner and what is to be learned. Throughout this book, we offer theory and research that support inquiry as well as detailed suggestions for how to organize and maintain inquiry in classroom learning communities. We have included illustrative examples that feature specific teachers' and their students' classroom experiences. In each chapter, we provide detailed ideas, strategies, and examples for keeping the cycle moving smoothly. We also answer anticipated questions about troubleshooting when things seem to bog down or become confused.

The chapter descriptions below include what to expect in each chapter with a brief illustrative example taken from Mrs. Fremont's Science class. For the examples we use throughout the book, we have drawn upon our own experiences as classroom teachers as well as our work with pre- and in-service teacher education students as well as many of their sixth through eighth grade students. Both of us take pride in the fact that much of our professional work is done collaboratively with teachers in their classrooms and with their school library media specialists.

Chapter 1 provides the foundations of our inquiry cycle. Chapter 2 begins at the top of the cycle with planning for inquiry. Chapters 3 through 9 follow the inquiry cycle from Phase A through Phase G. The concluding remarks for each of these chapters includes a list of the strategies that have been shared. Chapters 2 through 8 each end with an inquiry vignette written by a middle grades teacher. These teachers' stories range from one student teacher's experiences during her internship to a veteran teacher's work of 20 years. Five content areas plus a reading class are represented: Science, Social Studies, Mathematics, Language Arts, and Spanish.

Chapter 1. Inquiry: A Framework for Teaching and Learning

In this chapter, we introduce the inquiry framework and discuss the theoretical underpinnings that support it. We examine the interdependent relationships between and among inquiry, literacy, and learning. We discuss the need for both teachers and students to maintain a continuous focus on the four efficacy elements of confidence, independence, metacognition, and stamina that middle level learners need to develop and strengthen as they grow as learners.

Chapter 2. Planning for Inquiry: Building From the Known and Adding the New

The cyclical nature of the framework suggests that the learning process is non-linear and that students can enter or exit at various points throughout the cycle as warranted by the demands of the work they are doing and/or the content under study. The cycle always moves from the known to the new in order to provide the scaffolding necessary for lasting learning (Dewey, 1938; Vygotsky, 1978). Thus, new knowledge is meaningfully connected to prior understandings.

To plan for inquiry, we offer the following six questions as a guide. For example, by using these questions, Mrs. Fremont's plan for studying the environment leads her to offer multiple invitations to her students:

1. What is my role? What is the role of my students?

2. How will I maintain a collaborative learning community?

3. How do the major concepts and "Big Ideas" of this unit connect with the content and literacy standards I am responsible for?

4. What materials will I use? How will I choose and organize these? Where will I get them?

5. What instructional strategies will I arrange? What learning and literacy strategies will my students use and develop?

6. How will I assess my students' progress, growth, and development? What kinds of records will my students and I keep?

Chapter 2 ends with the voice of Meghan Luckett who is just beginning her professional career. She describes her planning process for the seventh grade Geography inquiry on Canada which she taught during her intern teaching experience in East Grand Rapids, Michigan.

Chapter 3. Considering and Connecting: The Importance of Browsing and Sharing

During this phase of the cycle the students consider broadly the possibilities within the inquiry concept, wander and wonder through the multiple materials, and take the time to connect prior knowledge and to make intertextual links across the multiple materials. For example, building from the known, Mrs. Fremont's students realize the impact of the environment on their daily lives. They dress as the climate of their ecosystem dictates, try to drink water from safe sources only, and participate in anti-litter projects by picking up trash as they walk home from school. As they browse the multiple materials, they consider ideas as they become acquainted with new terminology, new concepts, and technical explanations. They brainstorm questions and pose problems that arise as a result of connecting the known and the new. Some of the students wonder how a community responds to an oil spill. Others want to know measures used to prevent forest fires. And, still others delve into the ways in which the human population affects the plants and animals in a certain ecosystem.

Chapter 3 ends with the voice of Carol McNally who has been teaching for 8 years. Carol describes an inquiry focused on biography and autobiography that she did with her sixth grade Reading Exploratory class in Battle Creek, Michigan.

Chapter 4. Connecting and Collecting: The Importance of Personal Engagement

In this phase, the students are more deliberate and systematic about the connections they are making in order to decide on the kinds of useful and appropriate information they will collect. For example, after brainstorming, each student or group of students in Mrs. Fremont's class connected with an investigative goal (i.e., questions or problems). Within this environmental study, one group looked at the links between climate and the adaptations made by various flora and fauna. Another group investigated the interrelationship between and among the plants, animals, and humans living in a given region. After deciding on their goal, the students each gathered the particular materials they wanted to use to collect information. They also sought out other resources such as the Environmental Protection Agency, their local newspaper and TV news personalities, their public library, and a myriad of Internet sources. As the students engaged in the search for pertinent information, they each used a variety of literacy strategies for reading, recording, summarizing, and transforming the information they had gathered.

Chapter 4 ends with the voice of Vicki Sellers who has been teaching for 4 years. Vicki discusses the personal engagement aspects of inquiry as they play out in her eighth grade Social Studies class in Crosbyton, Texas.

Chapter 5. Collecting and Conversing: The Importance of Talk

In the previous phases, the students have collected lots of information using strategies that have encouraged them to record it and maintain it for purposes of analysis and synthesis. They are now ready to engage in substantive conversation in their groups about the data they have found. In these conversations, they share information, question accuracy and authenticity, and provide support to one another. One of the main engagements used in this phase of the cycle is discussion and more specifically literature circle discussion.

For example, several of the engagements in Mrs. Fremont's class's environmental inquiry included:

- a mini-lesson on different grammatical structures and writing styles as a way to focus her students' talk. As a result of the mini-lesson, her students could see how voice links to particular perspectives within a document such as one outlining a plan for the clean up of a toxic waste dump. They could then see how the different perspectives they each bring to a discussion influence their thinking and learning.

- two or three students interviewing a conservationist they had contacted. The students were involved in discussion both prior to and following the interview. These conversations include logistical matters such as writing questions, practicing interview etiquette and academic matters such as taking notes during the interview, and determining the ideas and perspectives gleaned from the interview.

Chapter 5 ends with the voice of Rebecca Miller who has been teaching for 7 years. She discusses how literature circles work in her sixth grade Social Studies class in Lubbock, Texas.

Chapter 6. Conversing and Constructing: The Importance of Interdependence and Collaboration

The conversations within the groups become more focused as they begin to construct a critical perspective from which to look at the questions and the information they have gathered to answer their questions or to solve the problems they have posed. For example, as Mrs. Fremont's students gathered information and ideas, they recorded them and began to organize the information into categories that allowed them to think about and to make sense of them in relation to broader concepts. They are using the content vocabulary with one another in their writing and their talking in meaningful ways. For example, the students began to look at the idea of pollution from a broader perspective and to categorize the major issues within this broader concept. It is here that students within their groups shared with one another in a planned and deliberate fashion what they had found, noting the similarities and differences, raising issues and questions, and sharing suggestions of resources to confirm their thinking. They then each returned to their respective investigations and continued to refine their answers and solutions.

As the students analyzed and synthesized the information and ideas, they took a critical perspective. They organized their work in ways that enabled them to be metacognitive and self-reflective in order to determine what exactly they would put forth as the product of their efforts. They began both individually and as a group to develop the method or methods for sharing the answers and solutions they had garnered. The goal was to create a product through which they shared their new knowledge and understandings and applied these in ways that also facilitated the learning of the other members of the classroom community.

Chapter 6 ends with the voice of Susan Lucas who has been teaching for 12 years. Susan talks about issues of investigation in her eighth grade Math class in Comstock, Michigan.

Chapter 7. Constructing and Co-Authoring: The Importance of "Going Public"

Once the students construct their knowledge and understandings, they are ready to co-author a presentation. The planning and presenting leads to their enriched learning. The presentation leads as well to the learning of their peers and teacher. It is in this phase that the students share the synthesis of knowledge, key understandings, and examples of particular applications with their peers and teacher. For instance, the group investigating the interrelationships between and among plants, animals, and humans in a particular region simulated an investigative television broadcast to present their findings.

Chapter 7 ends with the voice of Penelope Boyatt who has been teaching for 9 years. She describes a cultural inquiry entitled, "Life, Learning, Language, and Culture" that her students completed in their eighth grade Spanish class at Fuller Middle School in Framingham, Massachusetts.

Chapter 8. Co-Authoring and Confirming: The Importance of Assessment and Self-Reflection

The students confirm their learning through a process of reflection that focuses not only on what they have learned but also on how they have demonstrated that learning. Following the publications or presentations, the students along with Mrs. Fremont take time to reflect on and to assess the learning that has occurred and to evaluate the evidence of that learning. To accomplish this, the students think metacognitively about their work and the strategies they have used throughout the inquiry. They seek to describe what they have learned about themselves as inquirers. For example, Mrs. Fremont and her students look critically at their work and make negotiated decisions concerning each student's individual progress and the overall work of the classroom community.

Chapter 8 ends with the voice of Brett Sellers who has been teaching for 20 years. He discusses how he engages in assessment and negotiated grading with his eighth-grade Science students in Battle Creek, Michigan.

Chapter 9. Confirming and Continuing: The Importance of Negotiation and Transition

In this phase, the teacher and students take the assessment information they have gathered through the confirming process and made decisions about continuing on with the next inquiry. To make these decisions, they look at both the content concepts in the curriculum and the demands for various literacy strategies. At this point in the cycle, the community takes one last look at where they have been and make decisions about where to move next. This includes once again taking stock of the experiences and background they will bring to the next inquiry and the concepts and ideas that are an integral part of the new inquiry's content. The work of the community in Mrs. Fremont's class moved from the focus on environmental issues to a study of the Dust Bowl and the Great Depression in Mr. Newman's Social Studies class. To begin, the students thought about the interconnectedness of the environmental factors with the economic, social, and cultural factors affecting people's lives in the United States during the 1930s.

Our Intended Audience

This book is intended for all educators involved with middle grades learners who are committed to facilitating the intellectual, social, and emotional growth of their students in ways that support and foster the development of early adolescents' confidence, independence, metacognition, and stamina. For veteran teachers and veteran library media specialists who have been using an inquiry framework, we provide reinforcement and perhaps some new ideas. For veteran teachers and novice teachers who are new to inquiry, we provide a model, a variety of instructional/ learning strategies, and suggestions for developing sets of materials. In addition, we are anxious to be a part of strengthening the essential collaboration between library media specialists and teachers as they provide on-going information literacy instruction for their students. Collaboration between teachers and library media specialists is a powerful force in guiding middle grades students through inquiry investigations. For administrators and counselors, we provide ways to think about and to recognize learning-centered classrooms and the theories and practices that facilitate them, so that they may support and collaborate with their teachers and media specialists in joint efforts to foster continuous student learning both in and out of school. It is our hope that this book will inspire and guide the use of inquiry in every middle grades classroom and school.

Chapter 1

Inquiry:
A Framework for
Teaching and Learning

Inquiry as a curricular frame is grounded in the belief that the learner is the primary agent in the learning process. Lev Vygotsky (1978) and John Dewey (1938) both placed learning squarely in the lived experiences of the learner. The work of both educators suggests that rather than being an empty vessel to be filled, the learner constructs or builds knowledge and understandings by connecting the new learning with prior experiences and previously acquired knowledge and understandings. The growing independence on the part of the learner is scaffolded through the continuous development of an array of literacy strategies.

self scaffolding?

Learners strengthen their capacity to use both literacy and content knowledge through meaningful applications. An inquiry framework provides a variety of learning engagements that foster's the development of students as strategic learners. In essence, the inquiry cycle as a framework for teaching and learning provides the impetus for reading and writing as tools for learning because there is always something meaningful, useful, enjoyable, enriching, and empowering to read, write, and learn about.

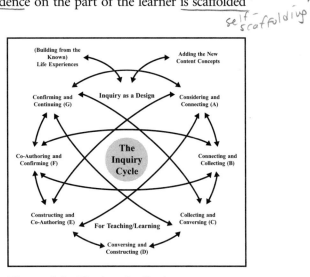

Figure 1.1 The Inquiry Cycle

impetus for reading & writing

"The first object of any learning act is that it should serve us in the future. Learning should not only take us somewhere, it should allow us later to go further more easily" (Bruner, 1960, p. 17). Inquiry as a curricular framework supports the idea of education for possibility as well as education for excellence. Inquiry provides students with the opportunity to become full participants in their own learning and the learning of the other human beings (both children and adults) in the classroom, school, and wider community. Inquiry includes the best of the knowledge base available in traditional content education, but makes use of the content concepts and accompanying information within a structure that is literacy-rich, democratic, and learning centered.

Through inquiry, the students *pose* questions and problems rather than merely answering and/or solving them. With help from the teacher and each other, students seek collaboratively to gain better understandings of the concepts under study. These understandings then lead to deeper questions and more critical engagements. Students move through multiple learning stances and perspectives as they reach out beyond textbooks and beyond teachers as the "transmitters" of knowledge. Students begin to see the complexities and ambiguities inherent within a given field of study. They think about ideas and information within a broader context, connecting and weaving facts and ideas with other facts and ideas gleaned from each other and previous experiences. The "ah-ha's" are audible when these tapestries of knowing emerge. The excitement is palpable.

> Instructionally, curriculum as inquiry means that instead of using the theme as an excuse to teach science, social studies, mathematics, reading, and writing, these knowledge systems and sign systems become tools for exploring, finding, and researching student questions. (Short, Harste, & Burke, 1996, p. 261)

This differs from traditional schooling practices that are grounded in a transmissionist view of learning that defines the learner as the receiver of learning. Figure 1.2 shows a comparison between an inquiry model and a more traditional model.

Inquiry Learning Assumes:	Traditional Schooling Assumes:
Intrinsic motivation	Extrinsic motivation
Collaboration	Competition
Teachers facilitate/guide/observe	Teachers lecture/test
Students are actively engaged/doing/talking	Students are silent/listening
Concepts are understood	Facts are memorized
Work is meaning based	Work is information based
Knowledge and understandings are applied	Knowledge is tested
Flexible curriculum	Set curriculum
Outcomes are scaffolded	Objectives are one size fits all
Authentic assessment	Standardized evaluation
Each student is a unique learner	Learners are sorted and labeled
A diverse community of learners	Students are tracked by "ability"
Progress is measured by growth	Progress is measured by grades

Figure 1.2   Inquiry Learning Versus Traditional Schooling

In this chapter, we discuss the underlying theory of our inquiry framework through an exploration of:

- Inquiry, literacy, and learning connections
- Inquiry as an appropriate curricular framework for middle level students
- Inquiry in a learning-centered classroom

Throughout this chapter, we will visit Ms. Lawrence's sixth grade Science class as her students engage in an inquiry on animal classification. We will refer to their work for illustrations and examples that support the foundations of inquiry in practice.

6ᵗʰ grade Science

Inquiry, Literacy, and Learning Connections

The IRA and NMSA Joint Statement "Supporting Young Adolescents' Literacy Learning (2001, p. 1) states:

> Continuous reading instruction requires that all middle school teachers understand reading and learning processes, realize the intricate and diverse needs of young adolescents, and know how to help students develop both the competence and desire to read increasingly complex materials across the curriculum. Reading strategies and skills are central to the success of the integrated, multidisciplinary middle school curriculum, and every teacher must possess the knowledge and skills to integrate reading instruction across the curriculum.

IRA
NMSA

Regardless of experts' theoretical stances on literacy development, all agree on one key point. Everyone—and we mean EVERYONE—agrees that the best way to become a better reader and writer is to read and write often and widely within a variety of contents, using a variety of genres, for a variety of purposes (Flippo, 1997). To accomplish this, students need to make choices and take ownership of their reading and writing outcomes. An inquiry framework supports teachers' creation of learning environments in which students forge networks between and among classroom materials, the human knowledge base within the classroom, and the extensive resources available to them throughout the community. "Literacy, therefore, requires active, autonomous engagement with print and stresses the role of the individual in generating as well as receiving and assigning independent interpretations to messages" (Venezky, 1995, p. 142).

Must read or write often (varied texts + purposes)

In order to facilitate learning in school, content and process must be intertwined. A responsive middle level curriculum and instructional framework must integrate the work of the classroom with the needs of the students and the concepts and ideas under study (Arnold, 1993). Figure 1.3 is a visual overview of the relationships between and among middle level students' development, an inquiry framework, and literacy uses.

Inquiry provides the impetus for middle level students to engage in sustained learning. Learning requires literacy and literacy development. Literacy, in turn,

Early Adolescence	Inquiry	Literacy
Range of intellectual development	• Focus on students' interest, prior knowledge, & background	• Variety of print material available for multiple purposes across a range of complexity
Moving from concrete to abstract thinking	• Scaffolds knowledge from concrete to abstract • Provides opportunities for exploration and discovery	• Connects abstract with concrete examples • Shifts between simple and complex engagements
Inquisitive	• Poses problems • Asks questions	• Seeks solutions & answers across multiple sources, for multiple purposes
Active	• Engaged • Self-directed	• Sets agenda for reading and writing
Social	• Collaboration within a community of learners	• Shares ideas, resources, strategies, & findings
Focus on reality & intertextual connections	• Investigations of real world issues & concepts • Provides opportunities for technology use • Offers connections across concepts & resources	• Develops comfort with expository text • Uses technology & internet • Uses literacy to record, create, & share connections
Emotional	• Encourages personal connections	• Covers all genres • Uses literacy to record and share responses
Capacity for seeing diverse perspectives	• Concepts viewed from multiple & often conflicting perspectives • Focus on diversity • Takes a critical stance	• Multiple print materials covering same concept or topic • Different points of view • Thinking critically about reading & writing
Focus on freedom & equity	• Democratic community • Focus on values & ethical choices	• Ownership of reading & writing processes • Choice in reading & writing • Materials used for authentic purposes
Need outlets for energy release, variety, & choice	• Free flow of purposeful activity in classroom	• Uses variety of literacy strategies & activities
		Continued

Figure 1.3 Connections Between and Among Young Adolescents' Inquiry and Literacy Uses

Strive for independence	• Variety of assessments • Responsibility for quality work	• Use of literacy for self-evaluation • Assess use of literacy
Experiment with identity	• Opportunities to try different roles & personal perspectives	• Uses literacy to experiment with voice & point of view
Need recognition	• Opportunities to share knowledge, understandings, & expertise • Opportunities to receive recognition for quality work	• Uses literacy & expressive language arts processes to be heard & acknowledged

Figure 1.3 Connections Between and Among Young Adolescents, Inquiry, and Literacy Uses *(Continued)*

requires the retention and application of strategies that enable the learner to inquire with increasing autonomy and independence. The learner must pose questions and problems, investigate possible answers and solutions, search among related and sometimes contradictory resources and determine what is accurate, what is true, what is meaningful in relation to other variables inherent in the problem or question. Inquiry requires thinking and the development of critical thinking. Middle level students are ready and eager to deliberately and systematically engage in questioning and critique.

Critical thinking is essential to the development of the kind of communication abilities our students will need to successfully negotiate the increasingly complex world of the twenty-first Century. Communication and learning are inextricably tied. From birth, we struggle to know the world and others in it as well as to make ourselves known through communication systems that are tactile, kinesthetic, visual, and verbal. Language as a sign system is critical to our development as human beings. Within an inquiry framework, "The prime value of reading and writing is the experience they provide through which we may constantly and unobtrusively learn" (Smith, 1998, p. 24). Although our focus is on language literacy, it is important to realize that students[6] use other sign systems as learning tools within the inquiry cycle. We use the term sign systems to refer to all the ways in which human beings communicate—language, math, art, music, and movement.

Inquiry as an Appropriate Curricular Framework for Middle Level Students

This We Believe (NMSA, 1995, p. 11) suggests,

"Developmentally responsive middle level schools provide:

- curriculum that is challenging, integrative, and exploratory
- varied teaching and learning approaches
- assessment and evaluation that promote learning
- flexible organizational structures
- programs and policies that foster health, wellness, and safety
- comprehensive guidance and support services

MS –
school
is
life

These six elements that responsive middle schools provide for students further suggest that school is not merely preparation for life—it is life. Thus, school experiences should be functional and useful for young people as they engage in the learning process. Middle level students learn to make informed choices when opportunities to get to know themselves as learners are encouraged and they are able to take more and more ownership of and responsibility for their own learning. The learner is the primary actor in acquiring knowledge, constructing understandings, and finding applications of the concepts she is investigating. As she does this, she will make connections to the worlds outside of school, often merging these various contexts of school, home, community, and beyond in ways that broaden and deepen her knowledge and understandings. With this widening of contexts, the opportunities for the student to apply the knowledge and understandings are multiplied.

Inquiry is predicated on the intrinsic motivation of the learner and assumes that the learner will be fully involved if the learning environment meets her needs (Gambrell, et al., 2000; Glasser, 1992). The assumption that the decline in the young adolescent learner's motivation upon entering middle school is developmentally triggered has been strongly challenged by current research, which states:

> The nature of motivational change on entry to middle school depends on characteristics of the learning environment in which students find themselves. That is, when students make a transition into a facilitative school environment, motivation and performance can be maintained or even improved. (Anderman & Midgley, 1997, p. 41)

Motivation is predicated upon the acknowledgment that all members of a classroom learning community are, indeed, learners. The concern is not whether students are learning; the concern is what they are learning. Rather than learning that animal classification concepts are "boring" and "hard" and that she is "lazy" and "stupid," the student in an inquiry community is learning that animal classification issues are "interesting" and have a real and meaningful impact on her life in ways she wants to explore and to share with others.

An underlying assumption of an inquiry framework is that all learners in a classroom including the teacher are afforded appreciation and respect. Therefore, inquiry encourages and necessitates a democratic approach to classroom management that assumes each member of the community can ask for and receive the space and attention they require. "Middle schoolers seek time away from others to reflect and try to make sense out of their own lives" (Mee, 1997, p. 62). From this reflection they bring back to the group their views and their voices. Working together, students and teachers develop the collegiality necessary to support one another. "They want to trust themselves, their friends, their teachers, and their families. For young adolescents to be trusted is a hallmark of becoming more mature" (Mee, 1997, p. 67). They negotiate the rules of the classroom with the teacher and each other so that everyone has the freedom they need to thrive as individuals.

Inquiry in a
Learning-Centered Classroom

To keep an inquiry moving smoothly, the impetus for the work of the classroom hinges upon the teacher incorporating the outcomes and what it is she/he wants the students to know, understand, and apply when the inquiry cycle is completed (standards and curriculum goals) with the best means for each student's achievement of these outcomes. With this in mind, we describe a learning centered classroom as one that operates on a continuum that borrows from Jeffrey Wilhelm's (2001) learning centered model based on Vygotsky's (1978) theories of scaffolding.

Our adaptation of Wilhelm's model puts the focus on the learner by using *I* for the student and *you* for the teacher (see Figure 1.4). For example, when Ms. Lawrence demonstrates a think aloud strategy of an excerpt on animal classification categories, the students watch and listen, but when the students are wandering and wondering in the text set, Ms. Lawrence is watching and listening.

I (student) WATCH >>>>>>>>>>>>>>>>>>>>>>>>>>> You (teacher) DO	
I (student) DO <<<<<<<<<<<<<<<<<<<<<<<<<<< You (Teacher) WATCH	

Figure 1.4   Learning-Centered Continuum

Throughout the inquiry cycle A–G (see Figure 1.1), the work of the classroom moves back and forth along this recursive continuum as the needs of the students and their learning demands. Through the use of this continuum the teacher maintains focus on the students' simultaneous growth and development in three areas: content acquisition, literacy development, and the four efficacy elements that enhance the first two (see Figure 1.5).

Content Acquisition	Literacy Strategies	Efficacy Elements
Knowledge	Writing	Confidence
Application	Listening	Independence
Critical Thinking	Speaking	Metacognition
	Thinking	Stamina

Figure 1.5   Student Growth and Development

Using this learning-centered model keeps the teacher's focus squarely on student learning rather than on the teacher's "teaching." Teaching is no longer simply "covering" the material established in the benchmarks, but ensuring that the students have a firm hand in their learning as they take control or "do" and the teacher "watches." It is allowing them to manipulate the material in order to discover and create meaning, not just listening to a teacher who seems to have all the answers.

While moving about her classroom, Ms. Lawrence guides, facilitates, questions, leads, prods, suggests, motivates, and, most importantly, maintains records. Thus the watching that she does is highly active, and more often than not interactive. The goal in this model is to spend the most time on the I DO/YOU WATCH side of the continuum where the student has primary ownership of her learning. The students manipulate, explore, and experience while you, the teacher, oversee and fill in gaps where specific students need more information, clarification, or guided practice.

The recursive nature of this model requires that the teacher shift easily back and forth between the two roles of guide/facilitator and participant/more-experienced learner. First, Ms. Lawrence provides information through a mini-lesson on classification. While her students are working in small groups, Ms. Lawrence joins each group periodically to offer insight, ask questions, and prod for further exploration. If individual students have misconceptions, she returns easily to the I WATCH/YOU DO and offers direct instruction; but the entire hour is never filled with direct instruction because that takes the learning out of the hands of the learner. Ms. Lawrence moves easily along the continuum to ensure that ALL of her students are learning in each of the three areas (content acquisition, literacy strategy use, and efficacy elements). This model demands much less time spent on a whole group focus and more time in small interactive groups and as individual learners. Because she is no longer standing in front of all the students, Ms. Lawrence's ability to "kidwatch" (Goodman, 1978) is enhanced; and she can easily keep track of where individual students are in their learning.

Kidwatching is

1. a continuous, systematic look at the process of how students learn;
2. taking what we know about students and turning that knowledge into effective instructional engagements;
3. reporting to students and parents about authentic learning;
4. valuing the contribution each student makes within the classroom learning community;
5. helping students to realize who is an expert at what and who they can turn to when they need assistance;
6. giving voice to students who might otherwise be silent;
7. getting to know each student in as many different contexts as possible;
8. an integral aspect of the curriculum.

(Goodman, 1978)

Figure 1.6   Kidwatching

This learning-centered model allows for strong student/teacher communication, which in turn offers the teacher honest and true insight into each student's educational growth. Knowing students well is one of the keys to the teacher's role in an inquiry process. If Ms. Lawrence stayed at the I WATCH/YOU DO side of the continuum and simply lectured, checked worksheets, and graded tests, she would never truly get to know the unique capabilities of each of her students. And since both content acquisition and literacy development are dependent on the student's continuous strengthening of the four Efficacy Elements (Freedman, Thomas, & Johnson, 2003): confidence, independence, metacognition, and stamina, it is essential that Ms. Lawrence know her students well.

All four of these elements are interrelated and interdependent for as confidence deepens, independence grows and stamina increases. As metacognition increases, confidence deepens, independence grows, and stamina increases (see Figure 1.7).

One of the things constantly in the zone of proximal development is our own self-image, including our beliefs about what we will and will not be capable of doing in the future." (Smith, 1998, p. 85)

Confidence:	attitudes, willingness to participate, level of active participation, willingness to collaborate, risk-taking, critical thinking, and questioning
Independence:	work habits, initiating questions, problem posing, willingness to seek answers and solutions, willingness to help others
Metacognition:	depth of self reflection, ability to think about and verbalize strategy use, knowledge of self as a learner and user of literacy tools, willingness to try new strategies
Stamina:	sustained reading, sustained writing, sustained discussing without direct and continuous prompting from the teacher or peers, self-regulation of time use, ability to organize time

(Freedman, Thomas, & Johnson, 2003)

Figure 1.7   Efficacy Elements for Learning

For an example of the learning-centered model at work see Figure 1.8 below.

Trevor watches and listens as Ms. Lawrence demonstrates browsing with a few books from the text set and together with the students' in-put fills in a knowledge chart.

Trevor wanders and wonders as Ms. Lawrence watches and listens to him and his peers:

- He skims through several sections of *How Nature Works*, *Hunters and Prey*, and *Defenders*.
- He slows down to read pictures, captions, sections of each text that draw his attention.
- He jots down on the form things he knows, things he's familiar with, and things that are new.

(Continued)

Figure 1.8   Trevor's Experience

Ms. Lawrence passes by Trevor's desk noting what he is doing and asks him to share something he has found that interests him.

Ms. Lawrence suggests that Trevor and Jack share with each other for a few minutes something of particular interest to each of them through a Say Something strategy.

Trevor is building:

- confidence through his active participation and willingness to share with Jack.
- independence though choosing materials that are stretching his learning through both reading and writing, and speaking and listening.
- metacognition by recognizing when he needs to slow down to ponder a new concept or what to do when he comes to an unknown word.
- stamina by maintaining focus and continuing to find purpose in his reading and writing and talking.

Figure 1.8   Trevor's Experience *(Continued)*

Concluding Remarks

Our inquiry framework is founded on the idea that "…no place…holds such power and promise for children's inquiry development as does the classroom" (Lindfors, 1999, p. 19). Therefore, we suggest that middle level classrooms be learning-centered environments in which the vehicle of inquiry employs the tools of literacy so that our middle level students see themselves as confident, independent, metacognitve, and strong learners and their learning experiences are rich, deep, intertextual, and lasting.

Chapter 2

Planning for Inquiry: Building From the Known and Adding the New

> The teacher understands the central concepts, tools of inquiry, and structures of the discipline(s) he or she teaches and can create learning experiences that make these aspects of subject matter meaningful for students.
>
> —INTASC Standards (1987)

Too often in too many classrooms, students and their teachers rarely get beyond teachers DOING and students WATCHING (see chapter 1). Within an inquiry framework this cannot occur as the teacher's planning deliberately limits the amount of time she/he is "doing and telling" by determining where, when, and how to embed mini-lessons and conferences in the daily processes of the classroom. Using the learning-centered continuum in daily planning helps Ms. Lawrence to see where she might be putting the emphasis and helps her to see when she is either "taking over" and doing too much for her students or "expecting too much" from them without adequate preparation.

In this chapter, we provide a six-question structure for planning for inquiry. We will return to Ms. Lawrence's sixth grade Science classroom for examples. The six questions fall into three categories: *6 Q's 3 categories*

- Supporting a learning-centered classroom

    1. What is my role? What is the role of my students?
    2. How will I maintain a collaborative learning community?

- Planning Curriculum
    3. How do the major concepts and "Big Ideas" of this unit connect with the content and literacy standards I am responsible for?
    4. What materials will I use? How will I choose and organize these? Where will I get them?
- Planning for instruction, learning, and assessment
    5. What instructional strategies will I arrange? What learning and literacy strategies will my students use and develop?
    6. How will I assess my students' progress, growth, and development? What kinds of records will my students and I keep?

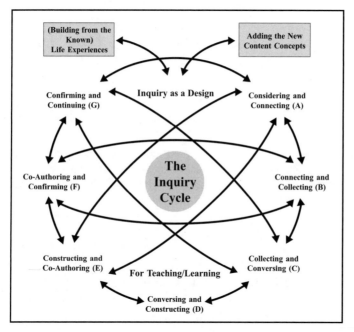

Figure 2.1 The Inquiry Cycle

Supporting a Learning-Centered Classroom

1. What is My Role? What is the Role of My Students?

In thinking about this question, Ms. Lawrence reminds herself that engaging students in the "classification of animals" inquiry requires that she reflect on her own practice. She must ask herself, "What is my role? And, what do I expect from my students?" In her planning, Ms. Lawrence anticipates many of her students' interests and *accountability*

needs. She knows it is her job to decide on the essential concepts that she should include and is prepared to insert these if the students don't come up with them in their own investigations. As guide/facilitator she offers information, provides direction, and manages classroom logistics. As participant/more experienced learner, she engages with the students in problem posing and self-reflection.

In a learning-centered, inquiry classroom the teacher leads from behind (Wells, *source of Wells??* 1986) by having and continuously acquiring an intimate knowledge of her students, their learning goals and the curricular outcomes delineated in state and local standards and benchmarks. Getting to know our students is a key to the success of inquiry. It is important for all middle school personnel to know the developmental aspects of this age group (see Figure 1.3 in chapter 1).

It is equally important to know each student as a unique individual who grapples in unique ways with growing up and becoming a decision making adult. Knowing our students means talking with them, observing them without prejudgment. One of the best ways to think about what we know about our students and what we need to still find out is to ask "why" questions instead of making statements about their behavior. For example, instead of stating to herself that Trevor has suddenly disengaged and is aimlessly wandering around the classroom, Ms. Lawrence wonders to herself why he might be doing this. While a statement could lead her to control his behavior without resolving the underlying problem, asking herself why would lead her to work *with* him on finding a solution. It may be that he simply needs a reminder to stay with it, or he might need redirection through a suggestion or a demonstration. Or it may be that he needs more intense one-on-one help. Asking why could also lead her to matching him with a peer, which could facilitate his staying focused. Asking why allows us to handle the problem constructively with the student. Making judgmental statements about students often stops our efforts to understand more deeply our students' motivations and actions.

Teacher Role

In a learning-centered/inquiry classroom, the teacher serves as guide/facilitator, scheduler, more experienced learner, resource expert, and assessor/record keeper.

As a guide/facilitator, Ms. Lawrence will take responsibility for organizing the patterns of classroom work as established through on-going negotiation. These patterns include such things as the use of time, materials, passes to the library, phone use. This assures that students are using time appropriately and productively. Guidance/facilitation might also include the teacher offering timely suggestions for instructional engagements that enhance students' use of strategies to accomplish their inquiry goals.

As scheduler, Ms. Lawrence is responsible for scheduling things like computer use, library use, as well as the use of other resources. Scheduling conferences, small group meetings, class meetings, and whole group mini-lessons are also part of this responsibility. Scheduling as part of the inquiry plan insures that students use their time and the materials with care, purpose, and efficiency in and out of the class-room.

As a more experienced learner, Ms. Lawrence demonstrates through mini-lessons strategies for learning new things as well as strategies for particular purposes. She makes this learning deliberate in order that students may benefit from her examples. Think alouds are one of many ways in which the teacher serves in the capacity of more experienced learner. Ms. Lawrence also makes certain that when she is demonstrating strategies, she gives the students an opportunity to reflect, to make comments, and to ask questions about the strategy.

As resource expert, Ms. Lawrence knows that she needs to be knowledgeable about the resources available to students and how to access those materials. For example, Ms. Lawrence works with her school's library media specialist to show the students who are investigating the major similarities and differences between desert life and ocean life how to access the web site of the National Science Foundation. In this capacity, Ms. Lawrence and the library media specialist move easily along the learning-centered continuum as both conduits to possible sources of information and as matchmakers between particular students and a specific source for information. Sometimes students merely need to be pointed in the right direction or offered a suggestion about where or what to research. Other times, students need to have specific sources given directly to them to get them started or to keep them going. In collaboration, the teacher and the library media specialist provide the students with on-going information literacy instruction (Public Education Network, 2003). The more inquiries the students engage in, the more the teacher and the library media specialist can support their learning about what is available to them and how they can access a variety of resources.

As assessor/record keeper, Ms. Lawrence assesses each student's progress and notes carefully what strengths each is exhibiting. From this information, she plans engagements that provide experiences for individuals and groups that help develop strategies the students lack or find difficult. Ms. Lawrence sets up the mechanisms for maintaining records that reflect the "finished" work within students' portfolios as well as records of the students' work in progress. It is important that these records reflect each student's growth as well as productivity.

Students' Role

Inquiry provides students with the opportunity to become full participants in their own learning and in each other's learning. It is important for early adolescents to have choices and to make decisions as they are finding their way into adulthood. As the teacher's role shifts from teller/director to facilitator/guide, the students' role shifts from memorizer/regurgitator to thinker/learner. "Useful learning doesn't occur when we take time out of our normal lives and knuckle down to serious study. Learning is an inevitable part of our normal lives, and it only takes place, in any useful way, when we are in a normal frame of mind. The main thing we learn when we struggle to learn is that learning is a struggle" (Smith, 1998, p. 13). This suggests students' motivation and engagement depend upon their being involved and having opportunities to activate their interest and to connect what is new to what they already know. "The nature of motivational change on entry to middle school depends on characteristics of the learning environment in which students find themselves. Thus, the teacher's role is less one of controlling students' learning and more one of supporting their efforts toward self-determination" (Anderman & Midgley, 1997, pp. 41 & 46). It is important to note, then, that much of the role of the student resides at the I DO/YOU WATCH end of the continuum. However, the student(s) and/or the teacher can initiate moves back along the continuum to the I WATCH/YOU DO end for demonstration and direct instruction as needed.

As thinkers/learners, the students initiate their desire to know and activate the search into their own inquiries through reading, writing, and discussing.

As negotiators they negotiate the schedule with the teacher to best facilitate their engagements. Through the demonstrations of more experienced learning offered by the teacher, students discover their own talents and preferences. They practice a variety of strategies though out an inquiry and share their investigative plans as they go. Together, they plan for peer-to-peer engagements where students take turns being the *I* and the *you* in the learning-centered model. These engagements can occur within the classroom and can also include cross age/grade collaborations. All learners are teachers and all teachers are learners.

As reflective learners, they take responsibility for getting to know themselves as readers, writers, speakers, and listeners. Along with the resource expertise of the teacher and the library media specialist, they take responsibility for getting to know each other and their teacher as collaborative colleagues. They learn each other's strengths and where they may be of assistance to one another.

As resource experts themselves, the students take responsibility for monitoring the atmosphere and work of the classroom by being full participants in a shared community of learners. This includes taking responsibility for self-assessment as well as personal record keeping. *self-assesst record keeping*

2. How Will I Maintain a Collaborative Learning Community?

As Ms. Lawrence facilitates the use of the inquiry framework, her students come to form a community of learners with each individual pursuing answers to her/his own questions at the same time each student is aware of his/her classmates' topics/content concepts/themes. Ms. Lawrence and her students share both information and the ways in which information is gathered, organized, and synthesized. She provides suggestions and engagements for the students as they use literacy strategies to formulate questions, choose materials, find and gather information, organize and synthesize the information and put it in a form to share in a meaningful and interactive way with their classmates. Inquiry requires on-going thinking and the development of critical thinking. Middle level students are ready and eager to deliberately and systematically engage in questioning and critiquing together.

Ms. Lawrence recognizes that inquiry demands that the learning community be a democratic one. As Maxine Greene (1988) states, "Democratic freedom [cannot exist] apart from critical thinking, hypothetical inquiry, the open exchange of ideas" (p. 43). To build an inquiry framework within an individual content classroom or in an integrated team, the teacher(s) and students must become consciously aware of a shift in their respective roles from the traditional role of teacher as disseminator and student as passive receiver. Ms. Lawrence realizes that for some of her students the shift to an inquiry framework will be one she will need to support them through. She knows that some students who have done particularly well within a traditional framework are fearful for their success within this new framework; some who get good grades without doing much are concerned that this new framework will require so much more from them that they may not be able to do it successfully. But she also recognizes that as they realize that the work of the class is learning-centered, she will be able to facilitate each student's use of a myriad of strategies for active learning.

The roles of the teacher and the students as described above are clearly known and practiced in a collaborative learning community. Together teacher and students negotiate the forms and functions of an inquiry classroom. This means that the rules of the community are democratically determined as much as possible and that what happens on a given day will never be a mystery to anyone. Rather a schedule has been carefully created with each student deciding on what they will commit to accomplishing. The overall processes of the classroom are negotiated at the beginning of the school year, but can be renegotiated when members of the community feel it is necessary. It is important here for the teacher to remember that she is a full-fledged member of the community and can call for renegotiations when she sees this as necessary. Just as with the schedule, specific forms and functions may need to be readjusted and new mechanisms may be required depending on the concept/theme/topic under study. For example, the classification unit incorporates a lot of concept vocabulary that all of the students need to be able to recognize and to use as they engage in the inquiry. Ms. Lawrence, therefore, has built into the schedule the development of a word wall beginning with Considering and Connecting, Phase A of the Inquiry Cycle. She has the students suggest words as they are browsing, and she has vocabulary that she knows will be necessary to their acquisition of the content. She also builds in many opportunities for the students and herself to use the words and to consider and connect them with the information and to concepts they are exploring.

Collaboration is at the heart of the work within an inquiry framework. Collaborative learning unlike cooperative learning focuses on the transactions between and among learners, transactions that empower thinking and enrich perspective. Cooperative learning tends to focus only on the exchange of information that the individual students will be held accountable to know primarily for testing purposes. Because learning always includes a social aspect, collaboration is more in keeping with how students learn. It is through our transactions with others that we discover what it is we know. What students know and how they know it deepens when they share it with others in and out of the classroom. "Even in the workplace, we're recognizing how much collaboration actually goes on in American life and how valuable group problem solving is, compared to perpetual competitiveness and isolation" (Zemelman, Daniels, & Hyde, 1998, p. 12). Hearing what others think and what their questions are only serves to broaden students' interests and their desire to know and understand more.

Through collaboration, students' intrinsic motivation is enhanced as they share ideas and viewpoints and question each other. So too, their curiosity grows as they seek to find answers to the questions that have grown out of these discussions. Through collaboration the resources that are made available to the classroom community grow exponentially because as students recognize each other as knowledgeable and talented, they can tap into these resource bases. In addition, each student connects to a world outside of school and within that world are resources that the community could potentially access.

Being a member of a community of learners is a powerful experience for students to have as it builds the four efficacy elements of learning through membership in the community. In many respects, learning becomes "effortless" not because the students work less, but because it is a fulfilling and confirming process that rewards students with increased confidence, independence, metacognition, and stamina (Smith, 1998; Freedman, Thomas, & Johnson, 2003). Through collaboration, busy work is eliminated. Students always have the opportunity to participate in meaningful engagements with others. The individual's responsibility to the group and the group's responsibility to the individual demands that each member of the community becomes actively engaged in work that holds immediate meaning for herself as well as long term meaning for members of the community. Because the work of the community becomes public through presentation, publication, and display, each member feels a sense of accomplishment and can take credit as either primary author/creator or community supporter.

In the course of an inquiry cycle, there are a number of reasons for and ways to group students. Groups can vary from pairs to groups of 10 to 12 depending on the purpose of the group. Duration of groups might be the entire inquiry or just for a few minutes conversation. Figure 2.2 shows several grouping formats, numbers of students, purpose of group, and so forth.

For example, during Considering and Connecting, Phase A of the Inquiry Cycle, Ms. Lawrence's students begin delving into the notion of classification of living things through browsing the materials in the text set. While in this phase of the cycle, the collaborative groups are primarily random or self-selected. Each group of students shares information in short bursts through an informal literature discussion established for as short a time frame as two minutes. In these brief discussions they

Type	Number of Students	Primary Purpose
Random	pairs to six	getting started, quick chat
Self selected	pairs to six	specific topic, initial sharing
Strategy Work	pairs to four	joint practice
Content specific	four to six	sharing information, organizing
Project	four to six	planning, job sharing, presenting

Figure 2.2 Collaborative Grouping Formats

share pictures and ideas and help each other navigate the use of information literacy supports such as an index, glossary, appendices.

Planning Curriculum

3. How Do the Major Concepts and Big Ideas Connect With the Content Standards and the Literacy Standards I am Responsible for?

Inquiry planning begins with the teacher building from the known (that is, building on what she finds the students have as background) and adding the new content concepts (see Figure 2.3).

Ms. Lawrence works from her school and district curriculum documents and her state's standards to list those content concepts every one of her sixth graders should know and be able to apply when the unit is completed. As they browse during the first few days of Considering and Connecting, she has her students fill in a

classification categories

vertebrates/invertebrates

cold blooded/warm blooded

flowering/nonflowering

reproduction

single-cell/multicellular

representative organisms

Figure 2.3 Content Concepts

knowledge chart that asks them to list in three columns the things they *know*, the things they are *familiar with*, and the things that are *new to them* (for more detail on the knowledge chart see chapter 6). These charts provide the connections between the unit outcomes and the information and prior knowledge that the students are bringing to the inquiry.

In planning her inquiry unit, Ms. Lawrence started with what she wants all of her sixth graders to know and be able to do when the inquiry is over and how she is going to assess this. Beginning at the end, so to speak, is simply keeping a focus on a target or routing a journey by knowing first and foremost where you are going. Therefore, planning for inquiry involves knowing the standards and benchmarks for both literacy and the content under study. The teacher brings together the standards and curricular documents with his/her knowledge and understandings of the students who will be involved in the inquiry. It is important for teachers to have a working knowledge of the literacy standards for students (IRA/NCTE, 1996; Moore, 1999) and for teachers (INTASC, 1987) and the literacy principles specifically addressing the needs of young adolescents (IRA/NMSA, 2002) as well as access through the school's library media specialist to the information literacy standards (AASL/AECT, 1998). See Figures 2.4, 2.5, 2.6, and 2.7.

(Note: While these standards may seem at first glance to apply primarily to the classrooms of English/Language Arts teachers, they are vital for the development of the literacy competencies needed and expected for learning in all disciplines.)

1. Students read a wide range of print and nonprint texts to build an understanding of texts, of themselves, and of the cultures of the United States and the world; to acquire new information; to respond to the needs and demands of society and the workplace; and for personal fulfillment. Among these texts are fiction and nonfiction, classic and contemporary works.

2. Students read a wide range of literature from many periods in many genres to build an understanding of the main dimensions of human experience.

3. Students apply a wide range of strategies to comprehend, interpret, evaluate, and appreciate texts. They draw on their prior experience, their interactions with other readers and writers, their knowledge of word meaning and of other texts, their word identification strategies, and the understanding of textual features.

4. Students adjust their use of spoken, written, and visual language to communicate effectively with different audiences for a variety of purposes.

5. Students employ a wide range of strategies as they write and use different writing process elements appropriately to communicate with different audiences for a variety of purposes.

6. Students apply knowledge of language structure, language conventions, media techniques, figurative language, and genre to create, critique, and discuss print and nonprint texts.

7. Students conduct research on issues and interests by generating ideas and questions, and by posing problems. They gather, evaluate, and synthesize data from a variety of sources to communicate their discoveries in ways that suit their purpose and audience.

8. Students use a variety of technological and informational resources to gather and synthesize information and to create and communicate knowledge.

9. Students develop an understanding of and respect for diversity in language use, patterns, and dialects across cultures, ethnic groups, geographic regions, and social roles.

10. Students whose first language is not English make use of their first language to develop competency in the English language arts and to develop understanding of content across the curriculum.

11. Students participate as knowledgeable, reflective, creative, and critical members of a variety of literacy communities.

12. Students use spoken, written, and visual language to accomplish their own purposes.

Figure 2.4   International Reading Association/National Council of Teachers of English Standards for the English Language Arts (IRA/NCTE, 1996)

The INTASC Standards (1987) in Figure 2.5 were developed through the work of the Council of Chief State School Officers for the induction and assessment of new teachers. As you read them, we think you will agree that they are certainly applicable to veteran teachers as well. These standards are ones that support the ongoing implementation of best practices in teaching and learning.

---

1. Content Pedagogy: The teacher understands the central concepts, tools of inquiry, and structures of the discipline he or she teaches and can create learning experiences that make these aspects of subject matter meaningful for students.

2. Student Development: The teacher understands how children learn and develop, and can provide learning opportunities that support a child's intellectual, social, and personal development.

3. Diverse Learners: The teacher understands how students differ in their approaches to learning and creates instructional opportunities that are adapted to diverse learners.

4. Multiple Instructional Strategies: The teacher understands and uses a variety of instructional strategies to encourage student development of critical thinking, problem solving, and performance skills.

5. Motivation and Management: The teacher uses an understanding of individual and group motivation and behavior to create a learning environment that encourages positive social interaction, active engagement in learning, and self-motivation.

6. Communication and Technology: The teacher uses knowledge of effective verbal, nonverbal, and media communication techniques to foster active inquiry, collaboration, and supportive interaction in the classroom.

7. Planning: The teacher plans instruction based upon knowledge of subject matter, students, the community, and curriculum goals.

8. Assessment: The teacher understands and uses formal and informal assessment strategies to evaluate and ensure the continuous intellectual, social, and physical development of the learner.

9. Reflective Practice/Professional Growth: The teacher is a reflective practitioner who continually evaluates the effects of his or her choices and actions on others and who actively seeks out opportunities to grow professionally.

10. School and Community Involvement: The teacher fosters relationships with school colleagues, parents, and agencies in the larger community to support students' learning and well-being.

Figure 2.5   INTASC (Interstate New Teacher Assessment and Support Consortium) Standards

In their joint position statement, *Supporting Young Adolescents' Literacy Learning: A Joint Position Statement of the International Reading Association and the National Middle School Association,* the IRA and the NMSA (2001) make it clear that every teacher must address and support the literacy development of every student in their content classroom. The third principle listed in Figure 2.6 is particularly applicable to our inquiry framework. It says,

> Schools for young adolescents must have ready access to a wide variety of print and nonprint resources that will foster in students inde-

pendence, confidence, and a lifelong desire to read. Because middle school students are a diverse group, care must be taken to include material that will appeal to linguistically and culturally diverse students. Librarians and media specialists are important partners who can ensure access for all adolescents. All school-based professionals must have sufficient knowledge of reading materials to provide guidance for adolescents in selecting reading materials. Students must have many opportunities to choose reading materials that are interesting and engaging. School-based professionals should model reading in various forms, have a love of reading, and possess the skills needed to help students progress toward mastery in all aspects of reading. (p. 2)

- Continuous reading instruction for *all* young adolescents.
- Reading instruction that is individually appropriate.
- Ample opportunities to read and discuss reading with others.
- Assessment that informs instruction.

Figure 2.6 *Supporting Young Adolescents' Literacy Learning: A Joint Position Statement of the International Reading Association and the National Middle School Association* (IRA/NMSA, 2001).

The American Association of School Librarians (AASL) and the Association for Educational Communications and Technology (AECT) developed the Information Literacy Standards for Student Learning (1998a) in Figure 2.7 below. The document "provides a conceptual framework and broad guidelines for describing the information-literate student" (p. v). These standards in conjunction with the ones listed previously make a clear case for developing and maintaining strong

---

Information Literacy

Standard 1: The student who is information literate accesses information efficiently and effectively.

Standard 2: The student who is information literate evaluates information critically and competently.

Standard 3: The student who is information literate uses information accurately and creatively.

Independent Learning

Standard 4: The student who in an independent learner is information literate and pursues information related to personal interests.

Standard 5: The student who is an independent learner is information literate and appreciates literature and other creative expressions of information.

Standard 6: The student who is an independent learner is information literate and strives for excellence in information seeking and knowledge generation.

(Continued)

Figure 2.7 The Nine Information Literacy Standards for Student Learning

---

Social Responsibility

Standard 7: The student who contributes positively to the learning community and to society is information literate and recognizes the importance of information to a democratic society.

Standard 8: The student who contributes positively to the learning community and to society is information literate and practices ethical behavior in regard to information and information technology.

Standard 9: The student who contributes positively to the learning community and to society is information literate and participates effectively in groups to pursue and generate information. (AASL & AECT, 1998a, pp. 8–9)

Figure 2.7   The Nine Information Literacy Standards for Student Learning *(Continued)*

teacher/library media specialist collaborations within all middle schools. Teachers and library media specialists need to continue to make clear to administrators and school boards that, "As a professional educator, each school's library media specialist collaborates with teachers and others to design, deliver, and evaluate information-based activities that engage students in active, authentic learning within the school's instructional program" (AASL & AECT, 1998b, p. 105).

The content standards and benchmarks that Ms. Lawrence uses to plan her inquiry on the classification of living things come from her state and district documents (see Figure 2.8).

Strand III. Use Scientific Knowledge from the Life Sciences in Real-World Contexts

Content Standard 2: All students will use classification systems to describe groups of living things; compare and contrast differences in the life cycles of living things; investigate and explain how living things obtain and use energy; and analyze how parts of living things are adapted to carry out specific functions. (Organization of living things)

Middle School Benchmark 1—Compare and classify organisms into major groups on the basis of structure. Key concepts: Characteristics used for classification—vertebrates/invertebrates, cold-blooded/warm-blooded, single-cell/multicellular, flowering/non-flowering. (Michigan Curriculum Framework, 2001–2003)

Figure 2.8   Michigan State Standards and Benchmarks (1996)

4. What Are the Benefits of Multiple Materials? How Will I Choose and Organize the Text Set? Where Will I Get the Materials?

Inquiry like a journey must begin with a plan that includes the acquisition, maintenance, and use of the appropriate materials. When a hiker plans a two-day journey through a wooded area, she makes sure she takes along plenty of water, food, rain and sleeping gear. She has to be sure that these supplies suit her ability to carry them and use them easily and productively. So, too, an inquiry journey must begin with the appropriate materials.

The amount of information that middle level students can now find in trade books written on their grade or reading levels (which range widely) makes the materials for inquiry topics far easier to find than in the past. Thus, middle level students can now enjoy using all types of texts for their inquiries, and the information they find in a trade book is often more engaging and more apt to be remembered (Johnson & Freedman, 2001).

We are using the "term multiple materials" to include such concepts as text sets and theme sets (Short, Harste, & Burke, 1996) as well as literature clusters (Hancock, 2000). Ms. Lawrence has realized along with her teammates and many of her colleagues that using multiple materials provides her with the resources to:

[handwritten margin notes: text sets / theme sets / literature clusters]

[handwritten margin note: value of text sets]

1. Validate each student's development level. A wide range of choices allows each student to determine how much prior knowledge they bring to the task and, therefore, the complexity of the reading material to accommodate their learning.

2. Spark interest, questions, and engagement. As students browse and read, the books add new information, trigger new questions, and engage the students as they work to find answers and to connect the new information to the old.

3. Offer information from a variety of perspectives. As the students are reading across the texts, they see the same information being used in different ways for different purposes. This stretches their understandings as they make connections between and among these various perspectives and their own views. Further, as they discuss the information and perspectives with one another, they are adding additional layers of perspective and viewpoint to their learning.

4. Offer information in a variety of genres and contexts. This allows students to see information presented in many formats. It allows them to become familiar with multiple styles and formats and to see models for their own organization and production of information.

5. Provide visual elements that reinforce and deepen concept understanding. Using graphs, charts, maps, photographs, diagrams, and illustrations

only enriches the learning experience of students. They are supported in their efforts to visualize the concepts as well as to construct explanations.

6. Support district curriculum as primary texts or as supplementary texts. Often text books have limited amounts of information on any given aspect of a concept or topic under study. When students become interested they want more information. Multiple materials provide this either as an addition to the textbook or as the primary print material.

7. Reinforces the interrelatedness of reading and writing (as well as speaking, listening, and thinking). Providing examples of different ways of expressing ideas enables the students to practice both receptive ways of understanding as well as productive.

8. Provide avenues for authentic assessment and evaluation. Using the materials as examples of ways to share learning and understanding, students can synthesize the information across the texts and share it in a way that is unique to them and their learning.

Choosing and Organizing a Text Set of Multiple Materials

Ms. Lawrence begins with a list of 10 questions (see Figure 2.9) to facilitate her pulling together the specific text set on the classification of living things (see chapter 3, Figure 3.2 for an abbreviated list of resources in the text set). These questions assure that the materials are authentic; accurate; represent a wide range of genres, styles, and levels of complexity both in ideas and in vocabulary; represent people from a variety of socio-cultural arenas; and provide strong intertextual connections.

- What is the organizing concept? Curricular focus?
- Are the materials authentic (written for real purposes)? Accurate?
- Is there a wide range of genres and styles?
- Do the materials accommodate students' interests?
- What demands does each text make of the reader?
- Do the materials represent a variety of socio-cultural factors (including ethnicity, race, gender, age, family structure, location, etc.)?
- Will the students be able to make connections between their lives and the materials?
- Do the materials help the students to widen and make sense of the world around them?
- Are there strong intertextual connections between and among the materials?

Figure 2.9   Questions to Guide the Selection of Multiple Materials

Locating Materials for the Text Set

Ms. Lawrence and her building's library media specialist work together to find suitable materials in the school's library/media center and public libraries in the area (Hughes-Hassell, 2001). They also use various review sources available to them such as *School Library Journal* and content area association journals and websites to locate materials to add to their collection. Ms. Lawrence and the library media specialist have also worked closely with their principal in order to use some of the textbook budget monies to purchase these materials. The principal understands the importance of students' information literacy development, and he sees supporting teachers' use of an inquiry framework as one way to embed information literacy into the curriculum. Ms. Lawrence also applies for—and has been fortunate to receive a few—grants that provide monies for the purchase of multiple materials.

Before she began the collaboration with the library media specialist, Ms. Lawrence pulled the materials together from what was available in her school's library, what she could find in her community public library's children's/adolescent and adult collections, went to used book sales, book club sales, and Amazon.com and Barnesandnoble.com. As she browses books for possible inclusion in a set of multiple materials, she often uses the Book Review Form below (see Figure 2.10 and Appendix 1).

Bibliographic Information: Bredeson, C. (1999). Tide pools. Photographs. 64 pgs. New York: Franklin Watts. ISBN: 0-531-15958-2.

Brief Summary or Key Ideas: "Describes the physical characteristics of tide pools and the organisms that inhabit them" (Library of Congress Cataloging-in-Publication Data). Tells what a tide pool is, what mollusks and crustaceans are, and how the organisms battle for survival.

Authenticity: The author has written many books for young people and has an M.S. in instructional technology/library. She is a strong supporter of information literacy in the schools.

Accuracy: The author includes a number of references, print resources, web sites, and videos and CD-Roms for information on tide pools.

Content Area Use: Exploratories   Science   Social Studies
                          Math   Language Arts   Other

Primarily science, but has aspects that could be used across the curriculum such as photography, descriptive language, geographical locations, ecological relationships and ratios.

Concept Load: The author uses clear, student friendly language, but also includes appropriate terminology. There is a glossary for support.

Vocabulary: Uses scientific terminology. Provides a glossary for support.

(Continued)

Figure 2.10 Book Review Form

Style: Clear, student/reader friendly.

Cautions: None

Support Material:
   Graphics (maps, graphs, charts, photographs, Illustrations, etc.): photographs
   Glossary: yes
   Index: yes
   List of sources used: yes
   List of references: yes
   Appendix material: no
   Other: Information about the author

Figure 2.10 Book Review Form *(Continued)*

Planning for Instruction, Learning, and Assessment

5. What Instructional Engagements Will I Arrange? What Learning and Literacy Strategies Will My Students Use and Develop?

Literacy strategies that support and strengthen content development are learned and practiced in an inquiry curriculum as an inherent part of the work of the classroom. "You can't think about nothing. We believe that we must teach our students to access content when they read as well as teach them the strategies they need to better understand text and become more thoughtful readers" (Harvey & Goudvis, 2000, p. 9). The following list offers several broad categories of strategies that we explore in detail in this book. For each category, we have listed some examples of specific strategies as well. We feel these categories make sense as they provide for the inclusion of all sign systems—language, math, art, music, and movement. For the individual strategies, we use the terms "constructing meaning" and "sharing meaning" to differentiate between literacy strategies that the learner uses primarily to seek input from others and those strategies the learner uses primarily to express himself/herself.

- Individual Strategies: Strategies for *constructing meaning* include browsing, skimming and scanning, skipping unknown words, using context, using support material such as an index, glossary, pictures and captions, and song lyrics. Strategies for *sharing meaning* include note taking, webbing, charting, listing, summarizing, formulating written questions, speech writing, song writing, and skit writing.

- Small Group/Paired Strategies: These strategies include written conversations, shared note taking, script writing, proving a point, Say Something, creating Venn diagrams and other graphic organizers.

- Discussion Strategies: Discussion strategies include literature circles, analogies and metaphors, issues and attributes, significant phrases or scenes, what have I learned?

- Publication/Presentation Strategies: These strategies include readers' theatre, writers' workshop, creating picture books, posters, brochures, pamphlets, formal timelines, essays, short stories, poetry.

Whether it is your first or your thirty-first inquiry, it requires time spent planning. Planning is the key ingredient to the overall success of any inquiry. Planning for inquiry takes two interrelated forms, Planning to Plan (Short, Harste, & Burke, 1966) and Planning for Daily Learning Engagements. Planning to Plan helps Ms. Lawrence identify all of the things that she needs to think about, organize, and set into place *before* the students ever enter the classroom. Planning for Daily Learning Engagements enables her to use on-going, formative assessments such as browsing sheets, prior knowledge/experience charts, and exit cards to determine and coordinate activities for individuals as well as groups of students.

Ms. Lawrence's planning for the entire inquiry cycle includes making decisions about the instructional engagements and learning/literacy strategies that will be incorporated into the unit. (It is important to emphasize that we are using *instructional engagements* to refer to those activities that are planned for and arranged by the teacher. *Learning/literacy strategies* are those practices used by the students as they continue their learning and literacy growth and development.) The following are engagements that Ms. Lawrence will use in the classification of living things inquiry:

- Mini-Lessons: Throughout this inquiry, Ms. Lawrence will have information and direction that she will provide to the students. For example, following the students wandering and wondering, Ms. Lawrence shares information with the students about the vocabulary of classification. As she puts up each word such as *vertebrate/invertebrate, mammal, amphibian, carnivore, herbivore,* and *omnivore,* she shares briefly information that will help the students get to know each of them. She uses visual representation as well as verbal cues.

- Strategy Demonstrations: It is important that Ms. Lawrence herself or individual or small groups of students demonstrate learning/literacy strategies that students will need to use and practice such as note taking, question posing, quick writes, skimming, scanning, using the glossary, using various maps, charts, graphs, and using the indices and appendices in the books.

- Small Group and Individual Conferences: Periodically throughout the inquiry cycle it is important that Ms. Lawrence meet with the students to discuss their progress, findings, successes, misconceptions, and concerns.

- Revisiting Text Structure: This is both an engagement and a strategy as it is often necessary to deliberately share information with the students about the ways in which information is organized. Students also need to keep track of the different organizational structures they are coming across and use them as models for their own writing and organizing of information.

- Learning Logs/Journals/Draft Books: Learning logs differ from notes in that they provide a place for students to make connections to the material, identify what interests them, puzzles them, intrigues them, confuses them. It is a place to pose and answer questions. It is also a place to think about themselves as learners of the content. What is coming easily; what is more difficult?

- Graphic Organizers: These can be demonstrated and then used by students as a strategy for keeping their information in a meaningful format. Venn diagrams for comparison and contrast of information, cause and effect charts, main idea and detail bubbles, and simple listing formats.

- Frontloading (Wilhelm, 2001): This again is an engagement in which the teacher shares with the students some of the major concepts they will be learning about. It is a kind of previewing of what is to come in the unit. It can also be an engagement that initiates students assessing prior knowledge and experiences with the concepts to be studied. Frontloading happens periodically throughout an inquiry and can take the form of a mini-lesson or small group or individual conference.

- Vocabulary Building/Word Walls (Allen, 1999): For continuous exposure to new vocabulary, terminology, and concepts, word walls are developed and maintained by both the teacher and the students. Having vocabulary up in a central location in the classroom provides easy access to the words both for initial study and as a reminder for usage. Words can also be illustrated, diagramed, and mapped, just to mention a few of the ways in which they can be used. The key is that both the teacher and students use the vocabulary repeatedly in their reading, writing, speaking, listening, and thinking.

- Providing Time for Sustained Silent Reading of Text Set Materials: This engagement is the heart of an inquiry framework. Giving students the time and support to use a number of literacy strategies from choosing a text to read and skimming what they already know, using the index to find specific information, slowing down for concepts less familiar, stopping to think about what they are reading, and jotting down notes or responses.

- Read Alouds (Opitz & Rasinski, 1998): It is important for both teachers and students to engage in this activity. For both, rehearsing the text to be read is essential. This engagement provides for the use of strategies that focus on structure, signals, and tone—the elements of expression that provide oral reading with meaning.

- Developing Questions and Problem Posing: Essential for inquiry is the strategy of question and problem posing. Students need to know both what they know and what they do not know. Part of becoming metacognitive learners is to be able to develop complex inquiries that facilitate continuous growth and development of knowledge, understandings, application, and critical thinking.

- Literature Circles and Other Discussion Strategies: Talk is essential to learning. It is essential to the learning-centered nature of the inquiry framework that students have ample time to talk in both formal and informal ways. Developing keen listening and speaking strategies is key to students' continuous development of the four efficacy elements—confidence, independence, metacognition, and stamina.

- Working Portfolio: This includes all of the student's work within the inquiry including self-reflective pieces. The working portfolio provides both the teacher and the student with an accurate record of the work each student has done, information collected, responses written, reflections written, words found, graphic organizers created and filled in, questions posed, and notes taken. Keeping track of their work and their learning develops students' ability to focus on their new learning as well as their learning processes.

6. How Will I Assess Their Progress, Growth, and Development? What Kinds of Records Should My Students and I Keep?

Throughout the Inquiry Cycle, Ms. Lawrence is an active listener and keen observer or "kidwatcher," (Goodman, 1978). Through observation, conversation, and portfolio reviews, she determines with the students what their needs are in terms of content and literacy learning.

Along with kidwatching, inquiry provides many opportunities for teachers to engage their students in demonstrations of their learning through authentic uses of both literacy strategies and application/critical thinking of content knowledge and understandings. We list several of the ways students can use and demonstrate learning below. (For a more detailed discussion of these as assessment strategies see chapter 8, Figure 8.3.)

Predict	Explain	Describe
Solve	Create	Infer
Discover	Compare	Estimate
Interpret	Perform	Synthesize
Respond	Inform	Relate
Invent	Communicate	Reason

Student Self-Reflection

It is important to note here that as teachers it is not necessary that we are ultimate experts on the content that we are teaching. In fact, it is important within an inquiry framework, and we would argue within any instructional practice, that we model our learning process as well as our knowing. It is too easy for our students to say to themselves, especially when they are struggling, "Yeah, I see you knowing/doing that; I don't see me knowing/doing that." But if we show them the ways in which we approach academic learning, then they can engage in the strategies we demonstrate for them and they can experience the learning more deliberately. This returns us once again to the essential nature of a learning-centered classroom.

Periodically throughout the inquiry, Ms. Lawrence has her students write self-reflections or talk self-reflectively during individual and/or group conferences. During this reflection, her students do "see themselves knowing" as a result of a learning process—a process they are becoming better and better at articulating. This, in turn, increases their metacognitive abilities, which in turn increase the development of confidence, independence, and stamina.

Record Keeping

Record keeping is an integral part of the logistics of teaching. For the smooth flow of the inquiry cycle, keeping accurate, detailed records is essential. It is through the information that is gathered and kept that Ms. Lawrence knows where her students are in their progress toward knowledge acquisition, literacy development, and pragmatic development, as well as where they are logistically in their inquiry work. (See chapter 8 for a detailed discussion of the kinds of records that are kept throughout an inquiry.)

Concluding Remarks

We often take a survey in our teacher preparation classes that goes something like this:

How many of you think you hate math? A number of hands go up.

How many of you think you hate history? A number of hands go up.

How many of you think you hate English? A number of hands go up.

How many of you think you hate Science? A number of hands go up.

And so on . . .

Then we have a discussion of all the ways in which these disciplines are embedded in our daily lives. It soon becomes apparent that it isn't the subject matter that our students "hate." Rather, it is the way these were taught to them that caused the dislike. As they talk with one another about their respective likes and dislikes of content areas, they realize how much overlap and connection there is between and among the disciplines. They begin also to see the ways in which interdisciplinary inquiries can be organized and planned, particularly within teaming structures.

Seventh Grade Geography

Meghan Luckett

When beginning my student teaching, my overall goal was to demonstrate that I was capable of creating meaningful instruction that engaged and excited my new students in challenging and motivating ways. I met with my cooperating teacher, Patti Woodruff on a warm summer day as she was cleaning and organizing her classroom for the following school year. Her enthusiasm and passion for teaching were immediately contagious, and I knew that my experience would be incredible. She showed me the curriculum for eighth Grade American History and we talked about our philosophies of education, which matched perfectly. As I left her classroom, ideas and activities for the following fall flooded my mind. I spent the rest of the summer searching libraries and book fairs for any materials dealing with the time periods of Puritans landing in the New World to the causes and implications of the Civil War. I called Patti 2 weeks before school was to begin to touch base with her and ask her a few questions about logistics. It was at this time that she told me that she had just accepted a job as the seventh grade Geography teacher in the same building. Even though I had gathered all the materials I would need to be successful in an American History classroom, I knew that working under Patti's expertise was more important than changing content. Later that night, I put away all my books, magazines, websites, and lesson plans and began thinking about Canada.

   With only a few days to plan for this new curriculum, I knew that I would have to enlist the help of the school's librarian if I wanted to accomplish the goals I had set for myself. I knew that I wanted to focus on inquiry and allow the students to delve into aspects of Canada that interested them and then share that newly gained knowledge with each other. I knew that I wanted the students to read, write, listen, discuss, and think critically everyday. I knew that I wanted to provide them with books, magazines, technology, and other sources to explore. I wanted them to walk away from my classroom with tools that they could use for the rest of their lives—not just the date that Eric the Red landed in Nova Scotia or that Nunavut was formed on April 1, 1999. I wanted them to have confidence and to trust their abilities to locate any information they desired.

As I sat down to create the daily lessons and the overall goals for the unit, I had to decide what my role would be in the entire process and the role I wanted my students to have. I knew what my role would not be, but labeling and defining my actual role was difficult. I knew I did not want to spend the minutes I had with the students lecturing and dispensing information. I knew I did not want them to read the chapters of the textbook and then take tests at the end of each section. I knew that I wanted the students to be active participants and have decision-making power over the kind of information they would be learning.

My role was hard for me to pinpoint, but I did know without doubt what I wanted the students' roles to be. The students were the key, the focus, and all of my energy went into assuring that we were partners in learning. With this in mind, I created an introductory lesson that allowed me to offer choice and ownership while also giving me the space I needed to figure out what my role was going to be in the process.

I began planning my unit on Canada by visiting the school's library. When I took the cart from my classroom to the library and asked for all the books they had on Canada, an odd look of shock lingered on the face of the librarian. I am not sure whether the look was more of a surprise to see a student teacher coming into the library seeking books instead of simply using their cooperating teacher's lesson plans or if she simply hasn't worked collaboratively with many teachers in the past. Either way, she was eager to help and together we gathered books on every subject dealing with Canada. We found books on the various peoples, languages, and cultures of Canada; books on the animal and plant life of Canada; books on the history, government, and economy of Canada; books on the landforms and physical features of Canada; books on the sports, music, food, and entertainment of Canada; books on the weather of Canada; books on the natural resources, farming, and industry of Canada and many more. With her help, I was able to gather even more materials than expected, especially since my curriculum changed shortly before the school year began. Without utilizing the expertise of the school's librarian, I would have been limited to the textbook and various Internet websites.

By using inquiry, the students were free to explore and experience many more aspects of Canada than the textbook had to offer. Of course, there are aspects of Canada that all of a the students were expected to know. In the inquiry cycle there is always a time and place for direct instruction where every student gains the same information, usually through a mini-lesson to help ensure understanding. For example, during our unit on Canada I was noticing that the majority of my students continually stereotyped the native people that lived in the northern reaches of the country. I wanted to address the issue in a way that would help all the learner's understand the unique and intricate aspects of Inuit life enabling them to gain a better understanding and respect for the people we were studying. To do this, I created a mini-lesson on stereotyping and embedded it into our inquiry cycle. I briefly talked with them about what a stereotype is, and then we discussed times when they have felt prejudged or stereotyped. Every student wrote a letter about the negative effects stereotypes can have and why people should remain open-minded.

My role changed daily from guide to research assistant, from talker to listener, from collaborative partner to evaluator, from observer to active participant. Once I was comfortable with my ever-changing role, I began to focus on how I was going to maintain a functional learning community and ensure that all students were learning and growing to the best of their ability. To ensure that I was creating and maintaining an environment that fostered collaborative learning, I implemented projects and assignments that focused on group cooperation. By grouping the students based on areas of interest, I felt better able to assure participation by all group members.

For example, when beginning our large project on the thirteen Provinces and Territories of Canada where the groups were to take the class on a detailed tour through the history, landscape, culture, economy, entertainment, weather, people, plants, and animals of a province or territory, I had the students first browse through the many books and magazines I had provided. First looking at the books and reading a little about the unique features of each province or territory gave the students the chance to choose a place that really piqued their interests. Whether it was British Colombia and the vast mountain ranges providing huge profits for the province's economy or Nunavut and its customs and traditions dating back thousands of years, the students had the freedom to pursue whatever interested them.

After browsing the materials, the students chose their area of interest and groups were formed. During the time afforded to them in class, the students worked in their groups creating a visual, museum-like display that appealed to all five senses that would eventually be shared with their classmates. At this point, each group was a mini-learning community, but I wanted more inter-topic discussion and sharing. So to create and maintain a larger collaborative community, I embedded mini-lessons that allowed the students to discuss and share with other classmates outside their specific interest group. For example, one lesson included an activity where the students were put in pairs and chose a few different books that interested them pertaining to Canada, but not necessarily their main topic. In these pairs, the students used all forms of literacy to think and share ideas, thoughts, feelings, and main concepts. One student would pick a passage or maybe a quote underneath a picture and read it aloud to their partner. They would then "Say Something" about the passage or quote, like how it made them feel or other thoughts it may have provoked. The partner listening would write down what was said, using his or her listening skills and questioning skills to gain more information from their partner. The reader then switches and this process carries on for about 20 minutes, with each student sharing, listening, writing, thinking, feeling, and gaining a stronger understanding of the material.

Mini-lessons gave the students the opportunity to interact with multiple and diverse partners helping them gain various opinions and ways of looking at the same subject matter. Having many different groups throughout the unit allowed me to see how the students interacted, and it also heightened the feeling of community. I also met weekly with the groups to ensure that they were on task and that each member of the group was participating and staying involved with the daily work of their group. Each day, I would call up the groups and ask them questions about their progress. The use of conferencing gave me short private time with each group away from their peers and allowed me to ask the hard questions and get them thinking more critically.

"Sam, Peter, and Alex, can you come up here?" I asked over the hum of hard working students. With nods, they gathered up their notes and headed towards my desk.

"Hey guys, how are things going?"

Sam, the most vocal of the group, gave me an odd, reluctant "okay."

"Well, how have you separated the topic into daily pieces you can tackle?"

"Um, Peter is doing the military and the Mounties. I am working on the physical features and um, Alex is looking up stuff on religion." Sam said looking at his scribbled notes.

"Okay, Alex let me see your notes." I said reaching for his paper.

"I am almost done," he said quietly.

"Let's see, looks pretty good. You at least have all the religions down."

"Yeah."

"But have you thought about why there are various religions in your province? Who settled each region and how does our theme of movement relate to the spread of religion?"

"Yeah, I'll look that up, too."

"Guys, it seems like you're on the right track. Make sure that you are thinking about the five themes of geography and relating them back to your topic. Ask yourself the why and how questions. Sam, how do people live in the various regions; how do they adapt to the environment? Also, remember that physical features have a direct affect on economy and culture."

"Okay, Ms. Luckett," they said almost in unison ready to get back to work.

"Thanks boys," I said, getting ready to call the next group up for a short talk.

Along with these weekly conferences, I also communicated with each member of the classroom learning community through daily journals. I would ask questions about their subject matter and also about how the groups were getting along and progressing. With these private journals, I could ensure honesty and always keep on top of any problems going on between group members. By being involved, either through conferencing, journals, walking about the room, asking questions, or daily progress checks, I was able to ensure that the collaborative learning community remained positive and truly functional.

When planning for the unit on Canada, I knew there were a few "Big Ideas" that I wanted all learners to know and fully understand. Some of these came from my own ideas and some of them came from the benchmarks and standards that I was responsible for during this unit. Having to plan the basic skeleton of the unit on Canada based on my desires to offer choice and my responsibility to address the benchmarks and standards, I had to strike a balance and decide what issues and lessons must be included and available to all learners.

The first content standard addressed locating and describing diverse people, cultures, communities, languages, religions, traditions, belief systems, gender roles, and how various regions affect people's daily lives. With this in mind, I began planning the first few lessons of the unit. One lesson involved each student creating two word cubes. A few days prior, the students had all browsed through the books, magazines, and technology, and listed words, concepts, or themes that were unfamiliar or that piqued their interest. It was from this list and from continual browsing that the students chose the words that they wanted to cube. Each cube consisted of six elements that the student had to include: define the word, describe the word, relate the word to their own lives, compare the word to something more familiar to them, contrast the word, and finally draw a picture or visual that represented the word.

Through word cubing, I was able to address each aspect of the first content standard. By adding on to each student's cube presentation with additional information, I was able to create a large group discussion that delved deeper into the material thus helping the students to gain a better understanding of the content. Through this lesson, the students first browsed through books and other sources; then they chose words that piqued their interest; then they completed all six elements allowing them to connect the word to their own lives; then they presented the words practicing their speaking skills and their listening skills while their peers presented; then they created original sentences of the presented words practicing their writing skills. Finally we hung the cubes from the ceiling so that they would be available as a reference throughout the unit.

The next content standard that I was responsible for teaching related to Human-Environment Interaction, showing the students how humans can negatively and positively affect the environment and the fragile and unique ecosystems of Canada. For this benchmark, I wanted to integrate some of the aspects the students were learning in Science about adaptation and changing to survive in a harsh environment. I was lucky to be part of a team of wonderful teachers who freely shared and integrated content. So, to address the second content standard, we used the novel *Julie of the Wolves* (George, 1972) to connect Language Arts and Social Studies. During this time, the students read the novel in Language Arts and in Social Studies we discussed, shared, and wrote about the many unique physical features of the northern reaches of the North America.

Each student was given a blank skeleton of notes that dealt with many physical features that would be seen in the novel and also in the northern reaches of Canada. There was a space for describing plant species, animal species, various landforms and landscapes, tools, clothes, houses, and traditions the people of the novel and the Inuit culture of Northern Canada would use to adapt and survive the harsh environmental conditions. There was also space for critical thinking about how the people in the novel and in Canada have negatively or positively impacted their environment. Each day the students would gather into small literature circles to discuss the various aspects of the packet and then share the information they discussed in a jigsaw format, where they are an expert on one topic and join a group of other experts on other topics and share the information they discussed in their original groups. We would culminate class with a large discussion on how the people, animals, and plants have adapted to their environment. Some days we would free write about our discussions with questions I would pose like: Why are Polar Bears white? Why do the Inuit people wear animal skins? How does technology and modernization impact, threaten, or help the Inuit culture? What natural resources are harvested and which of these are renewable and which are being destroyed? How have humans both positively and negatively impacted their environment?

When we finished reading and working with *Julie of the Wolves* (George, 1972), the students had gained a better understanding of how people interact with their environment both in positive and negative ways. To finish this section, we watched a video on the Inuit culture and how they have adapted peacefully to their environment for thousands of years. This video was accompanied with a video viewing guide that asked questions not only about the video to ensure the students were following but also prodded the students to think critically about the information.

Using the video viewing guide was a wonderful way to assess the students and their progress up to this point in the unit. To assess them with the first standard, I used the word cubes. To make assessments for this standard I used both the *Julie of the Wolves* notes packet and the viewing guide. By reading the students' answers to the viewing guide, I was able to see which students were finding the connections between nature, adaptation, science, and social studies and which were still thinking close to the surface. I liked using the Inuit culture to learn about human-environment interaction because they have been adapting and withstanding the elements for thousands of years. The way they have lived could be directly connected to Science and the major concepts the students were learning about classification, adaptation, and survival of the fittest. I also liked using the Inuit culture because their lifestyle truly illustrated a positive human-environment interaction, yet the way modern technology was seeping into the culture also vividly showed how industry can have a negative impact on human-environment interaction.

Because the Inuit's led the way to so many possibilities and offered so many lessons that connected directly to the Michigan content standards for geography, I chose to continue with the broad topic of Inuit culture. The third content standard focused on the theme of movement, location, and the basic interconnectedness of all people. To begin diving into this topic, I first used a mini-lesson on global interdependence. I had the students form groups and create a list of all the items they use on a daily basis, from food to clothes, from games to books, from technology to hygiene products. We then shared this enormous list and began to see that all of these products came from various places around the world. Shoes came from China, Polynesia, and Russia; clothes came from Japan, El Salvador, and Mexico; games came from China, Japan, and United States; food came via immigrants from Italy, Spain, China, Netherlands, and Mexico, as did many other products. We then mapped the globe with arrows pointing to the United States from the products' originating countries. We also found exports of the United States and drew dashes for products leaving the country. There were lines everywhere enhancing my point that we are all interconnected. Finally to finish off the lesson, I had the student's write a short story about their day and what life would be like if we were isolated and relied only on products produced, grown, or harvested in the United States. By connecting the material back to the student's lives, I had them hooked and could now begin to focus on the ways in which interconnectedness, movement, and location affected the lives of the people of Canada.

I wanted to continue with the Inuit culture to connect the themes of movement, location, and global connection, so I called a professor I knew at a local university and asked if he and his wife would come to school and talk about their adventures traveling through Nunavut, the newest Canadian Territory. The students had each prepared three questions to ask the experts and were able to see and touch artifacts brought directly from the Inuit culture.

One of the students asked about how the people lived and if they all lived in igloos and wore animal furs. This question gave our experts a chance to enlighten the students on traditions and also to help them eliminate some of their stereotypes. It also provided discussion on how the Inuits deal with their unique location using both modern practices of electric and oil heating and traditional ways of Caribou suits and dog sleds.

I had the student's write a letter to the speakers thanking them for coming to our school and also posing a few more questions that they would still like to have answered. One of my goals was to show the student's that there is always more to learn about any topic.

The fourth content standard deals with mapping and comparing and contrasting some of the major cultural, economic, political and environmental features of various areas around the world. To begin addressing this standard, I created a mapping assignment that began with the basic principals of mapping. For this activity, I brought in many books on geography, including but not limited to books on weather, landforms, regional environments, plants, animals, cultures, population, and much more. We began by creating a list of all the different types of maps we could create and what they would show to a viewer, from topographical to a population map, from a rainfall map to one that shows language distribution, from a physical feature map to a time zone map and many more. Once we had a list of various map types, I had the students pick a few and tell me how looking at that specific aspect showed its impact on the people, culture, environment, and economy of that region. We then discussed how a rainfall map shows the amount of rainfall and how that impacts where people live and what crops they grow and how a physical feature map shows the major landforms and how mountains and rivers impact economy through tourism and trade, respectively. We covered all the map types and the students thought critically about how all these elements affected culture, people, environment, and so forth.

After using the books to find information and then discussing the various map types, I introduced the mapping assignment. It is important to first show the students the connection the material has to their own lives before diving into subject matter that is so far from home. To do this, I had the student's pick a map they thought was cool and use that type of map to map their bedroom at home. I modeled this by mapping my own bedroom at home using a physical feature map. I had a mountain called Mt. Laundry Heap; a plateau called Sleepy Time (my bed); I had a small kettle lake, Lake Glass O' Water, next to a smaller mountain, Mt. Nighttabel; I had a Great Wall of Bedroom separating my room from the bathroom that was built by the ancient dwellers as a fortress of protection from floods; I had a picture rock, similar to the one in Utah (my window); and finally I had a mini tropical forest, my feng shui bamboo shoots. As I explained the assignment, I passed around my model, which because of the intended humor piqued the student's interest in the activity.

After the student's completed the bedroom mapping assignment, we then focused our energy on mapping Canada. Each student completed a basic political map, coloring the provinces and territories and labeling the capital cities. I wanted to spice up this assignment and returned to browsing the books, magazines, and websites I had gathered for the unit. Thus, I added a component where the students had to also find two unique facts or features about each province or territory to include on their map. I must admit that I learned a ton by reading the facts they uncovered, making this a wonderful activity for me as well.

Once this map was completed, we finished the mapping section of the unit by having each student choose one other map type and map Canada. They could chose from any of the list we had created earlier in the lesson or they could find a new type. For example, one student created a population map and in his definition explained to me that the reason for the distribution of population was the harsh weather conditions in the northern reaches of Canada. Another student created a natural resource and economy map and discussed how the changes in regional landscape affect farming and are very similar to the United States. He explained how in the far west there are vast mountain chains that allow for increased tourism; in the middle of Canada there are major plains that produce wheat and grain much like the states of Nebraska, Kansas, Iowa, and the Dakotas; and finally in the East where there is a large harvesting of fish and seafood, much like Maine.

Assessment

I believe that assessment should be as varied as the assignments. Just as not all students are interested in the same things, not all students can be assessed in the same manner. Brian, who loves history is a fabulous test taker, he can memorize dates and people without any problem; but Amy, who loves all aspects of culture, especially ancient traditions, is horrible at tests but can write intense and vivid poetry that expresses her deep thinking about Inuit traditions. Then there is Elli, who adores wildlife and all the flora and fauna of Canada and can create a project display with a Jell-O waterfall, containing goldfish crackers and the harmonious sounds of the true Canadian Loons in the background, but fails miserably when asked to take a multiple choice test on the same subject matter. Does Brian lack creativity because he can score excellent marks on his tests? Is Amy less intelligent because her skill in writing ends when she is forced to do oral presentations? Or is Elli a failure because she thinks abstractly and has raging test anxiety? Each student that walks through our classroom doors brings something to the table, and it is our responsibility to find their valuable addition to our learning community. Because I know that all my students shine in various areas, it is my job to make my assessments varied.

I assessed my students in a number of ways. I assessed them through daily journal writing. I assessed them on their work in class and whether or not they were on task each day. I assessed them through writing assignments; one on Inuit stereotyping where they had to write a letter to someone holding stereotypes and explain to them why they were inaccurate and detrimental; one on the newly formed territory of Nunavut using the computers, where they told me whether or not they would like to visit there on their birthday and why; one was a free-write to create a base to begin the inquiry cycle, where they wrote everything they knew about Canada; one was a poem, song, rap or short story about why people should visit their favorite province or territory. I assessed them through presentations, from the word cubes to their large group project (the museum tour guide). I assessed them through our weekly conferences. I assessed them through peer and self-evaluations. I assessed them through homework completion; browsing sheets; and in class activities, like "Say Something" and the Internet website treasure hunt on Nunavut, where each student used a laptop to search various websites gaining information on the newest territory and then applied that knowledge in answering how and why questions. I assessed them through one paper and pencil test that focused on applying their knowledge. They were allowed to use any notes they had, their textbook, and any other materials I had given them because each question required them to think critically and apply the information we had covered.

I used the RAFT approach (Role, Audience, Format, Topic) as an end of the unit assessment (see box on following page). I gave them a broad topic and then students decided what their role was, whom they were writing for, and which format they would use.

I assessed and I assessed, but to me, the thing that was the most important was using their work as a way to communicate with them. I required them to take the time to complete the assignments so I demanded of myself the same time commitment in responding to their work. My greatest enjoyment as a teacher is to see them reading the notes and comments I make on their papers and seeing their brows wrinkle as they ponder the questions I ask when seeking more thought or information. I even had one student comment to his neighbor how much he liked and appreciated the little notes. I admit it took time, many after hours at school and at home, but it was my best assessment tool. When something wasn't up to par or I wanted more, I simply asked the questions I wanted them to address and gave it back, waiting for it to be satisfactorily completed and returned. I communicated with each student this way; I got to know them personally, and it enhanced our learning community ten fold. I asked the students to keep their work in a portfolio, and periodically we went through it and looked back at progress. This was my best tool to challenge the students, by showing them what they had done in the past and helping them realize the leaps they had made during the course of the unit.

As a student teacher creating all these activities for the first time (my cooperating teacher had taught eighth grade American History and had no materials for Canadian geography), I was worried about classroom management. But using the inquiry cycle provided a framework through which I could offer my students choice, ample materials, flexibility, opportunities for individual investigation, a variety of learning activities, ample time for sustained reading, writing, and talking. Thus discipline problems were virtually eliminated. To me, the bottom line is advocating for kids and giving them every chance to be successful, to feel safe, and to be able to learn and grow. I was able to challenge my students to think critically and to find connections to the people and culture of far away places. My students joined Inuit hunters as they waited patiently, sometimes for hours outside a seal's breathing hole; they traveled with Eric the Red on his voyages to Nova Scotia; they rode alongside the Canadian Mounties as they made the streets safer for all citizens; they cheered as Nunavut gained its independence; they skied the slopes of Whistler Mountain in British Colombia; they panned for gold during the great Gold Rush of 1949; they trapped lobster and fish off the coast of Prince Edward Island; they even watched as nails were placed in the Canadian Transcontinental railroad system that mirrored the one in the United States. All these adventures and many more were made possible with books, choice, and well-planned activities within an inquiry framework.

ROLE   AUDIENCE   FORMAT   TOPIC

Now that we have seen all the wonderful, exciting places and aspects of each province or Territory, you are to pick one that you did not report on and evaluate (discuss) why that place is your dream Canadian land. You will choose a role, an audience that you are writing to, and the type of writing assignment you wish to write. Below you will find a list of roles, audiences, and possible formats for your writing.

Possible Roles:

1. You are a European traveler going to a specific province or territory.
2. You are a comedian doing a show in one of the provinces or territories.
3. You are a goose or a duck that is getting ready to fly south for the winter, but before you go, you have to write to your family in Florida and tell them all about the province or territory you are leaving.
4. You are a sports hero from a Canadian province or territory.
5. Choose your own adventure.

Possible Formats:

Letter	Essay	Song/Rap
Poem/Sonnet	Script	Speech
Short Story	Advertisement	News Column
Editorial	Memo/E-mail	Your Choice

Possible Audiences:

Teacher	Siblings	Politician
Parents	Family Member	Farm Animals
Principal	Sports Hero	Stuffed Animal
Friends	Pop Star	Family Pet
Your Choice		

Meghan Luckett

I am currently in my first year of teaching tenth grade Global Studies and ninth grade English at Portage Central High School in Portage, Michigan. My ninth graders much like my seventh graders during my student teaching experience reinforce for me that teaching is not only my chosen career, but also my passion as they bring new joy, laughter, insight, and excitement to our work in the classroom. The opportunity to write about my student teaching has helped me to look closely at my teaching experiences and to reflect on the lessons I have learned and my continuous growth into a stronger and more capable educator.

Canada: A Sample Text Set of Multiple Materials

Ash, S. (2002). *Sacred drumming.* New Delhi, India: Sterling.

Bernstein, M., & Kobrin, J. (1974). *How the sun made a promise and kept it: A Canadian Indian myth.* Illus. by Ed Hefferman. New York: Atheneum.

Bowers, V., & Hobbs, D. C. (1999). *Wow, Canada!: Exploring this land from coast to coast to coast.* New York: Owl Books/Maple Tree Press.

Brooks, S. (2000). *Canadian democracy: An introduction.* New York: Oxford University Press.

Chang, P. G., & Barlas, R. (1992). *Culture shock, Canada: A guide to customs and etiquette.* Portland, OR: Graphic Arts Center Publishing Company.

Colombo, J. R. (2001). *1000 questions about Canada.* Toronto: Hounslow Press.

Ferguson, W., & Ferguson, I. (2003). *How to be a Canadian: Even if you are one already.* Vancouver: Douglas & McIntyre.

Fleischner, J., & Fleischer, J. (1995). *The Inuit: People of the arctic.* Brookfield, CT: Millbrook Press.

Gutsole, M., & Gutsole, R. (1999). *Discovering Canadian pioneers.* Toronto: Oxford University Press Canada.

Hacker, C. (2002). *The kids book of Canadian history.* Illus. by John Mantha. Toronto: Kids Can Press.

Hall, B. G. (2001). *Spectacular Canada.* Westport, CT: Levin Associates.

Kalman, B. (2001). *Canada, the Land (Lands, Peoples, & Cultures), 2nd Ed.* St. Catharines, ON: Crabtree Publications.

Kalman, B., & Walker, N. (1999). *Canada from A to Z.* St. Catharines, ON: Crabtree Publishers.

Landau, E. (2000). *Canada.* New York: Children's Press.

Marx, D. F. (2000). Canada: Rookie read-about geography. New York: Children's Press.

Maybank, B. (2001). *National parks and other wild places of Canada.* Photographs by Peter Mertz. Hauppauge, NY: Barrons Educational Series.

Moore C. (2002). *The big book of Canada.* Toronto: Tundra Books.

Morton, D. (2001). *A short history of Canada,* 5th Ed. Toronto: McClelland & Stewart.

Must, J. (2001). *Toronto city guide.* Toronto: Firefly Books.

Parent, M., & Olivier, J. (1996). *Of kings and fools: Stories of the French tradition in North America.* Little Rock, AR: August House Publishers.

Patterson, E. P. (1983). *Inuit peoples of Canada.* New York: Franklin Watts.

Shilling, A. (1999). *The Ojibway dream.* Toronto: Tundra Books.

Thomas, D. M. (Ed.) (2000). *Canada and the United States: Differences that count.* Peterborough, ON: Broadview Press.

Ulmer, M. (2001). *M is for maple: A Canadian alphabet.* Illus. by Melanie Rose. Chelsea, MI: Sleeping Bear Press.

Chapter 3

Considering and Connecting: The Importance of Browsing and Sharing

Adaezia:	Did you know that some snakes can poison you and some snakes can crush you?
Jack:	Yeah! Like cobras bite you and . . .
Mallory:	Their venom kills you.
Jack:	My friend's cousin has a boa constrictor. It's huge. He feeds it mice and it swallows them whole. It's really cool.
Trevor:	What was that book we read in Language Arts about the cobra?
Adaezia:	You mean "Rikki Tikki Tavi"?
Trevor:	Yeah, that's it. That's about a cobra and that animal that's quick enough to kill it. I don't remember what it's called.
Mallory:	Maybe it's in here, in this book about nature.
Ms. Lawrence:	See if you can find mongoose in the index?

—*Sixth Grade Science Class*

Sitting at a small table surrounded by open books, Adaezia, Jack, Mallory, and Trevor excitedly discuss the information and pictures that have captured their attention.

They interrupt each other as they explore the texts Ms. Lawrence has pulled together into a text set of multiple materials for their study of animal classification.

In this chapter, we discuss Phase A of the inquiry cycle including:

- Wandering and wondering
- Stimulating and maintaining student interest, involvement, and commitment
- Vocabulary development
- Making connections

In the course of our discussion of Phase A of the Inquiry Cycle, we continue to illustrate our discussion with examples from Ms. Lawrence's sixth grade Science class.

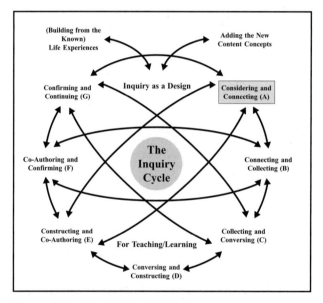

Figure 3.1   The Inquiry Cycle

Wandering and Wondering

As they begin their biology inquiry focusing on the classification of living things, the text set (see Figure 3.2) serves as the primary print resource for the unit. By giving the students the opportunity to browse the books she has selected for this study, Ms. Lawrence is putting the power of learning into the hands of each sixth grade student by facilitating their connections with the content through choice, connections with prior knowledge and experiences, and the development of interest. Rather than directing the students' progress through whole class lecture, textbook reading and recitation, worksheets, quizzes and a cumulative test format, she is giving the students individual ownership of their learning through an inquiry framework. Ms. Lawrence has told the students that for the next several weeks they will be engaged in a life sciences inquiry specifically focused on the ways in which living things are classified. She has told them that they will be doing this by comparing and contrasting different features and aspects of various groups and learning about the scientific categories.

In this initial stage of the inquiry cycle (Phase A—Considering and Connecting), Trevor, Jack, Mallory, and Adaezia have each chosen several of the books in the set and are "wandering and wondering" (Short, Harste, & Burke, 1996) by looking through the pictures, reading the captions, stopping to read sections of text that grab their attention, and informally sharing the information and their connections with it.

Berger, M., & Berger, G. (1999). *How do flies walk upside down? Questions and answers about insects.* Illus. by Jim Effler. New York: Scholastic.

Boyle, D. (1998). *Coral reef hideaway: The story of a clown anemonefish.* Illus. by Steven James Petruccio. New York: Scholastic.

Carlisle, M. W. (1993). *Let's investigate slippery, splendid sea creatures.* Illus. by Yvette Santiago Banek. Hauppauge, NY: Barron's Educational Series.

Crossingham, J., & Kalman, B. (2002). *What is hibernation?* New York: Crabtree Publishing.

Jenkins, S., & Page, R. (2001). *Animals in flight.* Boston: Houghton Mifflin.

Kim, M. L. (1992). *Polar bears and other arctic animals.* New York: Trumpet Club.

Markle, S. (1995). *Outside and inside snakes.* New York: Scholastic.

Mayes, S. (1997). *Mini monsters.* New York: Henderson.

McLeod, B. (2000). *Hunters and prey.* Illus by Antonella Pastorelli, Paola Holguin, Ivan Stalio. Woodbridge, CT: Blackbirch Press.

Parker, S. (1992). *How nature works.* New York: Scholastic.

Stonehouse, B. (1999). *Defenders.* Illus. by John Francis. New York: Tangerine Press.

Stonehouse, B. (1999). *Camouflage.* Illus. by John Francis. New York: Tangerine Press.

Figure 3.2   Classification of Living Things: An Abbreviated List

While "wandering and wondering" in *How Nature Works*, Trevor and Jack have shifted their focus from snakes to hunters and prey, and Mallory and Adaezia have moved from snakes to looking at hunters and prey, too, in a book called *Defenders*. Both pairs show an obvious curiosity and eagerness to play with the ideas, facts, and concepts in the books.

Trevor: I think it's weird how animals can change their color so they won't get eaten. Look at this rabbit—the mountain hare. It's brown in the summer and white in the winter.

Jack:	Look at that bug and that sea horse. They look like leaves.
Adaezia:	You think that's weird, look at this baby albatross spitting at that bird. It says it's some kind of bad smelling oil left over from their last meal.
Mallory:	That reminds me of what skunks do; only it's the other end.
Ms. Lawrence:	It's interesting to think about the different ways that animals and plants protect themselves. Let's think about the ways we humans have used some of these same strategies.

During this time, the four students have also been writing down some of the information that interests them on the browsing sheets Ms. Lawrence has provided. They will keep these initial browsing sheets (see Appendix 2) in their working portfolios. (See Figure 3.3 for one of Trevor's completed forms.)

Name: Trevor   **Date:**

Title of Book: Animals in Flight

Author: Steve Jenkins and Robin Page

Pages browsed: Hummingbird, Honey Bee, Flying Frog

1. **Item of interest:** on each page they compare the main animal to ones that do the same things. Like the hummingbird hovers sort of like a housefly.

   Information: hummingbirds wings act like helicopter blades

   Response/questions: I think it's cool how you can't see hummingbirds wings move and how it can hold itself in one place.

2. **Item of interest:** Other kinds of animals that seem like they can fly.

   Information: They can't really fly. They are gliders.

   Response/questions: I wonder how far flying frogs, squirrels and fish really can glide?

Figure 3.3 Browsing Sheet

While the students are engaged in browsing, Ms. Lawrence moves freely back and forth between her role as guide/facilitator and that of participant/more-experienced learner (see chapter 2 for definitions). In her role of guide/facilitator,

Ms. Lawrence interacts with her students through such leading questions and comments as:

- See if you can find mongoose in the index?
- I think that book might have a section on lizards.
- Why do you think the king snake looks so much like the coral snake? Why do you suppose nature would do that?

In her role of participant/more-experienced Learner, she shares and demonstrates question posing through such comments and questions as:

- It's interesting to think about the different ways that animals and plants protect themselves. I wonder how many of these ways we've adopted as humans?

Stimulating and Maintaining Student Interest, Involvement, and Commitment

During this phase of the inquiry cycle, it is important to stimulate and maintain your students' interest, involvement, and commitment to the inquiry. A lack of initial enthusiasm is rare. Coming into a room with books, magazines, newspapers, brochures, and so forth all over the place pique's the most resistant kid's curiosity. But, this can quickly wane without additional stimulus. Part of this is making sure that the students have a grasp of the theme or topic under study. But most of maintaining student engagement is the use of several of the following strategies for reinvigorating the wandering and wondering. Most of these begin with a teacher demonstration and then can be done by students within small groups.

Book talks

Sharing with students the genre, content, special features, and tantalizing tidbits of the materials in your text set has a tremendous impact on students' willingness to go beyond the one or two materials that initially caught their attention. Ms. Lawrence begins the second day of the inquiry on animal classification by book talking several books in an Animal Behavior series published by Tangerine Press.

As students get into an inquiry, they will want to share books with others who are investigating the same or similar topics. By demonstrating the process you use and giving them the guidelines to follow, you allow students to take ownership. This builds their independence and confidence through collaboration with peers using "adult" methods, for example, such as the book talk in Figure 3.4.

How many of you have heard of :

- a snow leopard? (many hands go up)
- a numbat? (no hands go up)
- a three-toed sloth? (a few hands go up)

(She has the pictures on the overhead and shows again the one of the numbat.)

It says here that, "the numbat resembles a big, striped squirrel and lives in southwestern Australia in eucalyptus forests." What does that make you think of? (Student responses vary and she adds her own.)

This book explains that camouflage is how many animals protect themselves from predators or hide themselves from their prey. It offers a number of examples from all over the world. The numbat, snow leopard, and three-toed sloth are among the 20 animals they show and describe. The book has a table of contents and an index you can use to find the ones you are particularly interested in finding our more about.

I'll read one more example. (She reads about the diamondback rattlesnake.)

Figure 3.4   Ms. Lawrence's book talk on *Camouflage* by Bernard Stonehouse (1999)

Purpose:

Things to include:

Show pictures or other graphics or items of interest (This can be done holding the book or by putting some of the pages on an overhead or putting it on power point.)

Figure 3.5   Book Talk Guidelines

Read Alouds

Beginning each day of a new inquiry with a read aloud can keep the flow of enthusiasm going. You can read one book for a week or so several chapters at a time; you can read several shorter books, such as picture books; or you can read excerpts from books, magazines, newspapers, or items off the internet. Encouraging students to choose sections of materials they are browsing to rehearse and read aloud to their group or even to the whole class can stimulate and reenergize even the student who is convinced he/she is bored. Also, reading what they themselves have written as a read aloud can ignite their peers' interest as well as reinforce their own interest in the work at hand.

- All oral reading is rehearsed.
- Be sure your audience knows what they are listening to (looking at) and why.
- Read the whole piece if it is short enough.
- Decide what parts you'll need to edit out if it is too long for the time allotted.
- If it is a long piece or is a book with multiple topics, read excerpts that are of special interest or importance to the concept under study.
- If there are visuals, make sure to show these.
- If there are captions that are critical to understanding the text, be sure to read these.
- Provide your audience with a way to respond: written or spoken, with others or alone.
- Complete a self-evaluation of your read-aloud.

(See *The Read Aloud Handbook,* 5th ed., by J. Trelease (2001) for a detailed discussion.)

Figure 3.6   Student Read Alouds—General Guidelines

Interviews and Surveys

Encouraging students to find out what "the experts" think or what their peers think can have an enlivening impact on their interest in the inquiry. Talking with people almost always generates the need to know more or to find out what is accurate or to delve deeper into an idea or a concept. It is often a good idea to model and practice interviews before students go out and conduct them with experts in the wider community. It is also important to stress with students issues of confidentiality and to explain that some people do not want to be named and that they need to respect that.

Interviews:
- These may be completed over the phone, via e-mail, or in person.
- Set up the interview ahead of time.
- Be specific about what kinds of information you are going to be asking.
- Have a list of prepared questions.
- Be prepared to ask follow-up questions based on the interviewees' responses.
- Have a note taking strategy in place so that you can record the information easily and quickly.
- Respect interviewees' right to privacy and confidentiality.

Surveys:
- These may be completed through e-mail, regular mail, or hand delivered.
- Set up the time to give the survey ahead of time.
- Provide the purpose and what you hope to learn from the survey in writing (or verbally) as part of an introduction.
- Keep the survey relatively short, no more than 10 questions.
- Open-ended surveys will give you more information, but forced choices may be more efficient to score.

Figure 3.7   Guidelines for Conducting Interviews and Surveys

Responding to Video Clips

Showing video clips and then having students respond to them is useful in getting their thinking going. You can demonstrate a think aloud, write a response, or generate questions and discussion. The students can do this in small groups or you can do it with the whole class. Small groups can watch video clips or students can bring in videos they think will apply and share them with a partner.

Making Connections

At the end of the first day, Trevor, Mallory, Jack, Adaezia, and their classmates are CONSIDERING the possibilities surrounding the curricular concept of classification. They are using this initial class time to CONNECT their prior knowledge and experiences with the intertextual links between and among the materials. They use various strategies:

- to think about: they think aloud, read aloud
- to talk about: they turn to neighbor, use abbreviated say something, do a one minute sharing
- to ask questions about: they use index cards and draft books
- to discover what they know about: they fill in a knowledge chart or concept map
- to share experiences about: they say this reminds me of or look at this.
- to write about the concepts, facts, and vocabulary integral to the classification of living things: they take preliminary notes or engage in a KWL
- to begin to develop questions about the classification of living things: they use exit cards and group questioning.

Knowledge Chart

As students wander and wonder, it is important for them to keep track of what they are finding and metacognitively measure their connections by determining what they know, what is familiar, and what is new. By doing this, students are building background by connecting the new and familiar with what they know.

Name: Jack		
Things I know	**Things that are familiar**	**Things that are new**
snakes are reptiles	differences between snakes lizards	lizards have eyelids snakes don't
snakes are cold-blooded	how snakes swallow whole	snakes try to catch birds
cheetahs are fastest animal on earth	three-toed sloths are the slowest	beavers have see-through eyelids

Figure 3.8 Knowledge Chart

"Say Something" and Metacognitive Awareness

Middle level students often do not understand that they should be monitoring their reading comprehension. To us, reading is meaning making; so if our students do not understand what they are reading or have read, then we find that knowing about what's on the page is a difficult task. One way we ask students to become more aware of what they are reading is through metacognitive awareness. We ask our students to "think about" what they are reading, and to become aware of when they are and are not comprehending while they read. As our students read, we suggest that they ask themselves the following questions:

- Does this make sense to me?
- Does this sound like language?
- Could I summarize what I just read?
- What is missing from this passage?
- What is the author trying to say?
- How does this connect to my own life?
- What does this remind me of?
- What other ideas are related to this?
- What else would I need to know to understand this?
- Why am I not understanding this?
- What questions come to mind from this selection?
- Could I explain this to someone else?

By asking these questions, students come to realize that what they are reading is important and that understanding what they are reading is critical to their learning. To help them with metacognitive awareness, we use a strategy called "Say Something" (Short, Harste, & Burke, 1996). "Say Something" allows students to talk through some of their thinking about the material they are consulting so they can realize that when we comprehend a text, we are thinking about it while we read. We ask questions, levy judgments, and make connections to what it is we are reading. Proficient readers rarely think about how they read; but for students who have difficulty with comprehension, "Say Something" is an excellent strategy for making meaning and the thinking that comes with it more conscious. We typically introduce this strategy as a mini-lesson and whole group activity; but with time, students learn to internalize this comprehension monitoring process.

The teacher introduces a short reading selection to the class and asks the students to predict what the selection will be about.

The teacher begins reading and after about a paragraph (teacher can decide) asks the students to "Say Something" to their neighbor about the connections they made to what was read, the questions the selection might provoke, or the responses they had to the piece.

Students talk about their connections, questions, or responses for about a minute.

Teacher continues reading and again asks the students to say something.

Students respond.

The process is completed to the end of the piece.

Once the reading is completed, teacher and students discuss the process and how their thinking was made conscious.

We typically practice this strategy with our students for a couple of weeks and then ask them to internalize. With each practice, we read longer portions of the text, but also look for places where responses may be more easily made.

Figure 3.9 "Say Something"

Vocabulary Development

As middle level students progress through an inquiry cycle, they often rely on their prior knowledge to make connections from the known to the unfamiliar. The same principle applies to vocabulary. Addressing vocabulary issues in the pursuit of content knowledge can be frustrating for students and teachers alike. Most of us don't read with a dictionary by our chair, nor would we expect our students to. We hope the text will teach us what it is referencing when we find a new word or concept, but often this is not the case. Using particular strategies to assimilate new or unfamiliar words is one way to expand our knowledge of a topic and also a way to build our vocabulary in general. (See chapter 6 for further discussion of vocabulary development.) Students, however, must become aware that when they begin a study of a topic that interests them, they may need to learn new vocabulary along the way. They can do so by being aware of new language as they read while we, as their teachers, encourage them to explore new or specialized vocabulary that is essential to the topic and to understanding it. We encourage our students to think of themselves as mathematicians, scientists, historians, geographers, and writers who are just entering the field of study that interests them for a specific inquiry. By learning the language of that field, they are becoming members of that "club" (Smith, 1998). As apprentices within a Civil War club or a wolf biology club, they need to have the language that club speaks so that others will be aware that they do have the expertise or knowledge that membership in those clubs require.

Once we have discussed this issue of vocabulary with our students, we find that they are often proud of their new language and feel a sense of ownership about what they are learning through their personal engagements.

Word Wall

Providing students with an idea of the words they will encounter in the inquiry under study is a key to their making connections in meaningful ways. The key to a word wall is that the words are constantly seen and heard and used by the students. Having a word wall up in the classroom that both you and your students can add to and use also reinforces the students' keeping a personal inquiry glossary in their working portfolios (for an example of this, see chapter 6). Reminding the students to make use of both of these is a part of guiding the inquiry in ways that support your students' continuous literacy development.

Concluding Remarks

In this initial phase of the inquiry cycle it is particularly important to provide ample time for students to wander and wonder. This time is well spent in facilitating students' deepening interest in the content concepts and broadening connections with prior knowledge and experiences. It is also significant in that it is the time when students will generate individual and shared involvement in and commitment to learning about the concepts being studied. As Frank Smith (1998) suggests, our role as the teacher in this phase is "to ensure that opportunities to engage in interesting and productive activities are always available" (p. 98). Further, he suggests that teachers "demonstrate commitment to a satisfying and absorbing activity, and have the patience and sensitivity to share their involvement with someone who is not as experienced as they are" (p. 99).

Strategies Discussed in Considering and Connecting

- Wandering and Wondering
- Book Talks
- Read Alouds
- Interviews and Surveys
- Responding to Video Clips
- Knowledge Chart
- Say Something
- Word Wall

Sixth Grade Investigations in Literacy

Carol McNally

The sixth grade "Investigations in Literacy" class was implemented through a fed-
eral GEAR UP grant partnership between our district and Western Michigan University. All sixth graders except music students take this class as one of the 9-week
classes in their exploratory rotation. I had taught sixth, seventh, and eighth grade
"reading" rotation classes for several years previously—classes that had been based
on facilitating study skills, content area reading strategies, and involving students
in independent reading workshop. The major difference between the Investigation
in Literacy class and these others was the use of the inquiry framework—an approach that I had begun experimenting with in some of the earlier reading rotation classes the year before. One of the purposes of the Investigations in Literacy
class is to support students in acquiring skill with comprehending general and
technical material as well as focusing on meaning and communication (Michigan
English Language Arts Content Standards 1 & 3, 2001–2003). More importantly,
the class would be a forum where students could "demonstrate, analyze, and reflect upon the skills and processes used to communicate through listening, speaking, viewing, reading, and writing" (Michigan English Language Arts Content
Standard 7, Michigan Curriculum Framework, 2001–2003).

The summer before the "new" sixth grade class began, the other literacy coaches
in my district, Lauren, and I met for several days to begin planning goals, objectives, and assessments for the class. We collaborated and decided upon appropriate
text sets to assemble for use in the class—text sets that would broaden our students' understandings of concepts they would be studying concurrently in their
science and social studies classes. These sets, naturally, would change throughout
the year with each new 9-week rotation of sixth graders since each group would be
studying a different concept in science and social studies when they were rotated
into the reading class. The first 9 weeks' rotation would use text sets built around
Canada and physical science concepts, the second 9 weeks would use text sets built
around Mexico, physical science, and cells/heredity in the life science area, and
rotations three and four would use text sets built around Central America/Life
Science and South America/The Caribbean, and earth science, respectively.

Each of the 9 weeks of the pacing guide was laid out meticulously—too meticulously, I would find upon implementation. But the process of putting the components of the class together in a logical fashion proved to be a worthwhile activity
for us as we pondered just what was important enough to fit into this short 9-week
class. There were, of course, non-negotiables that we all agreed upon that were laid
out from the beginning: teacher read-alouds, student rehearsed read-alouds, activities to introduce students to the concept of reading process, pre- and post-
surveys of student attitudes towards reading, mini-lessons as needed on such topics

as text features, development of vocabulary via word walls, small group discussions (literature circles), and student presentations. All of these components hung upon a framework of inquiry: book browsing, silent sustained reading in the text sets, question development, note taking, evaluation of information collected, and development of ways to share individual gained knowledge with the group as a whole so that each student could benefit from all of the others' inquiry. Intermingled within the day-to-day workings of the class lay countless opportunities for the teacher to conduct individual reading conferences with the students in the class, the purposes for which could range from clarification of some aspect of the inquiry process to miscue analysis.

The goal for the class was simple: increase students' reading comprehension processes while at the same time increasing their confidence in their own literacy skills. The objectives, as they were met, would all contribute to this goal. Student rehearsed read alouds, silent sustained reading of informational text, information gathering and sharing with teacher modeling as needed, and summary writing would all contribute to the students' increasing literacy expertise.

During the first 9 weeks of implementation, I attempted to meet the lofty expectations of our comprehensive pacing guide. What I found, however, was that the pacing guide seldom allowed me to be responsive to my students' needs. What if the students needed a mini-lesson on "re-reading for context to support vocabulary development" in week two, rather than week three where it was originally scheduled? What if some students were ready to give preliminary presentations to the group in week four rather than in week six? Right away, I learned that, though the component parts of the pacing guide were always important "pieces" to keep in mind as I taught the class from day to day, the order, even whether or not particular things were "taught" (my last group proved to me early on that they were proficient in using an index, no need for that mini-lesson) had to depend upon the needs of my students.

Another reality I had to face the first year of this class was the fact that there were not always, despite the generous funds provided by the grant which allowed this class to be developed in the first place, enough books available on the topics we had decided the students would inquire into because the content teachers were using them as well. This was *not* a big problem! It meant that the content teachers were valuing the use of inquiry via text sets in their classrooms, too! This has been an easy dilemma to assuage. For example, when the social studies teachers have the "Canada" text sets in their classrooms, I have my students doing inquiry with a text set built around the indigenous people of the Americas. Since indigenous peoples is a related topic, the information gained from this inquiry helps broaden the students' understandings of their study of Canada.

I learned that first year that a single text set—as opposed to the multiple text sets (i.e., "Mexico, physical science, and life science") we had originally planned on providing for our students—was much easier for me to manage and easier for the students to deal with, than providing them with too many topics and books from which to choose at one time. With a single text set built around a single theme or topic, students find small group discussions much easier to participate in. Students share books with each other more often, especially once they've internalized what each student is researching. And whole-group mini-lessons can be drawn from texts that are directly related to the concept that the students are *all* reading about.

Though I tweak the flow of the class with every rotation, a typical day in sixth grade "Investigations in Literacy"—a 50-minute block—class might look something like the schedule shown in Figure 3.10.

- Teacher Read Aloud—15 minutes
- Sustained Silent Reading Time—15 minutes
- Work Time—10 minutes
- Discussion Time—5–7 minutes
- Debriefing Time—3–5 minutes

Figure 3.10 Daily Schedule for Investigations in Literacy Class

Class Begins Daily With a Teacher Read-Aloud

I've found that this should be a high-interest text, probably at a more difficult level than the typical student's independent reading level so as to allow for plenty of opportunity for the teacher to use the "think aloud" strategy to point out her own interactions with the reading process as well as to allow instances for the teacher to encounter new vocabulary which she subsequently models "figuring out" via use of context clues, root words, prefixes, and so forth. This is in keeping with Vyygotsky's (1978) "zone of proximal development" wherein students are supported by the teacher in experiencing the use of strategies that are just beyond what the students would have a grasp of within the realm of their own individual independent reading strategy repertoire. Words may be extracted from the teacher-read aloud for display on the word wall.

Currently, I am reading Nancy Shore's (1989) biography of Amelia Earhart to my class. Word wall words we have gleaned from this text include: aviator, aviation, transatlantic, transpacific, and transcontinental. Through teacher read-aloud time, I can effectively model reading strategies for my students. For example, every day, I model and emphasize the strategy of going back a few paragraphs and re-reading some of what I read yesterday to get me back into the mindset of the book as I begin my read-aloud time. This is a strategy that I encourage them to also use as they begin their independent reading. Recently, I asked my class to tell me what reading strategies they have observed me using during read aloud time. Besides the above-mentioned "backing up strategy," they brought up re-reading until it makes sense, reflecting (their word, I swear), connecting to other information they know, and looking back in the book to make connections or just to remember specifics. I let them in on a "secret" strategy that I use when I'm reading out loud: When I miscue, sometimes, instead of going back, I re-word the rest of the sentence so the syntax is maintained and it doesn't sound like a miscue. I promised to let them in on my "secret" the next time I did this when reading aloud! Of course it wasn't long before that happened. While reading aloud about Teddy Roosevelt to the class, I said, "One of his good friends, a reporter who was traveling with the Rough Riders, wrote stories that made headlines." The actual text, however, had said, "One of his good friends, a reporter, was traveling with the Rough Riders, and when this reporter wrote stories, they made the headlines," (Fritz, 1991). My initial miscue was to insert "who" after "reporter." Subsequently, I unconsciously made further corrections to syntax in the sentence so it would end up making sense. Kids need to know that doing this is okay. They need to know that good readers do it all the time without even thinking about it. Teachers who point this out to their students will help their students become more confident oral readers.

I have the students keep a reading log in which they write down a few key things from the read-aloud each day. Once a week, we do shared writing of a topic sentence that pulls together the week's log entries. Then the students each complete their summary paragraphs from the notes in their logs. When the read-aloud is complete, the students then have four or five

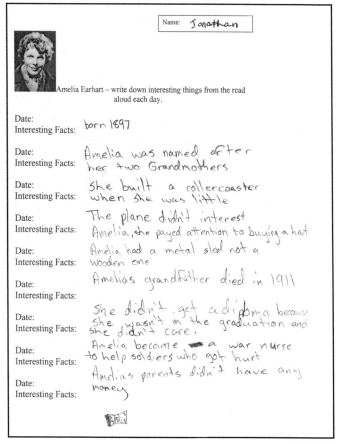

Figure 3.11 Example from Amelia Earhart read aloud

chronologically-arranged summary paragraphs that they revise and proofread. The result is a summary process paper that is used as a model for other summary writing the students do on their topics from the inquiry.

Teacher Read-Aloud Time is Followed by Silent Reading Time

The students know to move right into this as soon as their log entries are complete. Once the students have browsed the available books in the text set and decided on what they are interested in reading and finding out more about, time is reserved daily for individual, silent reading. I have learned that focused time for ONLY reading needs to be provided daily. During this time the students are JUST READING! They're not working on notes. They're not conferencing with a member of their discussion group. They're not simply book browsing at this point—they are participating in quality sustained, silent reading. Books are open, eyes are on texts, and the room is quiet. As this time begins daily, I also read silently in the book I've chosen from the text set. After a few minutes, when students are settled into their books, I use the time to do one-on-one reading conferences for a myriad of purposes including miscue analysis, oral retellings, and just talking with the students, one-on-one, about the problems and successes they're experiencing with their books. During this time, students use sticky notes cut to about half inch lengths to mark places they want to come back to during work time.

As a side note—but a very important one—I've often seen other teachers I've worked with, in my capacity as the building literacy coach, end up very disappointed with the results of their students' inquiry endeavors when they, the teachers, don't provide significant time for sustained silent reading in the books from the provided text set. One science teacher that I have been working with on using multiple materials to integrate inquiry into his science classroom has now done a life science inquiry 2 years in a row where students use multiple materials to research body systems. This year, he mentioned that he wasn't as happy with the results the students ended up with. The projects seemed to lack depth. They just weren't, as he put it, "quality." We put our heads together and analyzed the situation and found that, probably because he felt more confident doing this sort of inquiry this year, he rushed the process along faster than he had last year. He allowed students to jump right into note taking and working on their final projects (posters about the various body systems) after they had devised the questions that would guide their inquiry, without designating a specific amount of time daily where the kids would just read silently—just ponder the information without having to write anything down, free to re-read and peruse the text in pursuit of their interests. This science teacher came to a hard-learned understanding that silent reading time is imperative in sustaining a quality inquiry cycle.

Work Time

This is a broad category, but it does sum up what the students are doing during this time after silent reading, depending upon where they are in the inquiry cycle. Some students may be taking notes using graphic organizers, two-column notes, or answering questions they have written about their various topics. Some students may be drafting summary papers on their topics. Other students may be working on visuals (posters, overhead transparencies, or tangible items such as ship models or clay figures) that they will use in their presentation of what they have read about to the class. Some students may be working on the computer, looking up extra information or putting together a Powerpoint presentation to share with the class or their group. This might also be a time when a mini-lesson on a related literacy skill or strategy might fit in well for a small group or the whole class.

Currently, my students are all reading biographies. I developed a graphic organizer based on elements of biography that Margaret Mooney (2001) outlined in her book, *Text Forms and Features: A Resource for Intentional Teaching.* As my students fill in information on these biography graphic organizers, they are internalizing the elements of biography so when they do their culminating project and actually write biographies, they know what types of information should be included (see Figure 3.12). You may be thinking that this seems a particularly small amount of time to spend on "working." But, I assure you, that students who are focused on what needs to be done (i.e., they know what sections of their graphic organizers are not filled out yet or they know what questions from their SQ3R notes are not yet answered) and who have spent quality time reading to gather information are able to accomplish a great deal of "work" in this short amount of time, especially given the fact that they will be sharing this "work" with their peers during discussion time.

Discussion Time

This is also a broad category. Some days the students may participate in literature circles to discuss what they've been reading. Some days we may have a whole-group discussion. Often, the students will do rehearsed read-alouds for their peers in which a student reads a portion of the text he or she has been reading. The student has chosen a particularly significant portion of the text and has rehearsed reading it before he shares it with the class. Rather than impose the kind of tangible fear and dread that "round robin" reading may cause, students enjoy doing rehearsed read-alouds and particularly enjoy answering questions that their peers may ask about the text. The "rehearsed" aspect of this strategy recently came to fruition when Patricia, a sixth-grade student who was involved in a literature circle discussion with her peers, wanted to share an excerpt from her text with the group. Before she would read it aloud, she said, "Just a minute. I need to look it over first before I read it out loud to you." She has made this strategy her own!

Another reading strategy that I have had students use is reader's theater. Whether performing a student- or teacher-developed reader's theater, preparation time focused on "maximum dramatic effect" always yields an enjoyable read-aloud experience for the students who read, as well as for the students who make up the audience for the reader's theater. One rotation of sixth graders I worked with earlier this year

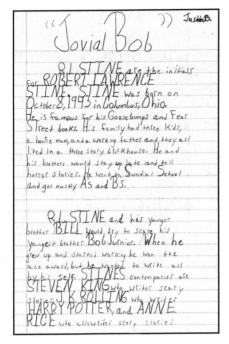
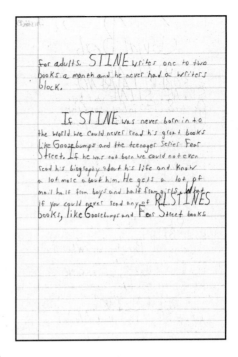

Figure 3.12 Biography Graphic Organizer

was using a text set on indigenous peoples in the Americas. Several students lifted lines from the readings and put together reader's theaters on the "Three Fires." (For those of you not familiar with the Ojibway, Odawa, and Potawatomi groups of Michigan, this is a good opportunity for you to do some inquiry of your own!)

Debriefing Time

This is a time to reflect back on class as a whole group and verbalize the thinking skills and the social skills that the students used that particular day to be successful or not so successful. This is an approach Harvey Daniels (2002) advocates in the second edition of *Literature Circles: Voice and Choice in Book Clubs & Reading Groups*. Daily reminders about using particular learning strategies as well as using good manners and group skills reinforces the goal of working together to create the kind of classroom we all want and brings a comfortable closure to our class day.

The first year I taught this class, I put great emphasis on the students' "final presentations" of their findings from their inquiries. Much time was spent in preparing visuals or computer presentations, and several days at the end of the class rotation was needed for making formal presentations to the class. And that was OK. But now I'm much more inclined to have the students do several "mini-presentations" as they work their way through the inquiry cycle. For one thing, this allows more time for the inquiry itself—and that's the thrust of my class. "Mini-presentations" take the form of many of the activities I've already described: reader's theater performances, rehearsed student read-alouds after which other students have the opportunity to ask questions of the reader, literature circle discussions, and so forth.

Grading for this class is simple. Our district uses a computerized grading program that automatically calculates grades consistent with the parameters input by the individual teachers. "Daily assignments" (as I've specified they be called in my grading program) are worth one point (graphic organizers, note sheets, etc.). If the student does the daily assignment, she gets the point. "Projects" are worth anywhere from 10 points (for doing simpler projects like rehearsed read-alouds) to 25 points (for say, the biography project where the students had to read a biography, complete a graphic organizer, write a summary process paper and read it to the class, and create some type of visual aid to accompany their oral presentation). These larger projects are scored via rubrics that the students are made well aware of at the beginning of the project. In fact, the students are often involved in developing the rubrics for the projects. When all the points are tabulated in the end, the percentages that calculate the final "grade" follows the traditional scale. Students are asked to self-evaluate many times throughout the course of the class as well.

In short, what I've found from teaching this class is what I've really known all along: The best way to become a better reader is to read more. To that end, I've used the inquiry framework to provide as much independent reading as possible while still making sure that the supports that students need to grow as readers (such as teacher modeling and focused writing and discussion) are firmly in place. Students increase their literacy skills by reading and writing in meaningful contexts for real purposes.

Carol McNally

I am a Literacy Coach at Springfield Middle School in the Battle Creek Public School District. Formerly a Title 1 teacher, I have had extensive training in and experience with coaching teachers in their quests to embed authentic literacy practices into content area teaching and learning. A fellow with the Third Coast Writing Project arm of the National Writing Project, I have facilitated professional development in literacy/inquiry focused instruction within my district as well as other districts in Michigan.

Biography and Autobiography: A Sample Text Set of Multiple Materials

Allen, P. G., & Smith, P. C. (1996). *As long as the rivers flow: The stories of nine Native Americans*. New York: Scholastic.

Cart, M. (Ed.) (2003). *Necessary noise: Stories about our families as they really are.* Illus. by Charlotte Noruzi. New York: Joanna Cotler Books.

Coburn, B. (2001). *Triumph on Everest: A photobiography of Sir Edmund Hillary.* New York: Scholastic.

Cooney, B. (1996). *Eleanor.* New York: Viking.

Dahl, R. (1984), *Boy: Tales of childhood.* New York: Puffin Books.

Dingle, D. (1998). *First in the field: Baseball hero Jackie Robinson.* New York: Hyperion Books for Children.

Douglass, F. (1845, 1989). *Narrative of the life of Frederick Douglass, An American slave.* New York: Anchor Books.

Dungworth, R., & Wingate, P. (1996). *The Usborne book of famous women.* Illus. by Nicholas Hewetson. New York: Scholastic.

Engel, T. (1996). *We'll never forget you, Roberto Clemente.* New York: Scholastic.

Freedman, R. (1997). *Out of darkness: The story of Louis Braille.* New York: Scholastic.

Freedman, R. (1987). *Lincoln: A photobiography.* New York: Scholastic.

Fritz, J. (1994). *Around the world in a hundred years: From Henry the Navigator to Magellan.* Illus. by Anthony Bacon Venti. New York: Scholastic.

Fullick, A. (2001). *Louis Pasteur.* Chicago: Heinemann Library.

Haskins, J. (1992). *One more river to cross: The stories of twelve Black Americans.* New York: Scholastic.

Hopkins, L. B. (Ed.). (1999). *Lives: Poems about famous Americans.* Illus. by Leslie Staub. New York: HarperCollins.

Krull, K. (1996). *Wilma unlimited: How Wilma Rudolph became the world's fastest woman.* Illus. by David Diaz. San Diego: Voyager Books.

MacLeod, E. (1999). *Alexander Graham Bell: An inventive life.* New York: Scholastic.

Palacios, A. (1994). *Standing tall: The stories of ten Hispanic Americans.* New York: Scholastic.

Pinkney, A. D. (1994). *Dear Benjamin Banneker.* Illus by Brian Pinkney. San Diego: Voyager Books.

Rockwell, A. (2000). *Only passing through: The story of Sojourner Truth.* Illus. by R. Gregory Christie. New York: Alfred A. Knopf.

Stanley, D. (1998). *Joan of Arc.* New York: Morrow Junior Books.

Stanley, D., & Vennema, P. (1992). *Bard of Avon: The story of William Shakespeare.* Illus. by Diane Stanley. New York: Mulberry Books.

Weidt, M. N. (1994). *Oh, the places he went: A story about Dr. Seuss.* Illus. by Kerry Maguire. Minneapolis: Carolrhoda Books.

Weiner, E. (1992). *The story of Frederick Douglass, voice of freedom.* Illus. by Steven Parton. New York: Dell.

Chapter 4

Connecting and Collecting: The Importance of Personal Engagement

As David begins to read, he finds himself lost in the words—the ink spots—on the page. What is a silo? Where could he find one in Tucson? How would a silo help his life? How does it connect to what he knows? He understands the questions he should ask himself: How does this information connect to other texts he has already read? How does it connect to his world? How does it connect to his life? David can't answer these questions, however, because he doesn't know what a silo is, nor does he think he's going to need one in the near future. He knows he could find the answer in the dictionary or by asking a teacher or friend, but David really doesn't care what he will find out. He doesn't care enough about silos, the book he is reading, or the subject of the arms race, nuclear war, or missiles to find out. And he has no personal experience with silos to make any heartfelt connections to the topic he's been required to research.

Students like David make up a large portion of middle level content classrooms across our nation. They have difficulty becoming engaged with many of the topics they are asked to study because they lack the interest or the prior knowledge it takes to understand why the information should or could be important or of interest to their lives. Their teachers—finding content material not only a curricular essential, but personally engaging—become frustrated when their students lack the passion that often accompanies real learning. We must remember, however, that students need to connect current learning to their existing schemas (Anderson & Pearson, 1984) as well as their own interests or experiences. They, too, need to become personally engaged with the content under study. Teachers can create a correspondence between their students and the learning by creating inquiry experiences that evoke or provoke student interest or that connects the content to their lives, their world, or to something they already know. Such scaffolding (Bruner, 1990) constructs a springboard from which students can begin to inquire about the content and how it will enrich their personal or academic lives.

John Dewey (1938) suggests that "the participation of the learner in the formation of the purposes which direct his activities in the learning process" (p. 67) is of primary importance in education. Heeding this advice, we explore how teachers create classroom environments that allow for student choice under an umbrella concept that addresses students' inquiry questions or interests. We also share how teachers can use mini-lessons to teach their students how to locate and to record the information they access as they progress through their personal engagements with the content and materials they select and study for their inquiry research.

In this chapter, we discuss the importance of attending to students' prior knowledge, scaffolding their learning, and addressing students' interests and experiences through:

- Connecting Through Personal Engagements
- Preparing for Personal Engagements
- Collecting Information Through Personal Engagements

Our illustrations and examples come from Mr. Taylor's seventh grade Social Studies class.

Figure 4.1 The Inquiry Cycle

Connecting Through Personal Engagements

When middle level students are involved in the inquiry process, they work with their peers, their teachers, and with the community. They also work individually in what we call personal engagements, which allow students to document what they are learning, ponder the information, refine their question or topical interest, or question or problem pose in relation to their inquiry interest.

Personal engagement is a necessary part of learning. When we plan an inquiry around an umbrella concept or theme for our students, we want them to become personally involved in the topic (see Figure 4.2). We know, however, that they may need some personal time to reflect upon the topic or to generate an intriguing question within the topic parameters after they have wandered and wondered through the multiple materials we have gathered for the inquiry. Thus, really thinking about what they want to learn or discover is one of the most crucial elements of personal engagements.

An umbrella concept or theme is a word or phrase broad enough for students to generate any number of particular inquiry topics under it. For instance, the term interdependence could have students inquiring about global interdependence, symbiotic relationships in the animal kingdom, the necessity of family, alliances during war and peace time, the food chain, and so forth.

Figure 4.2   Umbrella Concept or Theme

Another decision students have to make during personal engagement involves how they will collect the information they want to learn. Determining their reading process and comprehension, and what questions to ask about their reading, is of critical importance during personal engagement time. It is at this time, that we plan for mini-lessons on note taking, record keeping, and "how to read a book" for information.

During personal engagements, students may also make decisions about working in pairs, working individually, or working in small groups—if the teacher hasn't already made this decision. We often decide the student grouping that we would prefer when planning a particular inquiry, but we also will negotiate with students who wish to work outside those parameters.

Ultimately, this stage of the inquiry process is when many crucial decisions are made; and students often have to have reflective time to ponder these decisions. Personal engagement, however, is not only about how to study or with what type of group to research. It is also about becoming involved with the topic itself. So, during personal engagements, students are also involved in reading and transacting more deeply with the materials available.

The Importance of Transaction

Many of us think of reading and learning as individual, solitary activities. Yet, when we think about what knowledge is and what books contain, we realize that there is always a "someone" at the other end. There is an author, who presents to readers the information she has found or the passion he wishes to share. Thus, even while middle level students may read alone, they are engaged in what could be considered a conversation with an author's text, which is an extension of the author. Even in the most solitary reading of a text, then, there is an aspect of the social involved (Vygotsky, 1978). The conversation that exists between an author's text and a reader underlies the theory of transaction (Rosenblatt, 1995).

With the theory of transaction, the reader and the text "condition" one another. The reader is changed by the reading of the text, and the reader according to the reader's prior knowledge and experiences interprets the text. The reader and text come together to create what Rosenblatt (1978) called "the poem," which means "new creation" in Greek (see Figure 4.3). Each reader brings something different to the reading and, thus, creates a unique text or "poem." It is this new creation that readers respond to, not the actual text itself, because they respond to what they have created. That is why young people as with all readers can read the same book or essay and get different meanings from it. They can also have different stances toward a text or topic before they even begin to study it.

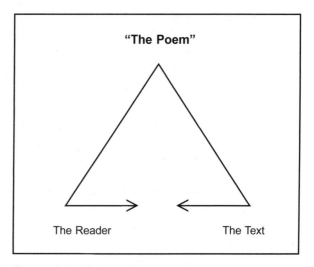

Figure 4.3 Transaction

For instance, when Mr. Taylor asked his seventh grade social studies students to read about ancient Egypt from the textbook, many of his students complained that "there is nothing interesting" about Egypt. Mr. Taylor then presented a series of book talks (as discussed in chapter 2) about trade books that addressed specific topics about Egypt, including a smart little book entitled, *Mummies, Tombs, and Treasure: Secrets of Ancient Egypt* (Lila Perl, 1987). His middle level boys found the book fascinating. Their fascination created a change within them, and they were then able to consider other aspects of ancient Egypt that at first eluded them. Many of Mr. Taylor's female students, however, did not find a book on mummies and tombs as interesting as the biographies of the famous pharaohs and queens who ruled Egypt. They found the books *Cleopatra* (Diane Stanley, 1994) and *Nefretiti and Cleopatra: Queen Monarchs of Ancient Egypt* (Julia Samson, 1990), as well as information about Ramesses, Akhenaten, and Tutankhemen much more interesting than treasure and tombs. Mr. Taylor's students found different aspects of Egypt engaging and would frequently ask how authors could write about so many different parts of one topic. This is the connection between individual reading, response, and stance. Although we may like only the tomb and treasure aspect of ancient Egypt, or the battles of the Civil War era, others will find alternate facets of the same time period more stimulating. Such is the connection between authors and readers—they both find similar ideas or features of a subject of interest, and they converse about it through the text the author has written.

We wish to note that although Mr. Taylor's students did divide somewhat by gender for their selection of inquiry interests for ancient Egypt, gender did not play a large role in their overall interest in the time period. Both boys and girls were equally attracted to their peer's findings as they progressed through this particular inquiry.

The critical aspect of inquiry that we emphasize involves combining students' personal interests and their literacy development. Although we suggest that students should begin with a personal interest and response to the subject under study, this does not mean that teachers should remain within the realm of the "personal" when teaching. We have discovered that middle level students need to realize how learning is contextual, and that the concept of "knowing" often fits within parameters of a larger community. Middle level students are old enough and sophisticated enough to recognize that some knowledge and ways of knowing (Belenky, Clinchy, Goldberger, & Tarule, 1986) are more privileged than others. They also need to confront the ways in which that knowledge is presented. And while we say this, we also encourage our students to feel free to voice their responses to what they are learning in ways appropriate for the classroom. Furthermore, we encourage our students to embrace the reality that not all people think alike, nor should they.

In an inquiry curriculum, where so many of the classroom engagements allow students to discover, first for themselves and then for others, new understandings about their interests, the need for reader-response is especially salient, as are the multiple ways in which students can respond.

The Importance of Reader Response in an Inquiry Curriculum

Reader response is the practice of allowing readers to first find what the piece means to them personally before attempting to find an accurate answer (Rosenblatt, 1995). Allowing for a more spontaneous response to the words on the page gives students a sense of ownership about their thinking and reading. It also paves the way for learning about multiple perspectives and the diversity found within the experiences and understandings that others bring to the text. When students work either alone or in groups on inquiry projects or through a classroom inquiry curriculum, they think through and discuss what they are learning. In response, they understand more deeply that which they have read.

Rosenblatt (1995) suggests that "when the young reader considers why he has responded in a certain way, he is both learning to read more adequately and to seek personal meaning in literature" (p. 67). We find this is a necessary part of the inquiry cycle since it allows middle level learners to realize what they know and to ask questions that push their learning further. Part of the process of coming to know, however, has to do with the metacognitive practice of identifying what it is we think we know before moving on. Thus, through engagements that encourage them to address their learning and reading, middle grades students are able to better understand what it is that they are discovering and constructing (see Figure 4.4). This in turn strengthens the learners' confidence, independence, and stamina as they are motivated to pursue that which may at first be confusing or difficult.

We use the word "constructing" because knowledge is created by people, and not just facts looking to be found. We use the word "discovering" because there are times, however, when we do discover what others have theorized, hypothesized, or created. For instance, students will discover that the earth is round, yet they may construct their own ideas of who, when, and how ancient peoples came to inhabit their areas of the world.

Figure 4.4   Constructing vs. Discovering Knowledge

Just as in our example of how Mr. Taylor's students constructed personal responses to texts on ancient Egypt, we find that when students are given the opportunity to respond to what they are reading, they are also discovering knowledge. They are discovering the content knowledge of social studies while also realizing how they may have constructed that knowledge based upon their own prior understandings (see Figure 4.5).

When students realize that they learn new information based on what they already know, they become more connected to the learning process. We often explain to our students that new material needs to connect to material they already know. Thus, building and accessing students' prior knowledge is a vital element of teaching. Short, Harste, and Burke (1996) assert that "learning is a process of searching for patterns that connect. We learn something new when we can make a connection to something we already know. When there are few or no connections, learning is difficult and easily forgotten" (p. 537). By asking our students the following kinds of questions, we can discover what their prior knowledge is and what we need to do to get them to the place where the new information they are learning will remain with them:

- What does this remind you of?
- What do you know about (particular topic)?
- Why would someone care about (particular topic)?
- What experiences have you had with (similar topic)?
- When I say (concept or topic), what comes to mind?

Figure 4.5   Importance of Prior Knowledge

Since we all bring something different to a reading, it is important for young people to understand that their own perspectives and ideas about a topic are heavily based on what they already know or think about a topic. For instance, before the boys in Mr. Taylor's class actually read the book *Mummies, Tombs, and Treasures* (Perl, 1987), Mr. Taylor asked them to write in their journals about their interest in the book. In their journal entries, a number of boys included information they had gleaned from "Raiders of the Lost Ark" along with other information about Egypt and pharaohs they had learned previously. Jackson, one of his students wrote the following in his journal:

> When I think about mummies and tombs and treasures they all go together for me because only rich people like queens and pharaohs got to be buried in like the pyramids. I don't know what happened to regular people. I think sometimes the servants of the rich people also got buried ALIVE with the pharaohs. I would hate that. But the other stuff I think about is "Raiders of the Lost Ark" and how they found all that treasure in the tombs. Why didn't people try to rob the tombs right after the pharaoh was dead? I think maybe there was some superstitious stuff involved, and traps, too, like in the tombs from the movie.

Mr. Taylor was not as concerned about what misconceptions his students had as he was excited about letting them discover for themselves some of their own misconceptions—their own faulty prior knowledge—through the reading of the book. Because they recorded their new findings and their reflections throughout their reading, his students' journals became a record for their discovery of knowledge along with how their misconceptions were corrected or their correct assumptions were validated. Through their journal writing, along with other strategies in which students can engage while involved in personal engagements with the multiple materials, middle level students can discover and construct knowledge that will broaden their own thinking and add to the expanded thinking of their classroom community. They are also continually developing the four efficacy elements. With validation their confidence strengthens; with discovery, their independence expands; as they correct the misconceptions, their metacognition deepens; as they focus ever more intently on their ideas, their stamina increases.

Preparing for Personal Engagements

As middle level students become interested in their own inquiry questions or topics, we have found that many need to be guided in their learning processes. What do they do? How do they record what they are learning? How are they expected to respond to what they are learning? These questions often become the topic of a class discussion, which we find is an essential part of scaffolding students' abilities to learn independently and along interests they have created. Preparing our students for personal engagements requires that we teach them about the materials available to them along with strategies that will support their learning. It is also about creating a learning environment where students have choices about what to study with an affirming teacher presence.

An Environment That Values Choice

With an inquiry curriculum, we find that our students are more involved in curricular decision making and negotiating. We may plan an umbrella topic or theme for our students to work within, but they make choices about what particular aspect of that theme most interests them. They also choose how to go about collecting information, what materials to use for that collection, and then how to present their discoveries or new understandings to their peers or other community members. We find that if we allow our students choice, most respond responsibly (Smith & Johnson, 1993). We do, however, guide our students' learning by helping them select an inquiry question on occasion as well as facilitating their decisions about how to collect data and what type of format their inquiry presentations will take (see chapter 7).

Our classrooms are frequently arranged in small group seating with areas where students can meet together as well as work independently when necessary. We also use library carts full of books or periodicals that our students can consult, and we also line our black/white boards with evocative book choices so our students will be sure to see them.

We encourage classroom meetings so our students can discuss issues or ideas with each other (see chapters 6 and 9). We also discuss—and on occasion renegotiate—classroom expectations before embarking on each inquiry cycle. Our students are prepared to work independently as well as collectively because we discuss "the rules" as a class at the beginning of the year.

By allowing choice, we do not suggest that students are given the liberty to not work or to not be responsive to the classroom community. "Respect" is our guiding principle: Respect yourself, each other, the teacher, and the learning that is created here. And while this principle may sound too vague for many teachers, we found that by talking about what respect may encompass, our students rarely pushed the limits of cordiality or appropriate classroom etiquette.

Multiple Materials for Inquiry

Our emphasis on text sets, theme sets, and literature clusters in chapter 2 does not go unfounded as all of these acknowledge multiple perspectives—differing perspectives on the content—and address the multiple reading levels within the classroom. The use of multiple materials available through different text combinations allows students to read and to learn at their independent reading levels while also inviting them to read materials that are written at a variety of reading levels (see

Figure 4.6). We have found that a reader allowed to choose their own material for reading can actually read at a higher reading level. We also suggest, however, that many texts written for "younger" audiences be presented in a middle level classroom. Picture books and beginning chapter books such as *Witch Hunt: It Happened in Salem Village* (Krensky, 1989) are great resources for middle level social studies classrooms.

We are often perplexed by the concept of reading levels since we find that middle level students, like all readers, will read a variety of materials as long as those materials address their needs or interests. Thinking of schooling, however, and how books are leveled according to concept load, grammatical structure, content, and vocabulary, we find that middle level readers read across a wide spectrum. Some of our students have difficulty reading texts written on their grade level, others can read far beyond the texts normally purchased for their grade level. When we select materials we look for books that can be enjoyed and used by all students, regardless of their reading proficiency.

Figure 4.6 Middle Level Students and Reading Levels

Finding a theme set that presents diverse perspectives also helps middle level students develop the critical literacy skills so necessary for the twenty-first century (see Figure 4.7). By selecting and presenting books that give opposing viewpoints, teachers scaffold student consumption of all types of texts. For instance, the book *Encounter* (Yolen, 1996) gives an account of Christopher Columbus from the Taino perspective. This deceptively simple picture book is a perfect example of a perspective that confronts our common ideas of Columbus' discovery of America.

Students should also become informed about how time periods produce particular viewpoints. This is also an aspect of the social construction of knowledge.

Critical literacy is the combination of decoding the words on a page as well as the social and cultural context of that particular text (Comber & Simpson, 2001). Comber and Simpson suggest that this usually means that students think about and question such ideas as:

- What or whose views of the world, or kinds of behaviors are presented as normal by the text?
- Why is the text written this way? How else could it have been written?
- What assumptions does the text make about age, gender, and culture (including the age, gender, and culture of its readers)?
- Who is silenced/heard in this text?
- Whose interests might best be served by the text?
- What is the author trying to say?
- How could the ideas about the topic be challenged by the reader?
- Who is the primary audience for this material?
- What other kinds of ways could this material be read/interpreted? Why would someone read/interpret this material in another way?

Figure 4.7 Critical Literacy and Middle Level Students

Books written in the 1950s are considerably different than books published in the late 1960s or early 1970s. Some ideas are more acceptable at different time periods than others, and middle level students would do well to understand this reality and perhaps why this happens.

Collecting Information Through Personal Engagements

When middle level students first begin an inquiry, they are expected to wonder and wander through materials that can help them solidify their inquiry question or interest (see chapter 3). Once they have selected a particular interest, they start to collect information that will help them to answer their question or to understand the topic in more depth. Yet, as many of us know through our own inquiries and our own studies, there can be a lot of material to wade through before we find what we really need or want. Most adults are adept at skimming and scanning texts, as well as browsing through materials to find what we need. Middle level students, however, still need help with their searching through materials. They also need help with how to record their findings and thinking about the information once they have located it. As part of this stage of inquiry, we use several strategies to help our middle level students with their data collection. We also address their metacognitive awareness for comprehension monitoring. It does middle level students little good to find a text that addresses their inquiry interest but is incomprehensible or inconsiderate.

Reading Text Structure for Skimming/Scanning/Browsing

Skimming and scanning is a strategy that allows a reader to review material rapidly with the intent of finding particular information. When students are interested in a particular topic, usually a textbook is not the best source to use for collecting data or information. Textbooks, however, are often accessible to middle level students in content classrooms, and there are trade books that cover much more of the topic than students would need for their inquiry question. We find that many of our middle level students have difficulty finding what they are looking for in reading material because they have not been taught that skimming and scanning is all right, nor have they been taught how to read an expository text by its structure (see Figure 4.8).

If middle level students are guided toward an understanding of text structure, they will be able to skim and scan material more quickly, thus becoming more efficient researchers and information gatherers. When teaching text structure, we find expository materials that present information in the five most common ways, but

Text structure is the organizational pattern that expository materials often follow to present information (Mooney, 2001). Just and Carpenter (1987) assert that texts "have both a content and a structure, with the knowledge of both entering into the comprehension process" (p. 241). The five most common text structures are:

- Simple Listing
- Chronological or Sequence Order
- Compare and Contrast
- Cause and Effect
- Problem/Solution

Figure 4.8   Text Structure

we also explain to our students that many authors use more than one organizational pattern or text structure to present information. Thus, we point out the language that authors use to give clues to the type of structures they are using. The lists in Figure 4.9 will help students determine the type of text structure they are referencing while skimming and scanning:

Sequence/Chronological	Compare & Contrast	Cause & Effect or Problem & Solution
First, second, third, etc.	Yet	Since
Next	Likewise	Because
Beginning with	In comparison/in contrast	As a result
Finally	Conversely	The outcome
Before	Other	Subsequently
After	Less than/more than	Consequently
Previously	Least/most	Therefore
Now	Similarly	If . . . then
Later	However	Due to
When	But	Accordingly

(Alvermann & Phelps, 2002)

Figure 4.9   Types of Text Structures

Power Notes

We help our students learn about text structure and how to find the information they want by introducing them to a modified form of Power Notes (Buehl, 2001), a strategy that helps students learn how to classify and to organize information. Power Notes can also be used to teach the skill of outlining when students want to subdivide the information they are gathering. Students are first asked to find the main idea of the material they are reading (Power 1). They then find examples or elaborations of the main idea (Power 2), and then they are asked to extend those examples or elaborations one step further (Power 3). Finally they are asked to give characteristics of the main idea (Power 4). From Power Notes, students can develop an outline or a concept map of the information. From the map or outline, they can then create an essay for use in their inquiry presentations. Figure 4.10 is an example of Power Notes that Mr. Taylor shared with his social studies students when they were studying the pyramids of ancient Egypt.

Name:	Date:
Topic: Building a Pyramid	
Reference: (include page numbers)	

1. Planning for a Pyramid
   2. Preparing the site
      3. Leveling the ground
      3. Site along the west bank of a river
   2. Finding the materials
      3. Granite from the River Nile
      3. Stones from a local quarry
   2. Having special arrangements
      3. Stone masons to cut the stones and granite
      3. Clay ramps to drag the stones up
      3. Water trenches to create a level surface
4. Pyramids were used to bury Pharaohs and Queens

Concept Map of Information:

Figure 4.10 Power Notes

Mr. Taylor asked his students to read information on the pyramids: What they were used for, who built them, and how they were built. The students were not asked to read the entire text, but to look at the headings and bold print of the material they were using. Then working together with the class, Mr. Taylor created an overhead (Figure 4.10) so his students could see how the information they gave him from their skimming and scanning could be organized into Power Notes. From their Power Notes, his students then had a choice about adding more details to create a concept map.

An important aspect of this strategy is that students can develop Power Notes from a variety of sources. Once they feel they have gathered enough information, they create an essay or presentation from the Power Notes they have gathered. And since each time they develop Power Notes students are expected to list the reference or source of information, they already have their bibliography started.

Question and Problem Posing

During personal engagements when students are reading for their individual interests, they still need to be critical consumers of those texts. We often find that when middle level students find something of interest to them, they voraciously ingest the materials without any real critical thought. By asking our students to be aware of how their interests may suspend their ability to disbelieve or to more objectively ponder a text and the author's perspective, we can alleviate some of the issues that result from texts that may lack accuracy and authenticity (see chapter 2).

One strategy we use for question and problem posing is a modified "Say Something." (See chapter 3 for a discussion of the original "Say Something.") Rather than "saying" something about what students read, we ask them to "question" something, such as the following:

- What perspective is not being represented?
- What is the dominant group represented and what does that group have to gain?
- Would this bother me, if it were happening in my country, town, neighborhood, home, family? Why or why not?
- What particular language does the author use to discuss this topic, and why would that matter?
- What is not being said in this material?

For problem posing, we ask our students to generate a list of problems that are embedded in the material. These problems could be about how the material is written, what group gets to speak and what group does not; or the problems can result from the content itself. For instance, when discussing Manifest Destiny, the problem in many texts is that the Indian populations are not represented. Other problems with the topic of Manifest Destiny could include:

- The lack of concern over the buffalo and how that effected the ecological balance of the plains
- The conditions of traveling across the country and how advancements such as the railroad produced further discrimination

- The attitude that expansion was just and right regardless of how many peoples were debilitated from it
- The issue of how to live with those the American government had "conquered"
- The lack of a balanced plan that would be democratic in terms of governance

When students are asked to question and problem pose from the materials they read, they are often at a loss when first beginning this kind of activity. Mr. Taylor worked with his seventh graders using the picture books, *Katherine and the Garbage Dump* (Morris, 1993) and *The Wartville Wizard* (Madden, 1993) to discuss not only the obvious problems in the book but also the embedded problems. These two books deal with trash and how it is handled within two communities. The obvious problem in each text is the garbage or the trash that people drop in inappropriate places. Yet, there are other problems that each of the main characters in these books must work through or recognize.

To help scaffold his students' ability to identify problems in the texts, Mr. Taylor read each book aloud, occasionally stopping and asking, "Is there a problem here? What is it?" After pointing out problems to his students, Mr. Taylor gradually turned over the responsibility of identifying the problems within other picture books so his students would learn to work independently on finding problems in other materials. Working in small groups, his students listed problems that occurred throughout each of the books and then discussed the underlying problem that caused the obvious problem. Often, the underlying problem had to do with people's attitudes and how they thought about their community and world.

By learning to question and problem pose, we find that middle level students become much more conscious and thoughtful readers. They engage the material more deeply and more personally, which is the purpose of personal engagements with inquiry topics and the texts that inspire their interest in learning.

Working Portfolios/Inquiry Journals for Note Taking, Record Keeping, Reflection, and Vocabulary

Creating journals that allow students to freely write their responses to what they are learning serves several purposes. Journals contain a record of what students have read, what they find of interest, how they respond to that information, and the new ideas that develop from their reading and response. For our middle level students, we created several journal formats to help them address what they have read, what they find of special interest, and how they respond to that reading. One format, Power Notes (Appendix 3) allows for note taking, another for a reflective journal (Appendix 4), a third for record keeping (Appendix 5a) and a Check List for Record Keeping (Appendix 5b).

Reflective Journal

This format allows students to pause and gather their thoughts, while also checking the information they have already collected. Since we find learning is a constructivist process where students build knowledge rather than simply collect it and retell it verbatim, middle level students need to be encouraged to think about their learning and how it connects to other ideas they have learned about or to experiences in their lives (see Appendix 4). We typically ask our students to write a reflective journal entry once a week throughout the inquiry cycle. We also know they need more guidance with this format, so we plan part of our time on Fridays for this activity. Students are asked to think about what they are learning and how it affects them, their community, or their world. We also ask them to connect what they are learning to other learning experiences. Finally, we ask them to think about the negative and positive aspects of this topic now that they have researched the topic in more depth.

With reflection, we hope our students will become more thoughtful and critical consumers of knowledge and of the materials they use. We also want them to see how what they are learning is of importance, and that the manner in which they go about this learning will help them in the future.

Record Keeping Journal

Typically, we ask students to create journals out of notebook paper and either three-ring binders or clip folders. We do this at the beginning of the year; and to teach them how to use this format, we often make the entry sheets for them. Later in the year, if they decide that the binder is too cumbersome or they need to think more about being organized, some students will use a spiral notebook to keep their journal all of one piece. Other students may decide to keep their journals on a computer disk, and so they will use a word processor to create their journal format and entries. Russell, an eighth grader who loved working on and with computers, kept his journal on a disk as well as on his hard drive at home. Figure 4.11 shows one entry from his inquiry journal during his interest in Muhammad Ali. Through the use of a computorized journal, Russell found that he could "make mistakes on the bibliography information and still not waste paper." We agree, but realize that not all students have access to computers.

As part of the "What I Read" section, Russell included bibliographic information. We ask our students to do this so they will eventually learn to think in terms of how a book is the creation of an author, is considered a source for inquiry, and thus must be referenced. By completing bibliographic information as part of their inquiry journals, middle level students come to understand how bibliographic information is formatted. We also include a place in this format where students can write further about what they are learning once they meet with others in pairs, small groups, or as part of a whole class discussion.

Name: Russell	
Topic: Muhammad Ali	

Information:	Response:
1. Muhammad Ali is from Louisville, Kentucky.	1. I would never expect him to be from Louisville. I thought he would be from New York City or another eastern place.
2. He was against the Vietnam War, and that made the government against him. They tried to get him to enlist in the army, but he wouldn't do it, so they took away his boxing title.	2. A lot of people were against the war, but because he was a black man while the Civil Rights was going on, he was in danger. I don't know if I could have said anything against the government or if I would be willing to go to jail for not fighting in a war.
3. His name was Cassius Clay before he became a Muslim.	3. I wonder if everyone who becomes a Muslim has to change their name or if they just want to?
4. Muhammad Ali used words to make people know that black was beautiful.	4. I still think people need to know that black is beautiful. Sometimes I think there is still a lot of racism in America.
5. As a member of the Nation of Islam he didn't feel like he had to integrate with white people, even though he did not hate white people.	5. Why do people always want to separate themselves because of their color? In the 1960s, life wasn't fair to black people so I kind of understand that. But why are we still having the same problems today?

What I Read: Myers, W. D. (2001). *The Greatest: Muhammad Ali*. New York: Scholastic.

What Else I Want to Know:
1. What was Muhammad Ali like when he wasn't in public?
2. When was his last fight?
3. Do people who become Muslims have to change their names?

Figure 4.11 Record Keeping Journal

We also ask our students to log what else they want to discover or find out. This section is the reason we call this a record-keeping journal. If they fill in the dates on each of these entries, they have a record of what they read, what they learned, and what other information they want or need for their inquiry research. This "record" then allows them to keep track of their progress through an inquiry. As a follow-up for record keeping, we also ask students to list all the information they want to gather or learn, and then check it off as they put it in their record keeping journal (see Appendix 5a and 5b).

Vocabulary Journals

Another type of journal we like our students to keep is a vocabulary journal. While not specifically an inquiry journal like the three journals we have previously discussed, this journal is still an essential part of an inquiry curriculum. Students are asked to be aware of words as they read; and when they encounter unfamiliar words, we ask them to write them in their journals and then share these new words with the rest of the class.

Writing the words in their journals, however, will not help our students learn new vocabulary. We also ask them to log the source of the word and what they can discover from the context. Thus, we are not asking them to look up words in a dictionary, but rather to think about the words as they are used in their reading materials.

Mr. Taylor rewards extra credit points to students who can "stump the teacher" with their new vocabulary. Often as the class begins, he asks if his students have a new word that they feel can "stump the teacher." Consistently, one or two students have a word they would like to share as well as use to attempt to earn extra credit points. This activity takes less than 5 minutes, and Mr. Taylor finds that his students feel a sense of pride when they can teach him something new.

We also create thematic word walls (see chapter 6) from the words our students discover as they progress through their inquiries. We arrange the words by themes, sub-themes, and often by their parts of speech. This way we feel our students learn not only how the word is used in a particular context, but also what kind of word it is in that context. With each new inquiry, our students generate more and more specific language that convinces them they are becoming members of the "clubs" (Smith, 1998) they may wish to join as adults.

Concluding Remarks

Personal engagements are an essential part of the inquiry process. When teachers create an environment where students are encouraged to ponder and question texts in ways that are personally meaningful to them, life long learning is often the result. Through such valuable experiences, middle level students learn that knowledge is its own reward, and that their interests have validity. Regardless of the topic or content, teachers can utilize personal engagement as a way of highlighting curricular mandates while also addressing the needs of the young adolescents who enter their classrooms. Furthermore, as middle level students personally engage with materials that reflect their inquiry question or interest, they find that reading and reflecting upon that reading are valuable skills to take with them as they continue in school and in their lives.

Strategies Discussed in Connecting and Collecting

- Skimming and Scanning
- Identifying Text Structure
- Power Notes
- Modified Say Something
- Reflective Journal
- Record Keeping Journal
- Vocabulary Journal

Eighth Grade Social Studies

Vicki Sellers

Inquiry is alive and well in my eighth grade classroom! When I take the time to stop and reflect on it, I marvel—not at its presence, but at how well it works. I recall my earliest experience with inquiry and remember wondering what role I would serve once my middle school students actually began their journeys into the unknown. Thoughts like "I guess I'll get caught up on my own paperwork" or "Gee, I may actually have an idle moment!" floated deliciously in my head. Little did I know that neither of these two ideas would surface—rather, I now realize how inquiry works, even in my small town classroom. In my seemingly limited rural setting, inquiry improves my role as a teacher and my students' roles as learners.

Once my "job" of exposing my kids to a general topic area is complete, I needn't think that my work is done. Yes, an exciting ride of unknown experiences awaits me! While some of my students seldom call on me for help, others make good use of my name, calling, "Miss . . ." or "Hey, Ms. Sellers . . ." this or that. I am available for whatever their needs may be; and, believe me, their needs often are wide in range, but never boring.

For example, Brooke, one of my inquirers, skeptically approached me about researching racist organizations in America and asked to interview a cross section of our school district's students and faculty. A social teen, she explained that people and their ideas would serve well as her major resource, but she worried that I would require her to limit her search to our school's library or to the Internet for her investigations. My own skepticism attacked my thoughts as I recalled Brooke's usual literal interpretations, her benign skill at worksheet-styled assignments, and her usual place as the last one to get a joke's punch line. I thought, "Oh my gosh, I can just see her running all over campus with the tape recorder, interrupting classes, and generally having a good old time while accomplishing nothing!" Then I put my fears aside and realized that Brooke's social needs had to be a part of her learning. Seeing real interest in her eyes, I found myself saying, "Okay, let's see what you can do!"

Surprised when I agreed to her request, Brooke became an investigator and our local expert on racism, surpassing her past levels of learning because she made her inquiry experience a personal one. Later in her search, Brooke uncovered information in our school's library and on the Internet that supported her interview findings. Because I allowed her to begin searching in the here and now of her social world, Brooke enthusiastically used high level thinking, sought parallels between racism's present and past, and applied historical facts and ideas to her interviews. In a traditional setting, Brooke may not have reached the pinnacle of understanding of racism in America; but thanks to inquiry, this eighth grader pulled out all stops to learning.

As a leader, I make sure that many sources are available for my students' use. In some cases, teachers may feel limited by the school's library sources; but I feel that, at the very least, students can explore there and find successful footholds of information, even in a small school library like ours. I work closely with our school librarian, Sherry, and discuss possible selections with her before my classes visit the library. When we arrive, she offers displayed books, magazines, and videos that pertain to possible topics of interest and warmly welcomes us to browse as long as we desire.

Browsing freely, some of my students have only a vague notion of interesting topics to investigate, but I remind myself to be patient at this stage. After all, not everyone is a Brooke whose interests and needs are certain. During our investigative library visit, I, too, wander about searching out topics that interest me, and I often find myself bumping into students or helping students locate information. I ask them questions about their interests and willingly share things that excite me, and together we seek and explore topics. This freedom to explore is not often felt by our kids, but the experience can be an exciting one. I can still hear one of my students, Isaiah, mention his plans to investigate slavery, change to his basketball hero, and finally resolve to research his inquiry topic, Jesse Owens. Enthused and confused by choice, Isaiah had difficulty in narrowing his research topic and did so only after taking the time to explore many topics.

Like Isaiah, Bobby expressed his interest in researching the African Slave Trade. Even our small library contains loads of pertinent information; and after 2 to 3 days of exploration, Bobby's discovery of the slave ship, *Henrietta Marie*, finally surfaced. Having begun his search with encyclopedias, reference books, biographies, trade books, and other non-fiction sources, Bobby first gained a foundation of information about the African Slave Trade before launching into his narrowed topic of the slave ship.

Who would have expected that students in our small library would parallel the proverbial kids in a candy shop? Yet, if allowed and encouraged to follow their noses, my students find that even a rural school's library is just such a candy store, not a limited resource but a place of almost limitless opportunities.

At some point during their inquiries, my students leap into their familiar world, the Internet, almost enthusiastically out of control. Before they bound off into its unknown, I remind them to look for credible sources and to document sources used. Yes, this is a problem area—teens who hear me do not necessarily follow my instructions! This situation may be complicated by the fact that the speed at which my students surf the Net is almost faster than the speed of light, or at least it would be if our server could keep up with them!

While I sometimes worry that they may disregard sources or may not maintain accurate lists of inquiry sources, I notice that with each inquiry process my students improve in this area. Perhaps providing them a folder in which to keep their printouts and other information helps prevent overlooking or losing sources, lack of documentation, and so forth. Also, I have issued index cards and required that students list source information on them, much as I did back *in my day.* Although this process worked for me, and still does, it seems outdated for them and is often left incomplete, lost, or undone. Several of my eighth graders have resolved this problem by copying and pasting their source addresses, quotes, and so forth into a document that they save in their own folder or on a disk. This works very well as long as the technology is in working condition. Yeah, right . . . only in a perfect world! As I see it, nothing is perfect and references and documentation have always been a challenge for teachers and students, but we must not let these challenges stop us from valuing inquiry research.

Other complications with technology can also be overcome with patience. One such hurdle is our school's strict filter. My student, Cass, had received little of value from the Internet about his topic, the Ku Klux Klan. Not exactly sure what he wanted to know, Cass felt frustrated and almost halted his search before it began. Why the frustration? "Bess," the filter, wouldn't let him explore searches for KKK due to connections to Nazis and other such topics. Agreeing that such restrictions are ridiculous, I helped Cass by rephrasing the query to "racial crimes," "racial discrimination," or "prejudice." Also, I shared a PBS site, *Forgotten Fires* by Bill Moyers. There Cass read and viewed an interesting clip about church burnings in the South. Finally, Cass's knitted brows smoothed, we congratulated each other with high fives; and I smiled as I heard him sharing his topic's information with his classmates.

Another search challenge proved difficult for Jay, an eighth grade inquirer. While using his own software at home to compose a "wowee" presentation about John F. Kennedy, Jay IM'd (Instant Messenger) me while I was online at my home computer one night. Searching for the Zapruder clip online, Jay wanted to find it in order to evoke an emotional response from his audience. As we both searched online, we continued chatting, and when I finally located the clip's site, I warned him of its graphic nature and that he might not want to use it in his presentation. Together online, we shared our emotions about the violent assassination of our nation's President Kennedy. Leaving Jay to explore and resolve things on his own, I wondered how this clip would affect his inquiry. Would he include the full clip for shock value or would he use the clip to expose his audience to truth, that death by assassination is a violent and horrific act? At school the next morning, Jay hurried by my door to tell me that the clip was not compatible with his software, but that he had found another one that worked and was also a legal source. This information brought smiles to both of our faces, and the outcome of his inquiry greatly moved his audience and demonstrated Jay's significant integrity and achievement in inquiry.

Near the end of my students' inquiry process, I always schedule a visit to Texas Tech University's library to locate additional information and to expose my kids to an academic world outside of our small rural school. After a morning tour of TTU's campus and a yummy dormitory lunch (ranked an A by my students!), we spend the afternoon in the library's modern computer lab led by a capable employee. Described as a "cool dude" by one of my students, the employee quickly teaches my kids how to use the library's search engines, to locate articles, to print documents, and to email the information to themselves or to my school email address. This field trip has become an annual daylong rite of passage for all of my eighth graders and validates the importance of inquiry research to our students, faculty, and administration.

As always, I have a few students who just cannot find the perfect resources for their inquiries. Recently, Rita complained to me that she had found quite a bit of information on the Internet, but our school and city library had no books about her topic, Faith Ringgold, the African-American artist. To overcome this obstacle, Rita and several other eighth graders traveled with me after school to again, the TTU library. Having done an online search, we had printed a number of possible books to find and take to my classroom for investigation. Not only did we find biographical information about Rita's topic, we located two videos about Ringgold. That night, our library experience took us up and down the elevators to many stacks of books, computer labs, and reserve desks and now we recall it as an evening of great fun. In fact, I am sure that my "Shh-h-h's" and our stifled giggles still echo throughout Texas Tech University's library. As we drove away from Texas Tech University's parking lot, I listened in the dark to my vanload of eighth graders sharing their giggles and their plans for higher education—I felt shivers of excitement tingle my spine, and I glowed with their hope.

I love feeling my students' excitement from inquiry-based learning. I feel their empowerment and academic growth as they ride the helm of their own educational experiences, and I also note their improved personal attitudes about themselves and education's purpose in their lives. Yes, I have taught without inquiry in my classroom and survived, feeling confident that I taught my students well. Now, I cannot imagine teaching without inquiry. Teaching with it helps my students make their own discoveries, and more importantly, ignites their enthusiasm for learning. As a teacher, using inquiry with my eighth grade students ignites, within me, hope for them all.

Vicki Sellers

I teach seventh and eighth grade students at Crosbyton Middle School in Crosbyton, Texas. With my M.Ed. in Language Literacy Education from Texas Tech University, I approach my Language Arts and Social Studies classes as opportunities for inquiry and social learning. As a teacher-researcher, I value the role educators can serve in motivating students to engage with the world that surrounds them through literacy.

Prejudice and Discrimination: A Sample Text Set of Multiple Materials

Bartoletti, S. C. (1996). *Growing up in coal country.* Boston: Houghton Mifflin.

Bunting, E. (1994). *A day's work.* New York: Clarion.

Bunting, E. (1988). *How many days to America?.* New York: Clarion.

Coerr, E. (1977). *Sadako and the thousand paper cranes.* New York: Putnam.

Coleman, E. (1996). *White socks only.* Illus. by Tyrone Geter. Morton Grove, IL: Albert Whitman & Company.

Cooper, F. (1994). *Coming home: From the life of Langston Hughes.* New York: The Putnam & Grosset Group.

Dash, J. (1996). *We shall not be moved: The women's factory strike of 1909.* New York: Scholastic.

Denenberg, B. (1991). *Nelson Mandela: No easy walk to freedom.* New York: Scholastic.

Denenberg, B. (1990). *Stealing home: The story of Jackie Robinson.* New York: Scholastic.

Dooley, N. (1991). *Everybody cooks rice.* Minneapolis, MN: Carolrhoda Books.

Ellis, D. (2002). *Parvana's journey.* Toronto: Groundwood Books.

Ellis, D. (2000). *The breadwinner.* Toronto: Groundwood Books.

Freedman, R. (1994). *Kids at work: Lewis Hine and the crusade against child labor.* Photographs by Lewis Hine. New York: Scholastic.

Filip, Z. (1994). *Zlata's diary.* New York: Penguin.

Haskins, J. (1998). *Separate but not equal: The dream and the struggle.* New York: Scholastic.

Hesse, K. (2001). *Witness.* New York: Scholastic.

Hesse, K. (1997). *Out of the dust.* New York: Scholastic.

Hoose, P. (1993). *It's our world, too!* Boston: Little, Brown.

Jeffers, S. (1991). *Brother eagle, sister sky.* New York: Dial.

Jimenez, F. (2001). *Breaking through.* Boston: Houghton Mifflin.

Jimenez, F. (1999). *The circuit.* Boston: Houghton Mifflin.

Lorbiecki, M. (1998). *Sister Anne's hands.* New York: Dial.

Meltzer, M. (2001). *There comes a time: The struggle for civil rights.* New York: Scholastic.

Meltzer, M. (1988). *Rescue.* New York: Harper & Row.

Miller, R. (1997). *Richard Wright and the library card.* New York: Lee & Low Books.

Park, L. S. (2001). *A single shard.* New York: Dell Yearling.

Strasser, T. (1981). *The wave: The classroom experiment that went too far.* New York: Dell Laurel Leaf.

Tillage, L. W. (1997). *Leon's story.* New York: Scholastic.

Volavkova, H. (Ed.) (1993). *…I never saw another butterfly…: Children's drawings and Poems from Terezin Concentration Camp 1942–1944.* New York: Schocken.

Warren, A. (2001). *We rode the orphan trains.* Boston: Houghton Mifflin.

Wood, D. (1992). *Old turtle.* Duluth, MN: Pfeifer-Hamilton.

Yolen, J. (1992). *Encounter.* San Diego: Harcourt Brace Jovanovich.

Chapter 5

Collecting and Conversing: The Importance of Talk

"Wait, wait! I wasn't paying attention. I was thinking about my book."

"I was just talking about how World War II isn't only about Europe, but about Asia, too. My book talks about what happened in the Philippines."

"Do you think as much bad things happened there as in Europe?"

"I can't say, but bad things happened all over the world during that time. I think we can sorta compare it, but not really."

"Yeah, but we should probably know about it."

It is through contact with others that we can begin to expand our knowledge of the world, to understand how others come to know and to negotiate what seems reasonable and good for the community. This is the essence of democracy. Learning as and through inquiry is central to schools becoming places where democracy is practiced. And thus, the social aspects of democratic learning—dialogue, negotiation, choice, and multiple ways of knowing—are necessary parts of a middle level classroom where teaching for a more responsive and responsible citizenry is desired. Contained within the concept of democratic teaching is Dewey's (1938) emphasis on experience and learning as an educative endeavor where the "most important attitude that can be formed is that of desire to go on learning" (p. 48). In an inquiry-focused curriculum, students have the opportunity to negotiate what subtopics or sub-themes they would like to study under the broad concept established by the content area, district curriculum, or teacher.

Selecting a topic by groups or as individuals, students still need to discuss what they are learning with others. They need to ask questions about their topic of interest, and they need to share with others what they discover with their questions. The social aspect of learning is an integral part of the inquiry cycle that allows students to discover their questions, pose those questions to themselves and others, and then have the time and space to investigate what they desire to know. Taking students' "wonderings" and creating within them the desire to know more about that idea, thought, or question is one of the primary purposes of education (Dewey, 1938). Inquiry as a social process allows individuals to investigate the topic from a personal context while also broadening their understandings by engaging with others who have different perspectives, ideas, and beliefs. Talking about what they each know, students can expand the collective knowledge of their classroom community. They share their passion, their interests, their questions, and their emotions.

In this chapter, we discuss the social needs of adolescents and the social aspects of inquiry and how to use these to enhance student learning. Using a number of middle level student examples, we discuss:

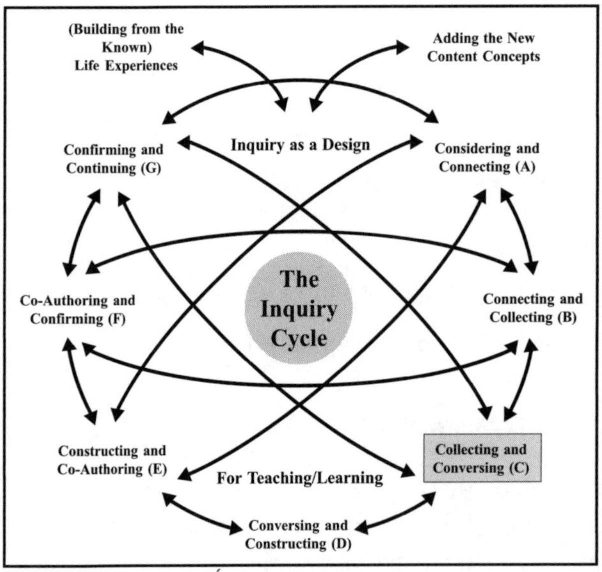

- Literacy as a Social Practice
- Reader Response and the Dialogic of Critique
- Enhancing Literacy Development through Social Engagements
- Comprehension and Social Construction of Knowledge
- Comprehension Breakdowns and Social Learning

Figure 5.1   The Inquiry Cycle

Literacy as a Social Practice

Peterson and Eeds (1990) assert that "where language and learning are concerned, other people are important. . . . Being together with others in a place outfitted for learning enhances opportunities for students to encounter the world through interesting, complex, and critical ways. It is through contact with others that meaning becomes intelligible to us" (p. 80). When we read books, periodicals, essays on the Internet, or excerpts from an encyclopedia, we respond to this knowledge and want to share it with others. With this sharing comes an "intensive experience . . . that support readers in thinking critically about books" (Short, Harste, & Burke, 1996, p. 479) and the information books contain.

Because the process of reading is a social activity and because social development is at its greatest during this time in their lives, we suggest that middle level students be given invitations to verbally share their discoveries with the classroom community. Through curricular engagements that encourage them to respond to what they are reading and learning, middle level learners deepen their comprehension of the material at hand and learn appropriate ways to share their understandings within the classroom. Through the use of dialogue in an inquiry curriculum, students develop a greater understanding of what they have read, what they might feel about that information, and a keener idea of how others think about similar content. Learning to share their ideas, however, is often a difficulty that middle level students can overcome with classroom engagements that encourage their talk. Responding to and sharing their reading with others, however, are integral parts of students' meaning-making and literacy learning.

Responding to what they have read in their textbooks, on the Internet, in an essay, periodical, or novel allows middle level learners to work through what they are reading and learning. They are able to tell themselves and others what they are learning, thus presenting what they comprehend while also "going deeper" into the topic. Through conversations and dialogues with others, students are responding to the topic under investigation while also evaluating, synthesizing, and connecting this knowledge to their own prior knowledge. Through this public discourse with others, students learn how to discuss their knowledge in appropriate ways and the ways in which informal presentations of "knowledge" can be critiqued by themselves and others. The following example illustrates how three sixth grade students, working together through discussion, come to understand the book *Tenement: Immigrant Life on the Lower East Side* (Bial, 2002):

Alicia: This book is different from anything I know, like, the way the people lived.

Cherie: I live in a house with my mom, and we live by ourselves, so I kind of thought of that when I saw that one picture with the woman and the baby.

Robert: This book reminds me of where I live. My family lives in an apartment with all these other families and sometimes it just seems too crowded. I can smell the food from down the hallway, and you can hear people walking around all the time.

Cherie: Oh! That reminds me of the people who lived in the tenements. We have people who came over from Mexico in our neighborhood. So, if they weren't living with their family on my street, they might live in a crowded apartment, too.

Alicia: Do you think there are still tenements in the world? I kind of think of these places for during a time before I was born, like way back before even my mom was born.

Robert: I bet there still are places like that, but we just don't call them that anymore. On one of these pages it tells what they looked like, and maybe we don't have buildings like that anymore.

Cherie: It says on page 12 that "with little or no space between the jumble of buildings and few windows, tenements were dark and airless." I think we have places like that in bigger cities, but not where we live.

Robert: I don't know. I think where I live is pretty dark, but I'm not sure what it means by airless.

Alicia: I don't know that, either. People need air to breathe. I think we should ask about this when the group comes together.

Through this brief excerpt, we can see how these three sixth graders made connections between their own lives and the content of the text they were reading. The students also realized that some of the words they thought they knew didn't seem to make sense in the passage they were reading. Thus, another strength of literature circles is the way they naturally create ways of looking at language usage and vocabulary.

Reader Response and the Dialogic of Critique

Responding to literature from a personal perspective is one way middle level students become engaged in what they are reading. Too often young people feel the need to find the correct answer or discover what they will be tested on that they no longer find reading a pleasurable activity. This happens all too often when students read the informational texts that are so critical for literacy learning and learning through inquiry in the same ways they read their text books. With all the extraordinary informational texts available to middle level students, it is disconcerting to see them resist reading. Yet, with a few strategies that allow for them to respond to their reading in a social environment that invites dialogue, middle level students can be drawn into engagements that push their thinking, enhance their comprehension skills, develop their abilities to critique their own perspectives, and motivate them to read further.

Allowing students to first respond to what they have read, and to then share it with others, opens up a dialogic relationship that welcomes critique. Students may share what they think, feel, or discover in a text while also being part of the larger social context where others may feel, think, or discover something different. Learning to share responses in an arena of discovery, expanding our understandings of the text, or of those within the classroom community, can be exciting but challenging for middle level students and teachers.

The following four strategies address ways in which middle level students can personally respond to the texts they read while also preparing to share with others. The first two strategies can work together in one binder, spiral notebook, or in one computer file. We often ask students to create separate journals for each inquiry they undertake so the information they are gathering or constructing doesn't become overwhelming or confusing.

Dialogue Journals

As we discussed in chapter 3, journals serve multiple purposes throughout the inquiry cycle. Another way middle level students can use their inquiry journals is by creating spaces for dialogue with others in their classroom community. Since the format of the inquiry journal is situated on one sheet of paper, when students decide to "dialogue" with one another through their journaling, we ask them to use the back of their papers for dialogue. If the dialogue continues beyond the back of one sheet of paper, students simply add more paper to this entry. If they are using a spiral, the students just continue to write on the following page. Because beginning to dialogue on paper, needs as much guidance as when students are talking in class, we created a form for students to use at the beginning of the year when they are going through their first inquiry cycle (see Appendix 6).

For example, Russell and Tony, two eighth graders in Texas, worked together on an inquiry project about Muhammad Ali. Reading different texts, they dialogued with each other about their findings. Thus, they were able to "go deeper" in their discussion of the boxer. Although many middle level students would rather verbally communicate than talk on paper, this paper dialogue becomes a record of information that can be used later in other parts of the inquiry cycle.

Individual or Topic Quotes

Another strategy that works well within an inquiry journal is a modification of a strategy called Character Quotes (Buehl, 2001). Although this strategy works with both fictional and real-life individuals, we use the same strategy for actual individuals only or text quotes about a specific topic such as volcanoes or the Holocaust. We use a similar format to the inquiry journal entries, but add a space where students can create a generalization from the quotes they collected (see Appendix 7). This strategy helps students gain deeper understanding about fictional characters or actual individuals. Students find quotes that can be either from speeches made by the characters or individuals or as part of an author's description. They list these quotes and then create a generalization or a personality profile from these quotes that describes the character and that character's place within a work, or examines an individual and the work that person accomplished in their time period or realm of accomplishment, such as science or math.

Because inquiry projects often involve an examination of the important people who were instrumental to that body of knowledge (e.g., wolves in Yellowstone) or to a particular time period (i.e., Benjamin Franklin during the Revolutionary War), by looking at particular information that either an author uses to describe a character or that the individual said, students can garner better insights into the person they are studying or the context in which the individual worked or lived. Figure 5.2 is an example of how Rita, a sixth grader studying Sojourner Truth, filled out an Individual or Topic Quote entry for her inquiry journal. Buehl (2001) suggests that middle school students be given an "opening stem of a template to assist [them] in organizing..." (p. 39). As students begin to work with generalizations, we find this to be especially beneficial. With the help of her teacher, Rita used this template to create a generalization of Sojourner Truth.

Topic: *Sojourner Truth*

Bibliographic Information: *Adler, D. (1994). A Picture Book of Sojourner Truth. New York: HolidayHouse.*

Quotes taken from Text:

1. *Isabella hated the way slavery tore families apart.*

2. *She said, "The rich rob the poor and the poor rob one another."*

3. *She preached on religion, spoke out against slavery, and stood up for the rights of women.*

Generalization: *Sojourner Truth* is/was the type of person/thing who/that *worked against slavery and injustice. She worked for the right thing for all people. She was for social justice.*

Other traits/aspects of this person/things include(d): *She wasn't afraid to sue white people if they did wrong things to her. She had five children and was married. She died in November and wanted white people to stop discriminating against black people. She wanted all women to have equal rights it didn't matter if they were black or white or Hispanic.*

Figure 5.2 Individual or Topic Quote Form

Jigsaw Reading and Response

A third strategy that middle level students enjoy is the jigsaw reading strategy. Students divide up the reading of a particular text by the number of members in their group, read their sections independently, and then meet together in a small group to discuss the text as a whole. We have found that at the beginning of the year it is better for the teacher to assign sections to particular students. As the year advances, students can self select the sections as they become more comfortable discussing their readings with each other. As part of the independent reading, we ask our students to summarize their reading and write their responses before meeting with their classmates so they are prepared to discuss their ideas with others. We also move about the room and talk the selections out with students who may be challenged by the reading material.

When students meet in a small group (typically between 4 to 6 students), they share what they have read and their responses to it. Students take turns sharing their summaries and responses with the rest of the group; but before moving on to the next group member, other group members are invited to respond to what the first group member has shared. Each student is encouraged to respond before moving on to the next reading section.

When they are just learning how to summarize and share responses with others, middle level students may not know how much to explain. Often they can't decide what is important or not. We ask them to select three things of interest and to respond to those on a short form we developed for this new work. We call this a "Summary and Response Form" (see Appendix 8), which is a scaffolding tool only. Students do not use this for long since we encourage them to write the information they are learning in their inquiry journals. Figure 5.3 is an example of Rita's summary and response form that she created during a unit on social justice.

On the bottom of the Summary and Response Form, we include a space for students to fill in information that they learned by discussing the reading with others. We incorporate this element into the form because we want our students to learn that other perspectives are valuable and that, as students, they can expand their thinking by listening to what others have to say about a topic or person. Too often students come to discussion with the idea of reporting rather than constructing knowledge. This space pushes them to think and respond to those with whom they talk.

Topic: Sojourner Truth

Points of Interest:	Response:
1. Her real name was Isabella and she traveled when she got free from slavery so she called herself Sojourner.	1. It would be fun to change your name to a different one so it could mean something. If I changed my name I think my mom would be sad.
2. She said women should take their rights not just sit around and talk about them.	2. How do people just take their rights when they aren't as strong as other people?
3. She sat where she wanted on a street car and soon the blacks and whites sat together and this was in the 1800s.	3. I thought that Rosa Parks was the first woman to make integration between whites and blacks during the Civil Rights times.

Ideas From Others:

1. Everybody's name means something. I just don't know what my name means.

2. Sojourner Truth was the first black woman to sue a white man and win.

3. She was born a slave and her freedom was bought by a Quaker who didn't like slavery.

4. She sued a newspaper because it said she poisoned a religious leader when she didn't. She won and got $125. That was a lot of money during those times.

5. She thought that freedom from slavery didn't mean freedom from poverty or hate because black people were still poor and white people still hated them during the time when she lived.

Figure 5.3 Summary and Response Form

Questioning the Author/Text

This strategy we use with middle level students to facilitate their critical thinking and their understanding of perspective. It can also be used to help students negotiate difficult text materials (Beck, McKeown, Hamilton, & Kucan, 1997). To question an author or a text, students need to understand that someone is behind the writing. Thus, discussing authorship is often the first step students need to take when reading. Typically, there is biographical information about an author on the copyright page of a text. Students can then either do Internet research to find out more about an author, or they can hypothesize about what type of person would write about the subject found within the text. Once students feel comfortable with the concept of authorship, they are better able to question the intentions of that person.

To scaffold this strategy, we listed the questions suggested by the strategy creators on a bulletin board. With the questions posted, it was easier for our students to access the thinking we are encouraging in their personal responses and in their discussions with others. These questions, which revolve around author purpose and intent, are listed in Figure 5.4.

- What do you think the author/text is trying to say?
- What do you think the author's/text's message is?
- What is the author/text talking about?
- What parts of the topic did the author explain clearly? Not clearly?
- Does each section of the topic make sense in connection to the other sections? (Does the author contradict him/herself?)
- What does the author/text assume you already know?
- Does the author explain why particular things happen/happened?
- Why do you think the author tells you this information in the order it is told?

Figure 5.4 Questioning the Author/Text

Once students start to read, we ask them to think about these questions. We also ask them to answer at least one of the questions in their inquiry journals about each of the texts they read. This way we feel students more authentically learn to think in critical ways. Tony, an eighth grader who is interested in Malcolm X, Muhammad Ali, and the Civil Rights movement, answered the question about the author's purpose in writing (question one in the list) in the following way:

> When I first opened [*Malcolm X: A Fire Burning Brightly* (Myers, 2000)], I saw those two quotes that talked about how revolutions aren't peaceful. And I thought about Martin Luther King, Jr. It made me think that the author was trying to show the difference between them and their ideas back during the Civil Rights. I also thought about how it made me want to read more because Malcolm X seemed more angry and willing to use violence than Martin Luther King, Jr. It made me curious about him, and I think that is what the author wanted.

Tony took this comment to a discussion with others, who then wanted to see the book he had referenced. Together, the group concluded that Tony was probably right, and that the author was about setting up a comparison between Malcolm X and Martin Luther King, Jr. so that young readers would become curious and read further.

Using strategies that encourage students to share their own thinking while preparing them for sharing with others sets up an environment where student participation is encouraged and expected. We also find that when students are invited to use journals that provide for a "second look" at their first responses, they are more willing to remain open to the various perspectives they will encounter in the classroom. Through the use of a variety of strategies, we push our students' thinking while also giving them opportunities to expand their ideas of the world, see the multiple perspectives through which a text can be viewed, and encourage a critical stance toward the information they consume.

> Taking a critical stance asks students to question. They can think about the author's purpose for writing, the information shared and left out, and the language used to discuss the topic.

Figure 5.5 Taking a Critical Stance

Enhancing Literacy Development Through Social Engagements

Once students learn that their personal response is encouraged and desired in the classroom, students will become more willing to share with others their ideas about the topic under study. Several strategies can be used to enhance middle level students' literacy development within a social setting. We suggest, however, that it takes time for young people to learn how to talk with one another in more formal ways than hallway chatter. Meeting in small, informal groups where they can share their ideas is always enjoyable for middle level students, yet they often need help in learning how to discuss information with their peers. Middle level students may have few opportunities to witness authentic discussions, and the challenging perspectives that often come with dialogue, in their daily lives.

Barnes and Todd (1995) suggest that discussion in the classroom is often "presentational talk" where students feel they must present their knowledge in a clear and concise manner. Discussion allows for more exploratory talk where students "can try out new ways of thinking and reshape an idea in mid-sentence, respond immediately to the hints and doubts of others, and collaborate in shaping meanings they could not hope to reach alone" (Barnes & Todd, 1995, p. 15). In whole group discussions, we frequently focus on the benefits and challenges of discussion since students are often reticent to engage in whole class dialogue that places them on the spot. As students practice in venues that are safe for risk taking, they become more comfortable with the process of sharing with each other in confident, compelling, and compassionate ways.

Practicing Discussion for Social Learning

Most students do not enter our classrooms with an understanding of discussion. Holly once asked her eighth grade students the purpose of discussion and was rewarded with the comment, "To get others to think like us." Middle level students need guidance throughout the year on group interaction, and we have found that if we create opportunities that allow them to practice dialogue, they are better prepared for the discussions that arise with inquiry. Through teacher scaffolding, middle level students can experience how to talk in small groups through the expectations the teacher establishes.

Some of the ways we have been able to accommodate students' learning to dialogue have been through practice with partners and in role playing situations. In Figure 5.6, we have outlined nine suggestions for helping middle level students with discussion. By addressing each one of these through demonstrations, whole group practices, and humor, middle level students and their teachers will become more familiar with dialogue and how beneficial it can be for literacy learning.

By using the following key processes, middle level students will be better prepared to use dialogue as a way of learning:

1. Bring something to the discussion.
2. Negotiate turn taking so all can feel free to speak.
3. Invite quieter members to add something to the discussion.
4. When the discussion has changed topics, referring to the preceding topic allows all participants to transition together.
5. Brainstorm topics for next discussion, if meeting again.
6. Ask questions of each other about the topic.
7. When disagreeing, suggest alternative perspectives with evidence when possible.
8. During discussion, don't take disagreement personally. Think of it as another way of looking at the topic.
9. Allow the topic to be the center of discussion.

Figure 5.6 Points for Learning How to Dialogue

Bowser (1993) suggests that teachers should "let students know that conversation is an essential component of [the] language arts, [a requirement] of functioning adults" (p. 38). Through discussions in literature circles, students' voices, questions, concerns, ideas, and intellectual lives become essential elements of the curriculum, which increases their active participation in their own learning (Johnston, 1992).

Middle level students agree that discussion is an important way to learn, whether it is for classroom topics or those they select for themselves in inquiry projects (Alvermann, Dillon, & O'Brien, 1987; Scott, 1994). By working with others in literature circles, students are able to work through their interpretations, their misunderstandings, and what they wish to know in more focused and involved ways. Additionally, students working together in literature circles are better able to scaffold each other's knowledge by using stories and metaphors that are relevant to their worlds; they support each other's learning in very real and concrete ways. Through reading and discussion, students are also expanding their vocabularies and their facility with language.

Discussion also gives English language learners the opportunity to learn the academic vocabulary they don't readily grasp when attempting to learn both the language and the content found in their classroom textbooks. By allowing student voice to become part of the curriculum, teachers create opportunities for marginalized students to become more active participants in their classrooms. "The discussion of themes with other students demonstrates how one's individual voice can be joined with other voices to effect social action on behalf of the community" (Ruiz, 1991, p. 224). Essentially, using discussion allows more students to be heard and creates spaces for all students to speak, thus enabling a community to develop among all those within the classroom.

Once students become more comfortable with discussion, either through teacher and student demonstration or whole group practice, they need guidance on how to interact with others in a small group. Through literature circles, we find that students can negotiate meaning making in a social situation that allows them both personal response and experience with other, varying perspectives that honors both.

Using Literature Circles in an Inquiry Cycle

Literature circles, a dialogue-based activity used most often with narrative texts, allow students to discuss a particular text in small groups (Peterson & Eeds, 1990). There are, however, ways in which literature circles can be used with all types of informational texts with an expository text structure (Johnson & Freedman, 2001). Literature circles support students' learning while addressing the teacher's desire for students to verbalize what they are learning in relation to their inquiry topics.

The number of students who meet in one literature circle often depends on its purpose or teacher directive. Scott (1994) defines literature circles as "groups of three to eight students who have read the same story or novel and have gathered to discuss their reading" (p. 37). While we agree that the number of students should remain between three to eight students, the literature discussions we encourage our students to undertake during an inquiry cycle are much more topic, concept, or subject based. Thus, students can come to a literature circle with different texts that touch on the same theme or topic. Through literature circles, students have the opportunity to become experts and teach each other about their favorite aspects or most interesting details of World War II, Sojourner Truth, Muhammad Ali, or the Civil Rights movement.

How Literature Circles Work

Literature circles work in multiple ways, but we have found that by asking students to meet for three times on the same topic, text, or theme, they are more likely to "go deeper" into the text, rather than completing a simple glossing over of what the text involved. The following three stages often happen with middle level readers and their discussions, which is why we want our students to meet more than once.

- First Meeting: "Dinner Table Talk"(Atwell, 1998): Students spend time working through the text covering their initial reactions and responses or clearing up misconceptions or comprehension difficulties.
- Second Meeting: "Issues Discussion": Students brainstorm and select issues they wish to discuss in connection with the text.
- Third Meeting: Continue discussion of issues or discuss the affective elements of the literature circle. The affective dimension might include the roles they filled, the way the literature circle worked, or the work they accomplished as a group.

As teachers we are always interested in what students focus on during the third meeting. We have had groups who have continued the issues discussion because their topic was so fraught with them (i.e., Civil Rights movement), but we have also seen a large number of students discuss their work together as a group. One way we facilitate this discussion is through a question matrix that allows them to reflect upon the types of questions they asked or the topics they covered (Johnson & Freedman, 2001).

Daniels (2002) suggests roles for literature group members when they are first learning how to discuss in small groups; but once students become familiar with literature circles, roles are no longer necessary. The roles we might assign for broadening students knowledge during an inquiry cycle would follow those created by Daniels and include having students attend to specific vocabulary, illustrating the concept or content under study, summarizing the content, question posing, bridging the content to other content or concepts, and leadership duties. Using role sheets may help students better understand what it is they are asked to do in literature circles and can be a handy reference to consult while learning how to dialogue about content area knowledge.

While we don't advocate the on going use of role sheets, or even student roles for literature circles, we have found that students need help in learning how to talk with each other about their topics and how they interrelate. One way we do this is through the use of an Intertextuality Sheet (see Appendix 9), which helps students see how their topics relate or how the texts they are reading relate to one another. Figure 5.7 shows how Marta filled out her Intertextuality Sheet after her discussion with Brandon, Felicia, and Betio on the topic of discrimination during their unit on Social Justice.

Marta listed three intertextual connections to other ideas or texts from the discussion and one hint at who these books highlighted. We usually only ask our students to make three connections and to fill in the sheet after the discussion. Through this practice, students pay more attention to the discussion than to filling out the sheet. Marta made quick notes during the discussion that included other group members' names and the information they shared. Concentrating on the connections made in discussions and then filling out the Intertextual Connections Form also allows readers to work on summarizing skills, computer skills, and bibliographic formatting skills.

Name: *Marta*

Topic: *Discrimination*

Text Read Before Discussion:	Connections Made:
Atkin, B. (1993). Voices from the Fields: Children of Migrant Farm Workers Tell Their Stories. Boston: Little, Brown and Co.	1. *My mom told me she worked in the fields when she came over from Mexico.* 2. *I liked the English and the Spanish in the book.* 3. *One of the boys talked about his large family and I have a large family, too. We both visit our grandparents and they help us.*

Titles of Other Texts Referenced in the Discussion:

1. *Tunnell, M., & Chilcoat, G. (1996). The Children of Topaz: The Story of a Japanese-American Internment Camp. New York: Holiday House.*
2. *Bridges, R. (1999). Through My Eyes. New York: Scholastic Press.*
3. *Park, F., & Park, G. (1998). My Freedom Trip: A Child's Escape From North Korea. Honesdale, PA: Boyds Mills Press.*

How These Texts Relate to Each Other:

1. *They all talk about kids being discriminated against.*
2. *Even though different kinds of kids like Black kids or Korean kids or Japanese American kids, they all had the same kinds of problems with the laws of their countries.*
3. *The kids all wanted something better for them and their families, and they had a hard time understanding why their were problems in their countries.*
4. *We didn't see any books about if white kids are discriminated against.*

Figure 5.7 Making Intertextual Connections

The Benefits of Content Area Literature Circles

The reasons to use literature circles are multiple and varied. They allow students to engage one another in real world ways while also providing an appropriate venue for students to learn. Literature circles also create conditions where students feel more comfortable in the classroom, thus creating a community of learners and readers who work with each other to produce more meaningful learning for everyone. Literature circles use discussion, which counters whole class recitation structure and students' fear of being "wrong" or of looking "stupid," which can be a powerful deterrent to participation for most middle level students. Exploring an idea in front of a large group or whole class involves a higher "price of failure" (Barnes & Todd, 1995). Seldom will students risk failure or uncertainty in front of a large group. As their teachers we may be losing opportunities for teaching at the same time some young people are losing an opportunity for authentic and life long, engaged learning about a topic or subject that interests them.

Other benefits of literature circles involve middle level students' reading comprehension. Short, Harste, & Burke (1996) assert that through the conversations and dialogues within literature circles, "readers have the opportunity to explore their half-formed ideas, to expand their understandings through hearing others' interpretations, and to become critical and inquiring thinkers" (p. 479). Through literature circles, students are able to explore their "rough draft understandings" (Burke & Short, 1991) in conversations where there are no correct responses, but rather a dialogue among readers who are attempting to negotiate the information found within texts. Barnes and Todd (1995) suggest "small group talk encourages exploration of ideas, rather than the presentation of certainties" (p. 15). In content areas such as science, social studies, and mathematics, learning is based on theories and ideas as often as factual information generally already proven. Teaching students to theorize and evaluate information are just two types of thinking that literature circles encourage.

Literature circles encompass both the social and the academic needs of the students while maintaining the curriculum. Because students address comprehension difficulties and expand their understandings of texts, content area literature circles help readers to become more literate, more articulate about content knowledge, and better critical thinkers (Robertson & Rane-Szostak, 1996; Short, Harste, & Burke, 1996). They can also explore and share such interesting curiosities as sea turtles, the Civil War, Muhammad Ali, Mozart, Civil Rights, and the percentage of any phenomenon on earth and make connections between and among them.

Strategies to Use in Literature Circles

With literature circles, students still need guidance in relation to what they should focus on in any one literature circle meeting. Once they have moved away from the roles that address vocabulary, illustrations or examples, and leadership, there are a number of strategies we invite our students to try so they will get more out of their sources and out of their discussions. The following three strategies we have found work well in encouraging middle level students to think about their inquiry topics in new and exciting ways. The first two strategies are especially good for encouraging middle level students to become more critical in their reading. The third strategy pushes students to consider other perspectives so they can "go deeper" in their understandings.

Proposition & Support Outlines

Often the texts middle level students read support a particular position. Learning how to recognize that position, or proposition, is the value of this particular strategy developed by Buehl (2001). Working together in literature circles, students fill out the proposition & support outline (Appendix 10). Completing the outline leads to discussion about the position the author takes and the support the author uses for reinforcing that proposition.

We realize that students may have a difficult time recognizing position statements or propositions, but when they are confronted with statements that can "be argued as true" (Buehl, 2001, p. 101) or false, they quickly become aware of how often propositions are used in texts, including the media. We have used the following statements with middle level students to bring about an awareness of propositions:

- The United States is the best country in the world.
- Women make better parents than men.
- Teenagers are bad drivers.
- Washington needs experienced politicians.
- Standardized tests are necessary.
- Classical music is better than rock music.

Once middle level students work with these statements, and how they can be either true or false depending on various perspectives, they are ready to work with the texts they encounter in their inquiry research. Working with the entire class, we select texts that have a clear format of proposition and support. We use the proposition and support outline on an overhead projector, and ask our students to find the proposition statements and the support for those propositions. In this way, we scaffold their learning, and then invite them to try another text with their literature circle members. Figure 5.8 is Alicia's, Robert's, and Cherie's outline for

Names: Cherie, Robert, Alicia
Topic: Social Justice and Living Conditions
Proposition Statement: "Many immigrants encountered hostility, even hatred, as they poured onto Ellis Island and other ports of entry on the eastern seaboard" (p. 9).
Facts: 1. The immigrants came from Scandinavia, Ireland, Germany, Italy, and eastern European countries and they were considered inferior, even less than human by people born in the United States.   2. Because they spoke other languages and didn't understand English the people in America thought they couldn't speak (mute) or they were ignorant.

Figure 5.8 Proposition and Support Form

3. They knew they were smart and they used to live in countries that persecuted them so they knew they could overcome the discrimination in the United States.

4. Because the Americans born in the United States didn't like them and didn't understand them, a lot of immigrants lived in the same neighborhoods and in rundown buildings like tenements.

Statistics:

1. From the early 1800s to the 1930s, 30 million immigrants came to the United States.

2. From 1880 to 1890, 60,000 Jews moved into the tenements of the Lower East Side that is in New York.

3. In 1910, the Lower East Side had 550,000 people living there. It's not that big of a neighborhood so people were crowded.

4. In 1864, 62% of the population of New York City lived in tenements and it was mostly the immigrant population.

5. New York City was the port of entry where 75% of the immigrants came.

Examples:

1. Ellis Island is where most of the immigrants came in the United States. Ellis Island is in New York City.

2. People lived in very bad conditions because they built tenements for them that weren't good places to live but the immigrants who lived there didn't complain. That's sort of like discrimination and treating immigrants like they aren't as good as other people.

Expert Authority:

1. The author, Raymond Bial because he researched for the book and listed other books he used for his information.

2. Lower East Side Tenement Museum (www.tenement.org) because it has an encyclopedia of immigrant life and how people were treated and the kind of living conditions the immigrants had.

Logic & Reasoning:

1. It doesn't make sense that people discriminated against the new people in country, but sometimes we treat the new kids who come to our school bad because we don't know them.

2. It does make sense that people would want to live with people who didn't treat them bad and who didn't discriminate against them.

3. It seems like today people who speak English are discriminating against people who speak Spanish and are from Mexico. That doesn't make sense, but maybe they just want people to understand them so they can learn at school and in the government.

Figure 5.8 Proposition and Support Form *(Continued)*

the book *Tenement: Immigrant Life on the Lower East Side* (Bial, 2002). This group was working on an inquiry project that addressed issues of social justice and the history of the United States.

Question and Problem Posing

Another strategy we encourage middle level students to use in literature circles includes question or problem posing. Both questioning and problem posing create more critically literate readers and learners by asking students to think not only about the position the author is taking, but also about the way in which information is presented. Almost everything they read or view is subjective in nature, and we want students to begin noticing that it is a rare occurrence for the "whole story" to be told. There is always a perspective that is missing or a dominant point of view. Learning to recognize the gaps in text, or what is not being told, creates more savvy readers and ultimately consumers of knowledge. Learning to pose problems invites young readers to look for multiple perspectives, which increases inclusiveness and understanding across perspectives.

In their literature circles, we support students in their question and problem posing through a list of questions they can ask while reading and discussing:

- Does this make sense?
- What argument could I make against this?
- Who is being affected by this?
- Who does this benefit?
- Who is not being heard?
- How could this hurt someone or someone's life style?
- Why would this matter?
- What other perspectives could be shared?
- Are all the perspectives present?
- Who gets to tell this story historically?

By asking these types of questions, students learn that the materials they consult for their inquiries may need to be challenged. We also suggest that they look for materials that contradict each other, or give alternative perspectives, so they can begin to see how broad ranging some issues are, and that not every problem, situation, or issue is easily solved. While we want our students to be problem solvers, we also want them to realize that solving problems can sometimes create new ones if we have not investigated the effects of our solutions on others.

Literature circle groups can create posters that address problems they encounter in a text or questions they ask in relation to their reading and inquiries. By sharing with others what they have discussed, the entire classroom can benefit. We have also discovered that through question posing, we discover what concepts or content our students do not understand as well as the vocabulary we need to cover to help them with their comprehension. Figure 5.9 is a list of questions one group of sixth graders asked about "Antonio, A Negroe," one of the profiles they read in *Building a New Land: African Americans in Colonial America* (Haskins & Benson, 2001).

1. What are European languages?
2. Why was his name Antonio?
3. Why did he have to have permission to get married?
4. Why did he change his name to Anthony?
5. Where is the Chesapeake Bay?
6. What does it mean to establish their own farm?
7. What does it mean about sponsorship of servants entering the colony?
8. Why did Anthony own slaves when he was a black person, too?
9. Why did Anthony not understand that his slaves wanted to be free?
10. Why were Anthony's rights slowly taken away when he was a free person?
11. What does "alien" mean in this story?
12. What does "repression" mean?

Figure 5.9 Questions

While we list only 12 questions from the 3-page excerpt on Antonio, there were other questions the students asked, which were based on their prior understandings of the world and experiences with other texts about colonial America. From these questions, however, we were able to work with students' comprehension about slavery, colonial America, and connections to current social situations.

Save the Last Word for Me

This strategy highlights how "different readers bring differing experiences and knowledge to a reading experience [and thus] will construct a different interpretation of a text" (Short, Harste, & Burke, 1996, p. 506). Students will garner two important concepts from this strategy: multiple perspectives and interpretations from one text or event and how texts have gaps that others may more readily see or question.

In this strategy, students follow these steps to discuss what they have read:

1. Read and select passages, quotes, phrases, sentences, or words in the text and write them down on index cards.

2. On the opposite side of the index card, students write their thoughts about the passage they selected.

3. Students meet in literature circles and one student starts the discussion by reading one of the quotes or passages on her index card. The student does not share her thoughts yet.

4. Other members of the literature circle share what they think about the quote and may give reasons why they think the first student selected the passage.

5. When everyone has shared something about the quote, the originator shares her thoughts about her selection.

6. The next student shares and the process repeats until all students have shared.

This strategy, while it increases student discussion and the sharing of interpretations of the text, also shows them how they connect to texts, which improves comprehension.

Comprehension and the Social Construction of Knowledge

Reading only really occurs when students comprehend what they are reading. Often middle level students can decode so well that we believe they can read quite well. By being able to summarize or retell what they have read, we are more apt to be sure that they can understand what they have read and can then work with the information in their inquiries. When students come together to discuss what they are thinking about, what they are reading, or what their questions are in relation to their inquiry topics, they are expected to tell something about what they are studying. Thus, comprehension is quite often informally assessed through social situations. What is often an added benefit, however, of these social situations where students construct knowledge with others is that comprehension is increased. Students bring their differing perspectives to the dialogue causing others to think again or in multiple ways about the topic they are researching.

> When students decode, they are pronouncing the words they see within a text. This pronunciation does not insure that they have understood or comprehended what they have pronounced. We suggest that when students comprehend and are able to discuss what they have decoded, they have actually read.

Figure 5.10 Reading or Decoding?

Strategies for Increasing Meaning Making

Three strategies we like to use with middle level students address synthesizing, inferring, and making meaning through drawings. By learning how to explicitly show the meaning they have made through their readings, middle level students comprehend the information they are gathering for their inquiry projects in a much more complete way.

Synthesizing

Synthesizing is a process of constructing meaning from the texts we have read, our life experiences, and our responses to our reading. We find that middle level students have a difficult time with synthesizing because they are often asked to summarize and can see little difference between the two processes.

To help students learn to synthesize, we work with them by using texts to which they can immediately relate. We select articles from teen magazines, stories or essays from collections, or show movies we know they will enjoy. We then ask them to address the following questions, either in their inquiry journals or on notebook paper:

- How did this connect to your life?
- How did this connect to other material you have viewed or read?
- How did this connect to what you know about the world?

From these questions, we invite students to write a piece that includes quotes from the original materials along with a discussion of other "texts" from their reading or their lives. We also must teach them how to quote or paraphrase texts, which helps them with understanding plagiarism. Synthesizing is a valuable strategy for middle level students as they proceed through their inquiries and their academic lives.

Inferring

One of the best strategies to teach inference is the Question/Answer Relationships, or QAR (Raphael, 1982). The QAR strategy focuses on where answers to questions can be found—in the book, in the reader's head, or in a combination of the book and the reader. Because students cannot rely solely on the book for finding the answers to some questions they will ask, or that we, as their teachers, may ask them, they need to learn about inferring. The following four categories explain text/reader relationships and QARs:

1. Answers found in the book:
   - Right in the book
   - Putting the answer together from different parts of the book

2. Answers found in my head:
   - Author and me relationship: Some from the book, some from me
   - On my own from my own experiences or prior knowledge

Through discussions of where the answers to questions can be found, students can work together in making inferences. We have created a chart (see Appendix 11) that middle level students can use while reading for their inquiries or in literature circle discussions to discover when they are using inferences or when questions only need a literal connection to the book they are reading. Figure 5.11 is an example of a QAR developed by Tamara, a sixth grade student, who while reading

---

Name: Tamara

Text: Coleman, E. (1998). The Riches of Oseola McCarty. Morton Grove, IL: Albert Whitman & Company.

Questions I Asked and My Answers:	QAR:
1. Why was she named Oseola? I think it might be a family name.	1. The answer came from my head and I still don't know if I am right.
2. Why did Oseola like to work alongside her grandmother at doing laundry? I think it made her feel grownup.	2. The answer came right out of the book and I found that out when I read a little bit more.
3. What is a menial job? It's a job like housecleaning where you don't get a lot of money for doing it.	3. The answer came from my head and the book so I did do an inference.
4. Why did she give her money for scholarships? She didn't get to finish her education and she thought it was good for young people to do that, so she gave her savings to a university so other young people could go to school in her place.	4. The answer came from my head and the book so I did another inference.

Inferences:

Oseola was happy to work for a living and thought people should be proud of their work. Money didn't mean that much to Oseola because she never took money out of the bank to buy big or expensive things for herself. Hard work can be done by men and women. Doing laundry without a machine is hard work and we don't do that anymore because we have machines. Oseola never complained about the hard work because she liked working with her family and they all did laundry. She cared so much about her family that she didn't even get married.

Figure 5.11 Question/Answer Relationships (QAR)

The Riches of Oseola McCarty (Coleman, 1998), developed questions, discovered where she made inferences, and where she found the answers right in the text.

From her answers and a later discussion with her teacher, Tamara was able to see how she connects what she knows and theorizes about people and the world to the information she learns through reading.

"Sketch to Stretch"

Sketch to Stretch (Short, Harste, & Burke, 1996) is a strategy that asks students to expand their meaning-making by creating something outside one sign system. Many of our middle level students are wonderful artists, performers, musicians, and mathematicians. Yet, school literacy often revolves around the language arts processes of reading and writing. By inviting students to expand their communication abilities to include viewing and visually representing and using other sign systems, teachers encourage more extensive meaning making.

"Sketch to Stretch" begins after students have read a text. They then sketch out the meaning they have made from that text. By asking them to sketch the meaning they made, we are asking students to think about theme and perspective, more than favorite scenes or characters. Once they have sketched the meaning they have made, students meet in literature circles to discuss their meanings, thus developing greater understanding of the text and the multiple perspectives others bring to the text as well.

Comprehension Breakdowns and Social Learning

Whenever a classroom of students read, there is bound to be at least one student who does not quite understand the text. Comprehension breakdown is an occurrence that middle level students encounter in their reading materials. Discussing what they have learned with others, however, can repair some of students' comprehension difficulties. By talking through what we know and what we don't with others, our misunderstandings and our misconceptions can be remedied. Students often discuss materials in ways that teachers would not. They create their own metaphors, their own illustrations or examples, and through common language, come to understand the texts they are reading and using for inquiry in accessible ways.

By connecting to themselves, their lives, to the world, and to other texts, middle level students improve their comprehension skills (Keene & Zimmerman, 1997). Furthermore, Wertsch (1981) suggests that peer-directed discussions are less rigid than the adult/child interactions that frequently take place in school. When students talk to one another, there is a common bond of adolescent culture which allows students to communicate in ways that may be more understandable to some students than the talk they hear from their teachers or the materials teachers frequently use. Because students can bridge the barriers often established in adult/child interactions where students may feel inhibited about telling the teacher they don't understand the information, more learning takes place that is relevant to more students' lives.

We also found that students bridge knowledge from one topic to another with a story from their lives. Cooper (1995) suggests "anecdotes are easier to remember because they carry more information in them than the average set of facts or research findings" (p. 122). By connecting the facts of content knowledge with stories from their lives, students help each other remember the information they found interesting, thus increasing the entire group's understanding of the topic.

There will be times, however, when the group does not understand what a particular text is attempting to say. With help from the teacher, the use of other texts, and with further research on the topic, students can overcome their comprehension breakdowns. With the use of the metacognitive questions we discussed in Chapter 3, students can come to better understandings alone or with others.

Concluding Remarks

Learning through social engagements is instrumental in an inquiry cycle. Middle level students expand their thinking, discover the gaps in their understandings, and build an appreciation for multiple perspectives. Because they are at an age where their social development is primary, allowing them to discover with others what they know, what they still want to learn, where sources of information can be found, and where these sources can lead them, this stage of the inquiry cycle "collecting and conversing," creates an excitement and a willingness to learn within most of our middle level students. This hum of excitement leads to deeper comprehension of the reading material, while also benefiting students' writing, listening, and discussion skills.

Strategies Discussed in Collecting and Conversing

- Dialogue Journal
- Individual or Topic Quotations
- Jigsaw Reading and Responding
- Questioning the Author/Text
- Intertextual Connections
- Proposition and Support Outlines
- Questioning and Problem Posing

- Save the Last Word for Me
- Inferring Through a QAR
- Sketch to Stretch

Sixth Grade Language Arts/Social Studies

Rebecca Miller

"Awwww Miss, that's not a good book." Inevitably, as soon as an informational text hits the desktop, the complaints begin to flow. I hear such comments as "This isn't a good story," and "This isn't real," and "There are no characters in this book." Normally, the complaints pass through one ear and out the other; however, "This isn't real" takes root in my brain. I can only think, "What do you mean this isn't real? Of course it's real. This is nonfiction. These are informational texts, not fictional stories." And then I realize that this student doesn't mean real as in fiction versus nonfiction. He means REAL as in how does this connect to my life. Why is this important? What am I going to get out of this? Real for a sixth grader is a synonym for relevant.

The idea that my students needed the informational texts to feel as real to them as fictional texts do was a teacher-changing event for me. I had been searching for some way to make informational texts more interesting to my students. I wanted them to get more from reading informational texts than dry facts. I wanted my students to be able to use the informational texts to build mood and tone in their writing as well as in their lives.

Although most teachers are familiar with the idea of discussing connections between the reader and the text when reading fiction, many teachers haven't discovered the power of using literature circles with informational texts. Fortunately, for my students, I discovered literature circles a couple of years ago and implemented them into my lesson plans whenever we use informational texts. As I teach an integrated Reading, Language Arts, and Social Studies block, we use informational texts quite often.

Using literature circles with informational texts does not take much additional planning on the part of the teacher or work on the part of the students. Mainly, using literature circles with informational texts requires a shift in thinking. I had to step away from the traditional view that informational text reading was for looking at text conventions and gathering facts to write a research paper and embrace the idea that informational text reading is the perfect way to allow students to use higher order thinking skills, develop questioning skills, and stimulate non-formulaic writing.

Literature Circles can be used with informational books from any content area. Consistently, the most popular unit in my class, every year, is the World War II unit which just happens to be the one with the most informational text reading required. One part of this 6-weeks unit deals with the Japanese-American internment camps in the United States. In addition to a selection of historical fiction books, my students read several informational texts including Shelley Tanaka's (2001) *Attack on Pearl Harbor*; Thomas B. Allen's (2001) *Remember Pearl Harbor*; Jerry Stanley's (1994) *I am an American*; and three selections from Nextext's historical reader, *Japanese-American Internment*.

Once the students choose the book they want to read first, they settle down to previewing the text by looking at the table of contents, pictures and captions, maps, glossary, index, and reading any author's notes that might be included. During this previewing process, the students note any questions that occur to them in their reading log. Their first literature circle is organized around this list of questions. The students, usually four or five per circle, share their questions with each other. They work together to hypothesize answers. While the students go into the literature circle with a set number of questions in their reading log, the discussions generated by listening to others' questions usually brings to mind several new questions for each. As the group finishes discussing the preview questions, they move on.

The students divide the pages of the reading by the days allowed for the piece to set a reading schedule. They then read their pages, either individually or as a group. During this first reading, each student is responsible for taking notes on their reading. The favorite note-taking method for my students is to use bright colored sticky notes. These, however, are not necessary. Plain paper is fine, just not as much fun.

While the students are learning the process of literature circles, these notes tend to be rather unfocused as the students feel they need to write something down. They will often note main ideas and supporting details because those are skills they are used to focusing on. As they develop a better sense of the purpose of the notes, they begin to focus on vocabulary that is unfamiliar; statements that make them go *hummmmmm*; and statements that generate an emotional response, such as anger, joy, or embarrassment. During this reading, the students are also beginning to notice patterns that connect to their lives. They will often note that they have read something about that topic somewhere else before; or they have seen a movie that talked about that topic; or that, they themselves, have experienced a similar situation in their own lives.

The notes that the students make during the first reading of their book are their own choice. They do not have an assigned number of notes to make or kinds of notes to make. They note what is important to them individually. The only assignment, other than the reading, that I give them during the reading phase of the literature circle is that they must find one quote from the reading that interests them. They write that quote on one page of their reading log. On the facing page, they discuss the quote in terms of why they chose it and how it impacted their understanding of the whole piece.

These notes are the foundation for the next literature circle. The students begin by discussing any notes that were written on sticky notes. They take time to discuss the denotations and connotations of the vocabulary and the statements that made them wonder about something. It is not uncommon to see rather animated conversations when they begin to discuss the statements that aroused emotional responses. The students all have personal stories that come to the surface during discussions in literature circles. These stories are the connections that the students make while they are reading. And these stories, connected to the informational texts, are what makes the material relevant and, therefore, a permanent resident in their brains.

After discussing their sticky notes, the students move on to their quotes. Each student shares his or her quote and reads their commentary on that quote. The discussion that follows will, in the early stages, usually be stilted agreement with what was read; however, as the students gain skill in listening and questioning, they move beyond mere agreement to requiring a justification or rationalization for the reader's position. "But, why do you think that?" quickly becomes the most often heard question.

The process of read, take notes, discuss, read, take notes, discuss, occurs as many times as necessary until the students have completed the reading. One thing that I have noticed during literature circles is that the students quickly become dissatisfied with only discussing the book with their circle members. They want more input from others who might add to their discussion. This desire to have more discussion has lead to a virtual bulletin board in my classroom. Unfortunately, my portable classroom is not wired for the internet so the students had to improvise. They took over one of the ten foot chalkboards, covered it with butcher paper, and began posting commentary to share with the other class that was reading the same books. They basically created a virtual discussion group without the computers. The first thing my students do when they come in my room is read the commentary that has been added to the board.

One of the most exciting things I have witnessed during literature circles is that the students will gradually move from asking, Why do you think that? to Why do you think the author thinks that? to Why do you think the author thinks I, the reader, should think that? and finally, to What do I really think about that? And that is the incredible thing about literature circles using informational texts. The students start with the ho-hum attitude that they have to gather some facts and regurgitate them in some form—on a test, in a report, or through a presentation of some kind. But through the interaction with others and the connections that the discussions make between the informational text and their own lives, the students begin to question their assumptions not only about the topic but about their lives and the world around them.

I started to hear discussions about hidden agendas and power positions and who was influencing whom and how. My students started looking at the big picture instead of just at the book. They moved beyond gathering facts to understanding how those facts affect their world. And there is nothing greater, as a teacher, to hear, 6 weeks, 12 weeks, or incredibly, the next year, a student shout out, "Oh, Oh, Oh! Remember when we read . . .? That's just like this."

Rebecca Miller

I have taught fifth and sixth grade for eleven years and currently teach sixth grade reading, language arts, and social studies. Through the use of an inquiry framework, I focus on facilitating my students' development of critical literacy skills. I have worked as an adjunct professor at the University of Texas at the Permian Basin and Texas Tech University. My research interests include Holocaust literature and education, adolescent literature, and issues of representation.

World War II: A Sample Text Set of Multiple Materials

Aaseng, N. (1992). *Navajo code talkers: America's secret weapon in World War II.* New York: Walker & Company.

Emert, P. R. (1996). *True Valor: Stories of brave men and women in World War II.* Los Angeles: Lowell House Juvenile

English, J. A., & Jones, T. D. (1998). *Encyclopedia of the United States at war.* New York: Scholastic.

Giblin, J. C. (Ed.) (2000). *The century that was: Reflections on the last one hundred years.* New York: Atheneum.

Greenfield, H. (2001). *After the Holocaust.* New York: Scholastic.

Hersey, J. (1985). *Hiroshima.* New York: Scholastic.

Korenblit, M., & Janger, K. (1995). *Until we meet again: A true story of love and survival in the Holocaust.* New York: Scholastic.

Krull, K. (1995). *V is for victory: America remembers World War II.* New York: Alfred A. Knopf.

Lawton, C. A. (1999). *The story of the Holocaust.* New York: Franklin Watts.

Lobel, A. (1998). *No pretty pictures: A child of war.* New York: Greenwillow Books.

Meltzer, M. (Compiler) (2003). *Hour of freedom: American history in poetry.* Honesdale, PA: Boyds Mills Press.

Mochizuki, K. (1993). *Baseball saved us.* Illus. by Dom Lee. New York: Scholastic.

Mochizuki, K. (1997). *Passage to freedom: The Sugihara story.* Illus. by Dom Lee. New York: Lee & Low Books.

Nieuwsma, M. J. (1998). *Kinderlager: An oral history of young Holocaust survivors.* New York: Scholastic.

Pausewang, G. (1992). *The final journey.* Translated by Patricia Crampton. New York: Scholastic.

Pettit, J. (1993). *A place to hide: True stories of Holocaust rescues.* New York: Scholastic.

Rubin, S. G. (2000). *Fireflies in the dark: The story of Friedl Dicker-Brandeis and the children of Terezin.* New York: Holiday House.

Sullivan, G. (1999). *100 years in photographs.* New York: Scholastic.

Sullivan, G. (1991). *The day Pearl Harbor was bombed: A photo history of World War II.* New York: Scholastic.

Uchida, Y., & Yardley, J. (1993). *The bracelet.* New York: The Putnam & Grosset Group.

Wiesel, E. (1982). *Night.* New York: Bantam Books.

Williams, L. (1996). *Behind the bedroom wall.* Minneapolis, MN: Milkweed Editions.

Chapter 6

Conversing and Constructing:
The Importance of
Interdependence and Collaboration

I was sitting in class
talking about the Civil War
and when they got done they were shot up
and there close was tore.
Little drummer boy's trying
to protect, one jumped
up and got shot in his neck.
Soldiers in the war eating werms and moldy bread,
then they went to fight the war
and now most of them are
dead.

—*Connor, Eighth Grade*

Prior to writing this poem, Connor, an eighth grade student, was seemingly unengaged in the Social Studies class's inquiry on the Civil War that was going on around him. In fact, he was completely absorbed in writing dirty poetry for the amusement of the other three boys at his table. When Ms. Dunlap became aware of Connor's activities, she offered him an alternative to "being in trouble." That alternative was to write a poem about what he was learning about the Civil War. As the poem indicates, Connor had gained quite a bit of information and understanding of the negative ramifications of war. He provides an example of what Frank Smith (1998) refers to as "learn[ing] from the company you keep" (p. 9). It is significant to note that Connor (as evidenced in his poem) though not engaged in the gathering of information or directly engaged in the discussion of what had been gathered, had gained a critical perspective from simply being in attendance as his group members shared with one another. His ability to glean not only information, but also ideas about the human suffering inherent in the Civil War, speaks to the power of adolescent peer collaboration and the interdependent relationships within inquiry groups. It also speaks to the engagement levels of his peers and the impact of a collaborative learning community versus a merely cooperative one, or a teacher directed one.

By this point in the inquiry cycle the students have formed cohesive groups and are supporting one another in their work. Students have a working portfolio or folder in which they keep their work in progress such as notes, log entries, graphic organizers, visual documents, and vocabulary information. The teacher's time is used to suggest venues for collaboration and to facilitate the students' in their individual as well as group work.

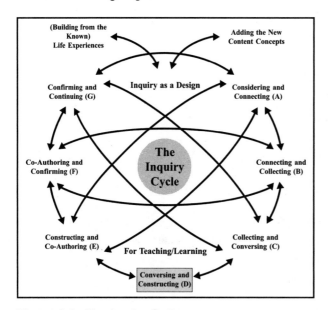

In this chapter, using examples from Mr. Hiedeman's seventh grade Social Studies class, Ms. Linden's seventh grade Science class, Ms. Dunlap's eighth grade Social Studies class, and Ms. Lawrence's sixth grade Science class we discuss:

- Interdependence and collaboration
- Taking stock

Figure 6.1 The Inquiry Cycle

Interdependence and Collaboration

The value and importance of Interdependence and collaboration are particularly evident at this stage of the cycle. For example, in Connor's group, each student has delved into a differing issue of the Civil War, yet, each member of the group is aware of the others' foci and share not only process ideas but information sources as well. John is focused primarily on gathering information about the weaponry used in the Civil War and reasons why so many soldiers died in battle. But as he reads, he comes across information about the Drummer Boys and the low amount and quality of rations for the soldiers of both the North and the South. He notes pages and book titles to pass along to Brian who is focused on these issues.

Through collaboration the students assist one another in organizing the information they are finding. In their study on explorers, a group of seventh graders in Mr. Heideman's Social Studies class helped each other develop charts providing information about the Aztec and Incan civilizations already in existence in the "New World." They also used Venn diagrams to make comparisons between the explorers in the fifteenth and sixteenth centuries and invasions that have happened in the twentieth century and land disputes continuing into the twenty-first century.

Through interdependence they facilitate each group member in his quest to gather enough of the right information and to think about the information in ways that allow him to create a whole body of knowledge and to apply it in a useful way. They learn to question each other and to suggest avenues of questioning. They help each other dig deeper and gain broader understandings.

In chapters 1, 2, and 9, we speak at length about the significance of building a learning community and establishing both collaboration and interdependence within inquiry groups in order to strengthen the community of learners. Each student has a stake in each other student's work. A piece of each of their group member's project is partly theirs. Through this community of learners, they strengthen each other's continuous development of the four efficacy elements of confidence, independence, metacognition, and stamina. It is worth revisiting these ideas here, as it is at this stage in the inquiry cycle that they manifest themselves and development shows.

A student's confidence grows as she is able to present material to her group and be heard, listened to, asked important questions, and know that she can find answers to her peers questions. Students realize that the key is not in simply knowing lots of facts, but in the knowing how the facts relate to each other and where to find more to fill in holes. They may not be able to answer each and every question posed to them, but they will be able to locate information that will facilitate finding answers.

Their independence grows as they are able to take the groups questions and go back into the materials, back to the sources and find answers and more importantly apply those answers to the bigger picture. They know how to use the index, glossary, and appendices. They can skim and scan and then focus on aspects of a text that are pertinent.

Their metacognition grows as they discuss with their group the processes they are using to not only find information but to record it and to connect it with what they already know, as well. To put together the big picture of their topic and see the threads that run through it. Further, they are developing deliberate ways to use the vocabulary they are learning and to talk about the material in disciplined ways.

Their stamina grows as they become bound up in the need to proceed and progress, to stay with their project until it is completed. They have a vested individual interest and a vested commitment to their group as well. They are not going through the motions to please the teacher or to just get the "work" done to receive a grade.

Up to this point in the cycle students have used a variety of strategies to:

Consider and Connect by wandering and wondering:

browsing, brainstorming, building background, accessing prior knowledge and experience, book talking, reading aloud, conducting interviews and surveys, watching video clips, making connections, saying something, gaining exposure to new concepts and terminology, beginning to keep records through logs, journals, notes.

Connect and Collect by personal engagement:

responding, analyzing text structure, making intertextual links across the materials, forming inquiry questions and problems, accessing resources, note-taking and gathering information, webbing and mapping, gathering and using key vocabulary, maintaining working portfolios, monitoring their growing use of these literacy tools.

Collect and Converse by engaging in talk:

dialoging in literature circles, keeping dialogue journals, sharing quotations, using jigsaw reading, summarizing, synthesizing, questioning the author/text, taking a critical stance, analyzing intertextual connections, proposing and supporting, inferring, sketching.

Figure 6.2 Collecting and Converse . . .

Taking Stock

Vocabulary

Deliberate use of content vocabulary

During the conversing and constructing stage of the cycle, students' use of the academic content vocabulary becomes a key ingredient in their ability to pull the information together; to add missing pieces; and to share a cohesive body of knowledge, understandings, analysis, and synthesis with a wider audience.

Vocabulary is at the center of academic learning. Our students must learn brand new words many of which hold enormous conceptual meanings. The words listed below are just a few of the new words Ms. Linden's seventh graders learned as they engaged in a science study of protists and fungi:

parasite	invertbrate
coral	polyp
regeneration	mycelium
lichen	amoeba
euglenas	hyphae
cytoplasm	

Our students must also learn specific meanings for seemingly simple words that are used academically in very specific ways. Some of the words used in Math for example fall into this category. Words such as pattern, equal, volume, product, cube, angle, and network have very specific meanings in a mathematics' context.

For our students to learn the academic concept vocabulary necessary to own their learning of the concepts, they must be exposed repeatedly to both new words and the new contexts for words. They must also use them repeatedly in multiple contexts for diverse purposes (Allen, 1999). Teachers need to be very aware of the ways in which they are using the content vocabulary and to do so deliberately and to call attention to their usage. The following are ways to make students' acquisition of and usage of vocabulary deliberate in the course of their inquiry.

WORD WALL

As you develop a unit of study one of the key components is the vocabulary that you will hold students responsible for. The class word wall would begin with these words. As individual students and inquiry groups begin to find additional words that support the ones on the word wall they can add or develop new lists that go up on the wall. In Figure 6.3 below is a sampling of the words chosen by both Ms. Dunlap and her eighth grade students as they engaged in an inquiry on the Preamble to the United States Constitution. The students investigated the meanings of the preamble and the purposes it provides for our constitution.

Ms. Dunlap's words	Students' additions
Union	secession, states rights, national
Liberty	civil rights, segregation, ACLU
Democracy	suffrage, free speech
Justice	turbulent, discrimination, censor
Defense	gun control, draft, atomic bomb, assassination
Welfare	waiver, health care
Tranquility	immigration, internment, peace corps

Figure 6.3 Word Wall for the Preamble to the U.S. Constitution.

GLOSSARY IN WORKING PORTFOLIO

It is also important for each individual student to have in their working portfolio a glossary of the terms they are coming across that relate to their topic. The glossary has several purposes. One, they are deliberately focusing on the language of their concepts and ideas. Second, they are creating a resource that provides ready access to the words and their meanings so that they can make use of them in their reading, writing, and speaking as well as listening and thinking. Third, this glossary will serve as a reminder to the students that they need to include the vocabulary in their public presentations and writing—presentations and writing that will have a wider audience than the teacher or their own inquiry group. Figure 6.4 below is a sampling taken from one of Ms. Linden's science students who was investigating protists and fungi.

Invertebrates—animals without a backbone

Mantle—covers a mollusk and produces material for a hard shell

Mucus—slippery trail left behind by snails

Parasites—organism that feeds on another organism

Regeneration—ability to re-grow lost parts

Spicules—tiny structures that form the sponge's skeleton

Figure 6.4 Student's Working Portfolio of Terms

KFN CHARTS

A KNOW/FAMILIAR/NEW chart (adapted from Allen, 1999) is similar to the one we saw in chapter 2. Students were using it there to assess prior knowledge. Here a KFN chart can be used by students as they are taking ownership of the vocabulary of the concepts under study. This is a metacognitive strategy that promotes each student's deliberately focusing on the words they will need and determining how well they know the words and their conceptual nuances. It is key for students to be able to differentiate between words they know (i.e., they use them correctly with ease in multiple contexts and could easily explain their meaning and usage to a peer) and words they are merely familiar with. Often students view a word they have heard or seen before as one they "own." But on closer thought or reflection, they realize that it is mere recognition without any depth of understanding and that they would be hard pressed to actually use the word. New words are also important for our students to keep track of as they will need to begin to make some deliberate connections through use of graphic strategies such as ones suggested in chapters 4 and 5 (i.e., individual and text quotations, summary and response, making intertextual connections, proposition and support outline, QAR). (See Appendices 9–11.)

The KFN chart below is a sample from one of Ms. Dunlap's student's investigation into the ideas of liberty in the preamble (see Figure 6.5). It is important to note here that students need to revisit their KFN charts regularly in order to move words over as they become familiar and known and as they add new ones. Each student should have several of these charts in their working portfolio as these shifts occur.

Know	Familiar	New
Colonies	Boycott	Ban
Crew	Civil Rights	Censor
Contains	Glimpses	Dispute
Statue of Liberty	Unique	Turbulent

Figure 6.5   Students' KFN Chart

CONSTANT USE

Once students are aware of the need to acquire the content vocabulary, it is incumbent on them and their teachers to insist that they practice using the new language as they are reading, speaking, writing, as well as listening and thinking. While reading and listening, they need to note unknown words; use the terminology in their notes and journals; and add words to word walls, working portfolio glossaries, and KFN charts. While speaking and writing, they need to make a concerted effort to incorporate the language of the content they are investigating. Figure 6.6 contains excerpts from students' working portfolios. The vocabulary is underlined. These are again from Ms. Dunlap's class's inquiry into the Preamble to the Constitution.

> The Ku Klux Klan started in about 1865 or 1866 in Pulaski, TN. The Klan was formed by a group of Confederate Army <u>Veterans.</u> It was mainly formed as a social group.
>
> People of color who were brought over from Africa had <u>virtually</u> no rights. They were sold like animals...on the selling blocks. They would make the colored person show their teeth. . . .
>
> <u>Censoring</u> is illegal according to the first amendment. Sometimes the fight to <u>ban</u> a book goes on for years. Some of the reasons a book is <u>censored</u> are: racism, sexist, bad language.
>
> The Korean War of 1950 to 1953 was not really considered a war, but was called a <u>conflict</u>.
>
> The FBI investigates more than 180 kinds of federal crimes including bank robbery and kidnapping. It also gathers information about individuals or groups that they believe are dangerous to <u>national security</u>.

Figure 6.6   Excerpts From Students' Working Portfolios

Mini-Presentations

Mini-presentations are made to the student's inquiry group and are a kind of dry run or way of determining what needs to be added or changed in order to move on to the development of a formal presentation. The mini-presentation begins with each student in the inquiry group sharing their information in turn. Once they have shared, they are to turn the floor over to their peers who will provide critique through questions, comments, editing, and suggesting. The student then must engage in a critical reflection of what has transpired so that they can revisit their resources and their working portfolios and make the necessary revisions.

Sharing information: In their small groups, the students share one-at-a-time the big ideas and supporting details and examples of the concept/topic they have been investigating.

Verbally: If they present the information verbally, they need to have prepared an outline to follow and have visuals to reinforce their ideas and information.

Read aloud of written work: If they read a report, detailed outline, or detailed notes aloud, they need to have visuals to reinforce what they say.

Peers read written work silently: If this procedure is used, it is important that the group members have access to the presenters working portfolio for support material such as pictures and charts, graphs, graphic organizers.

Peer discussion: This is the real bulk of the mini-presentations as it is through the peer discussion that the presenter has the opportunity to get feedback which will enable him/her to edit, revise, and add to their body of information.

Questioning: It is important that the presenter's peers write down their questions as well as offer them verbally.

Commenting: These also need to be written as well as verbalized.

Editing/Suggesting: If the peers have access to the presenters written work, they could edit and suggest directly on that work WITH THE PRESENTER'S PERMISSION ONLY.

Critical Self Reflection: Once the presenter has received this feedback, he/she needs to write a self-reflective plan that draws upon this feed-back.

Add, Edit, Refine: This work is completed based on the reflective plan the presenter comes up with.

Figure 6.7   Steps in Mini-Presentation

Revisiting Materials and Resources

Following the mini-presentations, each student takes their critical reflection based on their peers' review of their work and goes back into the materials to fill in the holes, make additions, and sometimes corrections or clarifications. They use strategies such as skimming and scanning and they use indexes and tables of contents to revisit texts they have already used and to glean more from texts not yet used. As they locate information, they add it to their notes or graphic organizers already in their portfolios. They add words to their portfolio glossary, and they make new intertextual connections to the already existing information.

It is here that, once again, ample time needs to be provided for the students to engage in sustained silent reading. This becomes an essential aspect, as it is through reading at this time that students begin to realize how much they have learned and how much they actually know and can, with increasing ease and readiness add to their bank of knowledge and understanding. They can become more critical of the texts they are reading, see where authors agree and disagree, and where there may be out and out discrepancies.

As they revisit the materials, they are refining their skills as critical readers and inquirers. They become focused on pulling together a cohesive body of information around a key concept. They are able to think about presenting this body of knowledge in ways that require application of their understandings through analysis and synthesis.

For example in a math class, revisiting a word problem and an original solution can be very effective for checking for "validity and accuracy" (Adams, 2003, p. 791):

> Looking back lets students engage in discussions about the problem-solving process to further enhance their reasoning skills and abilities to explain and justify solutions. The look back phrase also stimulates additional instruction by incorporating extensive problems and requests for students to solve the problem in a different way.

Working Portfolios

Although most of the information in the working portfolio has been gathered in the previous three stages of the cycle, it is important to revisit it here as a whole so that the ways in which students now organize and use this work becomes clear.

Along with student's individual glossary and KFN charts, working portfolios include log or journal entries; notes; quick writes; information from mini-lessons; a list of the references they have been using with notes as to pages and so forth, for easy return; primary source information such as news clippings; info received from experts; and various organizers for categorizing, analyzing, and synthesizing information.

At this stage of the cycle, the students are using all of this material to pull together a mini-presentation to assess where they are, what they have that is cohesive and useful, and what they need to add or change.

Summarizing

When deciding to present, one element a student should consider involves summarization. Summarization, which is "reducing text to its gist—to its main points" (Vacca & Vacca, 1999), enables students to condense information while also learning how to say it in their own words. By putting the information into their own words, students are actually involved in understanding and retaining important ideas (Kintch & Van Kijk, 1978). We often had our students summarize articles or book chapters as they went through the inquiry cycle. Using post it notes as they read or after they read a portion of a text allowed them to jot down notes and "post" them in their journals. From the notes, they were later able to pull together a summary or synthesis of the information.

Using any number of advanced organizers, students can learn to summarize the information they gather while undergoing an inquiry. To help students learn how to summarize, teachers might wish to use the Guided Reading Procedure (GRP) in Figure 6.8 as a reading strategy (Manzo, 1975). The GRP can be modified to work well as a strategy to support students as they move toward their presentations. Ask the students to take the information they have gathered in their learning logs and start with step number six. With questions that address how ideas or information is connected, students can begin to organize the main points of their inquiry presentation. By asking questions about how the ideas or information are supported with details, the presentation material becomes more solid. Then, each inquirer or group decides what information should come first and they learn how to better reconstruct their ideas into a cohesive piece that can be shared with others.

---

1. Prepare students for reading: Clarify key concepts, determine prior knowledge about content to be read, build prior knowledge if necessary, give purpose forreading.

2. Students select a reading selection of 500–900 words (approximately 5–7 minutes of silent reading).

3. Direct reading behavior: Read to retain as much information as you can.

4. When students finish reading, have them close their books. Ask what theyremember and log on a transparency or chalkboard as the information is given.

5. Point out that some information is inaccurate or missing. Suggest that further information is needed.

6. Have students return to reading selection and review to add information.

7. Organize the information into a semantic map or advanced organizer.

8. Ask questions, such as: "What are the most important ideas?" "How are these ideas connected?" "What order does the information follow?" "What are supporting details of the ideas given?"

9. Use questions to extend analysis of material and then ask students to synthesize this learning with other ideas/information they already know.

10. Reinforce new information by having students share written syntheses.

Figure 6.8 Guided Reading Procedure

After creating his semantic map, John took the information he generated and wrote notes on four index cards. Other students, who were thinking about written formats for their presentations constructed paragraphs that could be turned more easily into essays. By converting the semantic map to written notes or essays, we find students have the opportunity to retain the information in a more coherent manner. By summarizing the material from various sources, John was then able to think about his ideas in more coherent pieces or "chunks" rather than in bits that did not make sense when listed one after the other. With these pieces they then can decide how to synthesize the information for sharing with an audience.

		Gangs		
Like a Club	**Drugs**	**Weapons**	**Crimes**	**Loyalty**
join & initiation	not legal	not legal	stealing	take an oath
wear colors	cocaine	semi-automatic	rape	swear on it
handshake	marijuana	all members	killing	can't quit
brotherhood	heroine	have one	no narcing	
friends	alcohol			
protect each other				

Figure 6.9 John's Semantic Map

Conferencing

These can occur throughout the inquiry cycle, but become critical at this stage as students are shifting their focus from gathering and learning to sharing and informing. Throughout this stage of the cycle, teacher/student conferencing will occur both formally and informally with both individuals and groups. The teacher here is facilitating the ongoing work while also guiding and instructing both individuals and groups.

Individual Student/Teacher Conference

It is easy to build in individual conferences as, in the normal course of a class period, you are walking around making yourself available to guide your students' inquiries. When either you or an individual student feel a need to talk more deliberately about an issue, this can be accomplished either during class in a space everyone in the classroom community knows is reserved for such conferences or after class or after school when there is even more time and privacy.

For example, the following is a brief excerpt of a conference between Ms. Lawrence and Trevor, one of her sixth grade students.

Ms. Lawrence:	You seem frustrated. What's going on?
Trevor:	I'm trying to draw a map of this wetlands and I keep messing up.
Ms. Lawrence:	Let me see.
Trevor:	I threw it away.
Ms. Lawrence:	Well, let's get it. I'll bet you've got things on your paper that you can work with.
Trevor:	Ok. (He goes and gets the map out of from under his table.) Here.

Ms. Lawrence:	What books have you been using? (He goes and gets a couple.) Maybe you need to use one of the maps in here as a reference.
Trevor:	I'll try. I guess I had the parts of a wetlands here. It just doesn't look right. I'll use this one. (He points to a map in the book.)
Ms. Lawrence:	Good idea.

Inquiry Groups/Teacher Conference

Here the teacher might want to meet with an entire inquiry group as they are working. Sometimes the conferences focus on content issues such as negotiating disagreements over the accuracy of information or the "rightness" of each group member's opinion. Here the teacher facilitates the discussion, guiding the group members back to their references and the group process guidelines they have created for working together.

Literacy Strategy Groups/Teacher Conference

These conferences often arise spontaneously and more often than not cross the inquiry groups. These conferences can come up as an invitation from you to students who want to or as you feel the need to work on specific strategies or skills. It is during these conferences that you can work with students through mini-lessons or through a reading/writing workshop model. The duration of these conferences varies with the purpose.

Concluding Remarks

The power of interdependence and collaboration cannot be over emphasized. It is through their social relationships with peers and teachers that learners not only strengthen the efficacy elements of confidence, independence, metacognition, and stamina, they also are acquiring new knowledge and ideas that they can now connect with what they already know and apply in new situations. The research on "cooperative" [collaborative] learning supports its positive impact on "achievement, as well as motivation and self-esteem. Cooperative [collaborative] learning outcomes include retention, application and transfer of principles and concepts, verbal abilities, problem-solving abilities, creative ability, divergent thinking, productive controversy, awareness and utilization of individual capabilities, and the ability to understand and take on others' perspectives" (Kane, 2003, p. 42 [based on the work of Johnson & Johnson, 1999]).

Strategies Discussed in Conversing and Constructing

- Vocabulary: Word Wall, Student Glossary, KFN Charts, Constant Use of New Vocabulary
- Mini-Presentation
- Revisiting Materials and Resources
- Working Portfolios
- Summarizing
- Guided Reading Procedure
- Conferencing

Eighth Grade Mathematics

Susan Lucas

I have just completed my seventh year of teaching eighth grade students. The first 4 years were spent teaching language arts, and the past 3 years have been in the math classroom. I am part of a 5-person team of teachers who are responsible for approximately 125 students; 4 hours of the day are devoted to our eighth grade curriculum, and the other hour I am engaged with a section of algebra students. While I am constantly exploring new ways to explain concepts, my classes are teacher-driven the majority of the time. I know through professional reading and training that students benefit from collaboration and student explorations. While I have dabbled with these venues of teaching, I do not yet have a very high comfort level with them. I think this is partly due to the fact that each of the past 2 years we have adopted new textbooks, first for the general math classes and then for the algebra sections. One of these texts offers a wide array of student explorations, most involving cooperative group work. The first year I used this text, I conscientiously followed the recommended guidelines. At the end of that year, I was faced with two facts: We had only covered about two-thirds of the expected material, and many of the explorations we used had very little connection to the mathematical concepts the students were expected to glean from the unit of study. I was somewhat disillusioned about this "exploration" process.

This past year, I was more selective about which explorations to use, based upon the strength of their connections to the unit of study. I diligently provided several opportunities each week for partner or small-group work, but this was generally used to reinforce concepts, not to discover them. I have this underlying fear of "letting go" and perhaps "losing control" in the classroom. However, being convinced that student collaboration is a critical component in learning to converse effectively on mathematical topics, I have taken the first steps through cultivating a community of trust, tolerance, and respect for each other's ideas. I model this by always giving credence to a question or an answer by finding some aspect to comment positively upon. "I think I know where you're trying to head with this" or "you're on the right track." When students feel belittled or even slightly embarrassed in the classroom, it is likely they will shut down further attempts at communication. This, in my opinion, is the moment they "turn off" to math, and I do whatever is in my power to prevent that from happening.

Why am I prefacing my section of this book with my teaching experiences? Because I am a work in progress, just as each of you are. Many of you are much further along the professional path than I, while others do not yet have classrooms of your own. No matter where we fall in the experience spectrum, we all have our comfort zones and our fears of leaving those zones. This section details how my past experiences as a language arts teacher and my current role as a math teacher have come together in a way that I find comfortable, yet exciting, and that seems to provide students with a new sense of mathematical power.

Last year, I participated in a graduate course titled, "Strategic Learning Through Texts for Middle School Teachers." Having previously taught language arts, I had already begun to recognize that there are many parallels between reading and mathematics, but this course took my perceptions to a higher level. Learning the language of math is similar to deciphering a foreign language; unless we understand mathematical "phrases" and "punctuations," we will not be able to clearly communicate with other mathematicians. We must first share a common language before we can share a common understanding. The development of this common language creates an interactive classroom community and, even more importantly, draws students into the worldwide community of mathematicians. This common language, "numeracy," is defined as a "shared language of numbers that connects us with people across continents and through time" (Anneberg, 2002).

In the conversing and constructing phase of the inquiry cycle, familiarity with content vocabulary benefits students by giving credence to their ideas and efforts. However, I find students are wary of using unfamiliar terminology. Putting them at ease with new vocabulary is a multi-step process. I recently discovered an article describing the variety of language uses in the math classroom (Herbel-Eisenmann, 2002, p. 100). These include "contextual language," "bridging language," and "official mathematical language." Students and teachers begin to describe mathematical processes through contextual language, then together begin to come up with terms and "bridge" between contextual and official language. For example, one teacher and her students described the slopes of lines by how "slanty" they were. Eventually, official language, or that terminology which would be recognized in the mathematical world, is established in the classroom. Lines that were once "slanty" now have a specific "slope." I have witnessed all three types of language in my classroom, and I enjoy the rich mixture of mathematical terminology that we both create and manipulate, which brings about camaraderie in the classroom.

I have been able to overcome some students' resistance to new vocabulary by simply immersing them in the beauty and enjoyment of language. This requires a willingness to get "off-topic" for a few moments when perfect opportunities arise. For example, while giving examples of a new math concept one day, a locker door slamming closed in the hallway outside our room startled an otherwise peaceful environment. Jennifer blurted out, "BAM!" Since our train of mathematical thought had already been broken, I responded, "Wow! Jennifer, that's a great example of onomatopoeia!" As expressions of confusion spread about the room, I explained that onomatopoeia is a literary term meaning a word that describes a sound. Marcel responded, "You mean like 'bang'?" Others began chiming in with other examples, "Meow! Crash! Buzz!" Suddenly, this formidable new term carried a very simple meaning. I have found that by taking advantage of such opportunities to relish our spoken and written language, students begin to lose their fear of new vocabulary— after all, many scary-sounding words have rather simple explanations!

Students also enjoy play on words. In our recent unit investigating linear graphs, several students became confused in the difference between positive and negative slope. Through discussion, we hit upon the following key fact. When determining positive and negative slope, we "read" the graph from left to right, just as we read text. If the line slopes upward, "things are looking up" (a positive connotation), so the slope is positive. If, on the other hand, the line moves on a downward slant, "things are going downhill" (a negative connotation), so the slope is negative.

Word walls play an important role in a classroom, and the math classroom is no exception. Oftentimes, I realize a student's difficulty in learning a new concept is due to misunderstanding a symbol or using the wrong definition for a word that has multiple meanings. For example, midway through the school year, we were approaching the unit in which students would learn to determine the volume of a cylinder. Earlier in the year, we had explored volume of a rectangular prism, so I felt confident there was prior knowledge to build upon. In order to gear the students' thinking in the right direction, I asked, "What do you think of when I say the word 'volume'?" I was pleased to see many hands fly into the air, and I randomly called on Eric. He responded confidently, "When I hear the word volume, I think about how loud or soft the music is on my radio." Around the classroom, his peers nodded their heads in agreement. I was dumbfounded by his response, because I had never made this connection between the two forms of "volume." There are other terms that also hold quite different meanings depending upon whether they are being used in mathematics or otherwise, and a word wall might even contain both uses of the word.

In math, as in writing, there are specific signal words that substantially benefit the mathematician. For example, the word *is* translates to the mathematical equal sign. The word *of* translates to multiplication. Therefore, a mathematical statement such as "50% **of** what number **is** 60?" translates to "50% **times** what number **equals** 60?" By including these signal words on the word wall, students will improve in their ability to convert written language into mathematical language. This past year, students in my class were given access to small white boards and dry erase markers, and they thoroughly enjoyed the experience. In fact, each day students would enter class and check the daily agenda to find out if they would be using the white boards. While these boards are used for honing different skills, one of the most effective is for mathematical translation. Expanding upon the previous example, students would write ".5 * x = 60." On the count of three, everyone holds up their board to compare answers. It takes very few repetitions before each and every student in the classroom has caught on to the concept. One word of caution when using white boards: students are easily distracted by creating original artwork. However, the effort to keep them "on task" is minimal compared to the benefits gleaned from the activity.

In the language of mathematics, symbols are an integral part of the vocabulary. Thus, math symbols deserve a prominent place on the word wall. Figure 6.10 contains examples that might be useful in a math word wall.

<	is less than
>	is greater than
≤	is less than or equal to
≥	is greater than or equal to
~	is similar to
≈	is approximately equal to
≅	is congruent to
%	percent
·	times
π	pi, a number approximately equal to 3.14 the digits 5 and 4 repeat
<A	angle A
m<A	measure of angle A
Δ ABC	triangle ABC
∟	right angle
$\overleftrightarrow{AB}$	line AB
$\overrightarrow{AB}$	ray AB
$\overline{CD}$	segment CD

Figure 6.10   Math Word Wall

At this point in time, the word wall in my classroom is created with brightly colored card stock, vibrant markers, and an appealing arrangement on a prominent wall space. Last year was the first time I used a word wall, and I must admit it was totally teacher generated. However, in the future, students will suggest new terms and design the cards. Students refer to the word wall frequently as we read, discuss, and write about mathematical ideas. Students take pride in correctly using these terms, and as I grow more comfortable with student collaboration and provide more group opportunities, I believe the word wall will play an even greater role in the development of mathematical language.

Each student in my classroom is responsible for keeping a daily journal. This journal is kept in a three-ring binder and is divided into specific sections, one of which is labeled "glossary." In previous years we have simply used the label "definitions," but the use of "glossary" sounds more "professional" and gives this section a necessary aura of importance. Other journal sections are reserved for daily notes, daily assignments, and graded quizzes. In an effort to hold students responsible for correcting assignments and keeping notes in order, I have periodic "notebook quizzes." A notebook quiz is comprised of five questions, the answers for which can be found in each student's journal. For example, I might ask, "What is the correct answer to Question 12 on page 273?" This question serves three purposes: first, students routinely bring their journals to class for the possibility of a notebook quiz; second, they are more apt to correct assignments when they may be held responsible for the corrected answer; and third, students tend to keep their journals more organized, including necessary labels, when they may need to find information quickly. Generally, at least two of the questions are taken from the note or glossary sections of the journal, such as, "What is the definition of a trapezoid?" Each of the five questions is worth one point. This provides incentive for those who need a little push to stay organized, and it serves as a reward for those who have kept their work updated.

As you will learn throughout this book, text sets are a key component to the inquiry cycle. Last year, I developed a text set centered around the mathematical concept of *pi*. Our school celebrates *Pi* Day on March 14 (to commemorate 3.14) each year through a wide variety of activities. My text set was designed to lead up to *Pi* Day by reintroducing geometrical concepts through children's picture books. Primarily through read-alouds, the class shared the brilliantly colored artwork of *Circus Shapes* by Stuart Murphy and the delightful tale of *The Greedy Triangle* written by Marilyn Burns. More difficult concepts specifically addressing geometry of a circle were reviewed through a series of books written by Cindy Neuschwander, detailing the mathematical adventures of Sir Cumference, his wife Lady Di of Ameter, and their young son Radius. Students were drawn into the topic through this approach, and I became convinced the use of text sets holds an important position in the math curriculum. I am presently exploring children's literature that will expand this text set as well as help to develop sets revolving around other math concepts. The enthusiasm of my students made it quite evident that I should increase the availability of pertinent books within my classroom.

The quality of conversing and writing about mathematical ideas is directly affected by the quality of understanding gleaned from texts and examples. Having drawn a correlation between the language of math and a foreign language, I have begun to examine potential effects of mathematical "miscues." In reading, a "miscue" is defined as an unexpected response during reading. If the miscue does not change meaning, it will not interrupt the reading process. For example, a text might state, "Jenny went to her *house,*" but the reader states, "Jenny went to her *home.*" In this situation, the meaning is the same and the miscue will not alter the reader's understanding. Conversely, changed meaning will interfere with reading comprehension—as in, "Gene's summer job was mowing lawns," which was mistakenly read, "Gene's summer job was moving lawns." Likewise, a mathematical miscue may or may not change meaning For example, $2x$ and $2 * x$ have the same meaning, even though the symbolism is different. On the other hand, (x) and $(x 2)$ may have entirely different meanings, depending upon the value for the variable x. One way that math miscues would likely occur is when a student is anticipating a problem to have an expected response and, therefore, jumps to conclusions without carefully following the prescribed steps.

As each new school year approaches, students nervously anticipate the expectations of their new teachers. Teachers, in turn, anxiously wait to meet their students and begin once again to build a cohesive classroom from these lively, impressionable youngsters. The inquiry cycle provides a unique platform upon which to build a classroom community rich in collaborative communication and critical thinking. This is the classroom I envision for my own students, and I anticipate the coming school year with a sense of excitement edged with nervousness at the thought of "letting go" of some of my classroom management strategies designed to keep students quiet and presumably learning. It will take small steps, but I am determined to provide inquiry experiences to my eighth graders so that they can discover firsthand the magic of wondering, exploring, and learning in the world of mathematics.

Susan Lucas

Susan Lucas graduated from Western Michigan University in 1996 and holds secondary certifications in English and mathematics. Her first teaching position was in 8th grade language arts at Northwestern Junior High School in Battle Creek, Michigan. She currently is teaching mathematics to 8th grade students at Comstock Northeast Middle School in Kalamazoo, Michigan. Susan is in her eighth year of teaching and is nearing completion of her Masters in Reading.

Geometry: A Sample Text Set
of Multiple Materials

Burns, M. (1995). *The greedy triangle.* Illus. by Gordon Silveria. New York: Scholastic.

Burns, M (1975). *The I hate mathematics! book.* Illus. by Martha Weston. New York: Scholastic.

Enzensberger, H. M. (1997). *The number devil: A mathematical adventure.* Illus. by Rotraut Susanne Berner. Translated by Michael Henry Heim. New York: Henry Holt.

Flor Ada, A. (1993). *El Reino de la geometria.* Illus. by Jose Ramon Sanchez. New York: Scott Foresman.

Hamilton, J. & Hamilton M. (1993). *Math to build on: A book for those who build.* Clinton: Construction Trades Press.

Hoban, T. (1983). *Round & round & round.* New York: Greenwillow Books.

Hopkins, L. B. (Ed.) (1997). *Marvelous math: A book of poems.* Illus. by Karen Barbour. New York: Scholastic.

Juster, N. (2001). *The dot and the line: A romance in lower mathematics.* New York: SeaStar Book.

Lasky, K. (1994). *The librarian who measured the earth.* Illus. by Kevin Hawkes. Boston: Little, Brown.

Mlodinow, L. (2002). *Euclid's window: The story of geometry from parallel lines to hyperspace.* New York: Free Press

Murphy, S. J. (1998). *Circus Shapes.* Illus. by Edward Miller. New York: HarperCollins

Neuschwander, C. (2003). *Sir cumference and the sword in the cone: A math adventure.* Illus. by Wayne Geehan. Watertown, MA: Charlesbridge.

Neuschwander, C. (2001). *Sir cumference and the great knight of angleland: A math adventure.* Illus. by Wayne Geehan. Watertown, MA: Charlesbridge.

Neuschwander, C. (2000). *Sir cumference and the dragon of pi: A math adventure.* Illus. by Wayne Geehan. New York: Scholastic.

Neuschwander, C. (1997). *Sir cumference and the first round table: A math adventure.* Illus. by Wayne Geehan. Watertown, MA: Charlesbridge.

Pappas, T. (1993). *Fractals, googols and other mathematical tales.* San Carlos, CA: World Wide Publishing/Tetra.

Peterson, I., & Henderson, N. (2000). *Math trek: Adventures in the mathzone.* New York: John Wiley & Sons.

Schwartz, D. (1998). *G is for googol: A math alphabet book.* Berkeley, CA: Tricycle.

Sciesczka, J. (1995). *The math curse.* Illus. by Lane Smith. New York: Viking.

Silverstein, S. (1976). *The missing piece.* New York: HarperCollins.

Tang, G. (2002). *Math for all seasons: Mind-stretching math riddles.* Illus. by Harry Briggs. New York: Scholastic.

Tang, G. (2001). *The grapes of math: Mind-stretching math riddles.* Illus. by Harry Briggs. New York: Scholastic.

Chapter 7

*Constructing and Co-Authoring:
The Importance of
"Going Public"*

"How do you want me to do this? I don't have to write stuff, do I?"

"What do you think would be the best way *for you* to demonstrate what you have come to know about homelessness in America?"

"Well, I like acting. Maybe I could pretend to be a homeless person and do a skit for the class. Then they could ask me questions about my life."

"Great idea."

A s our students proceed through the inquiry framework, we find that they have lots to share with one another and with us. We find also that this informal sharing is not enough. As teachers, we want to know not only what our students have discovered, but also how these discoveries fit together within the broader conceptual framework of the inquiry unit and the mandated curriculum.

The "constructing and co-authoring" phase is a time when students take their understandings and learning and transform them into a cohesive body of work they can present to others thus making their learning public. This transformation into another format is "co-authoring" based on Rosenblatt's (1938; 1995) idea of transaction where a reader and an author's text join together to create a "poem." As discussed in chapter 4, this "poem" is not a poem often thought about in connection to a poet such as Jack Prelutsky or Shel Silverstein, but rather as a "new creation" which is the Greek meaning of poem. Thus when students co-author, they create something new in the form of a synthesis. Co-authoring also works in the inquiry cycle through the transaction that takes place between the inquirer's presentation and the audience. When the audience hears or views the presentation, they, too, "co-author" by taking in the information from the presenter and connecting it with their own prior knowledge. What results is new knowledge for all students.

Planning for a presentation, however, involves several decisions. Middle level students may find making decisions about "constructing and co-authoring" inquiry presentations as complex as deciding what they originally wanted to explore. Michael, an eighth grader in Ms. Sawyer's Language Arts class explored a number of options about his presentation on prejudice in a small town. Many of his ideas were good, but most had to do with standing in front of his classmates. Discussing his ideas with his teacher, Michael realized that his primary audience may not be the eighth graders in his class, but fifth graders who would be entering middle school the next year. He wanted students entering middle school to think about how they talked about and treated each other because of racial and ethnic differences. Deciding that a younger audience was his primary audience, Michael made changes to his presentation style and format.

In this chapter, we share the complex decisions teachers and students face when students set about to transform their knowledge into products that can be enjoyed by a wider audience. Using Ms. Sawyer's eighth grade Language Arts Class for examples, we discuss:

- Defining and describing Inquiry Presentations
- "Going public"
- Explaining What Students Need to Know about Presenting
- Determining Presentation Genres
- Presentations
- Presentation Issues and concerns

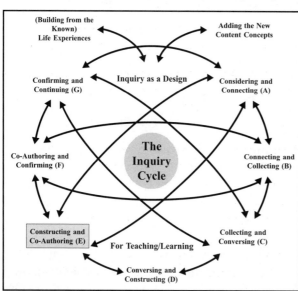

Figure 7.1 The Inquiry Cycle

What Are Inquiry Presentations?

When working through a particular inquiry, one of the final processes of the cycle revolves around the concept of "going public with what [students] currently know and understand about their inquiry" (Short, Harste, & Burke, 1996, p. 279). Going public allows students to share what they know with their peers, their teachers, and other interested members of the school and outside community. This aspect of the inquiry cycle does not come without questions of process or procedures. For instance, how do we get our students to display what they have learned in ways that will benefit them while also engaging their classroom community and allowing others to know, evaluate, or assess what has been learned? What might students "do" to show they have learned something? How do students present salient or interesting information from the wonderland of information they have been studying and absorbing?

Short, Harste, and Burke (1996) suggest that inquiry presentations "reflect formal, but not final, drafts of [students'] thinking about their inquiries" (p. 279). In Ms. Sawyer's eighth grade language arts classes that worked on various inquiry projects throughout the year, students often shared informally with others as they proceeded through their research. They shared new discoveries, momentary frustrations, and budding realizations as they gathered answers to their first questions or realized they are much more interested in new questions they are formulating. This informal sharing, however, does not allow students to fully develop what they are beginning to understand in the larger sense of learning and formal inquiry. Inquiry presentations allow students to gather a sense of their discoveries for themselves and others. They also allow students to share what they are learning even as they continue with new questions or stay with the one idea that has absorbed their curiosity and attention. There are a variety of ways to present and a number of skills that can be learned while students attempt to transform their understandings into another form of knowing that can be communicated to and beneficial to others. Barry Hoonan (1995) suggests, "the more experience students have with multiple response invitations, the greater the chance students will push into new territory" (p. 162).

"Going Public"

"Going public" is a way of thinking about inquiry presentations that incorporates the reality that most schools and parents expect to see something concrete that shows students are learning specific pieces of information about the content area or about the world in general. Going public serves several purposes. It can precipitate a student's desire to move on to another question, because she has already fulfilled her desire to know about the present inquiry at hand. In Ms. Sawyer's eighth grade Language Arts class, Leticia, who fell in love with the work of Jane

Goodall, decided to find out more about chimpanzees. As she was researching, she came across the book, *Walking With the Great Apes* (Montgomery, 1992), which chronicles the lives and works of primatologists Jane Goodall, Birute Galdikas, and Dian Fossey. Wanting to move on to a study on orangutans, Leticia decided that she would present what she discovered about chimpanzees to the class. Leticia's desire to go public had to do with her desire to move on to a study of another primate.

Going public may also facilitate or support young people's learning when they appear lost in the inquiry and need the time to find out what they have come to know. John, an eighth grader interested in gangs, researched for weeks before figuring out that he really didn't know what he wanted to learn or know about gangs. He gathered information on gangs throughout U.S. history, current statistics on gangs, and the personal writings of gang members in prison. When Ms. Sawyer asked him about his process, he replied, "I don't think I have a clear idea of what information I have and what it all means. I don't know what to do from here." Ms. Sawyer suggested that John revisit his information and categorize it, finding out what he could discuss the following week. John took the opportunity to slow down, rethink his inquiry questions, and formulate what he had come to know.

Other times, going public offers a meaningful stopping point when teachers may feel it is time to move on to another question or to regroup and plan where the classroom community might go next. While students' questions may not be fully answered—especially for themselves—they should be encouraged to still share what they are coming to know about the topic or theme studied. As with John, Ms. Sawyer noticed many of her students were "getting lost" in the information they were gathering and that to restore a sense of the process, it was time for everyone to wrap up their inquiries and move on to a more class centered question. By doing this, Ms. Sawyer believed that her students could go through presentations; and with the next inquiry cycle, she could guide them more closely with information gathering and categorizing.

Through the request for sharing their presentations, Ms. Sawyer's students were then able to practice transforming information to different genres or sign systems and for different audiences, even if their inquiries weren't quite finished. She explained to her students that presentations are a time when inquiries become public if only for a short time, but their effects on the lives of a classroom community can be life changing and long lasting. Going public through inquiry presentations does not necessarily mean that students' "wonderings and wanderings" are over or that a new topic needs to be introduced. Even if the class moved on to a more class-centered inquiry, Ms. Sawyer encouraged individual students to continue their own inquiries throughout the semester by giving them "Friday time" to work individually. Through this compromise, the students and Ms. Sawyer were able to address their respective needs.

What Students Need to Know About Presenting

Learning to transform their understandings into a format that others will enjoy and learn from can be a difficult task for many young adolescents. Throughout their inquiries, students have shared informally with small groups; presentations are more formal experiences where the notes or learning logs students usually keep while traveling through the cycle need to be converted into a format that engages a larger audience. While informal sharing in small groups may be enjoyable and tax students very little, a formal presentation takes more work and can be much more intimidating. Separating presentations into before, during, and after segments can help students manage the complexity of presentations. By engaging students in particular experiences at each stage of a presentation, teachers can help students accommodate the strategies needed for presenting well—a necessary life skill.

Inquiry presentations can be individual efforts or a small or large group endeavors. While we often encourage collaborative presentations, the engagements and activities we suggest are appropriate for either individual or group presentations. We share these invitations with middle level students as well, believing that not all strategies need to be taught directly, but can be shared through mini-lessons, in small group tutorials, or adapted to individuals depending on students' ideas, interests, and needs. The following pages explore the different aspects of presentations students might want to address before, during, and after they "go public." The strategies we share are not necessarily to be learned in one inquiry cycle, nor are they "steps" to follow one right after the other. We see students needing to think through their presentations and the experiences we suggest might best be thought of as part of a whole presentation experience. Choosing what students need along the way is what often guided us in our own middle level classrooms.

Before the Presentation

Throughout the inquiry cycle, we have suggested that teachers support students' learning with mini-lessons and engagements that connect to reading with a purpose, being metacognitively aware while reading, writing syntheses, and selecting books and web-sites about the particular topics or themes under study. With presentations, we suggest similar advice. There are three elements to consider as students plan their presentations:

- the information on the topic
- the inquirer and the particular talents and skills possessed
- the purpose for the presentation

For instance, Abel is one of Ms. Sawyer's "most social learners." By his own account he is a good reader who enjoys "conversing" with the information in a book and especially likes to share new information with his classmates verbally. Often he can't wait to meet at the classroom discussion table to talk about what he has learned. Abel also despises writing. When asked to write, he jots perfunctory notes, and limits his essays to superficial information. Knowing himself as a literacy learner and inquirer, Abel knows he must keep notes as he journeys through an inquiry cycle, but he doesn't want to "write a long report at the end." Knowing his strength as a more verbal learner, Ms. Sawyer suggested that Abel should think about ways he could use his orality in presenting. Abel decided he should dramatize his research on homelessness. Abel chose to do a monologue as a homeless person and then answer questions at the end of his presentation. Because Ms. Sawyer knew Abel as a learner, she was able to guide him toward a presentation format that fit his personality. Writing the monologue for his own use also helped him to see the value of writing as a purposeful and useful tool.

To help students understand presentation, teachers need to allow themselves time to teach mini-lessons on the three aspects of presentation listed above. One of the first issues Ms. Sawyer addressed with her students concerned presenting information in the best ways. By best ways we mean that students should become aware of how some topics are better shared through a brochure that their classmates can take home. Other ideas can be dramatized to get the best effect. Still other themes or topics can be shared through a question/answer panel, an oral presentation, or a written essay. As Abel's dilemma showed, however, it is not only the information that needs to be considered when planning a presentation.

The second aspect of presentations that Ms. Sawyer addresses with her students is the inquirer and the inquirer's skills and abilities. Some students are marvelous and entertaining actors and should be encouraged to use their drama skills to create captivating and enlightening presentations for their classroom community. Other students are excellent artists; and they should be prompted to use their artistry to present the information they have learned through paintings, drawings, cartoons, or murals. Still other students connect well with music and should be encouraged to think about how their topic could be shared through that particular sign system. Because middle school students possess a wide repertoire of talents and skills, they need to understand that they should use these strengths in their presentations. Often, however, they don't know how to use these gifts to inform and to entertain others. They need to become aware of themselves as learners and presenters. In essence, both the information and the inquirer should be important elements for students to consider when creating an inquiry presentation.

However, considering the purpose of the presentation should be utmost in the presenter's and the teacher's minds. Students should ask themselves what is it they are attempting to share, why they wish to share this particular information, and what do they want their classmates to understand or be able to do as a result of the presentation.

Discussing his presentation plan with Ms. Sawyer, Abel determined that he wanted his audience to understand the plight of homeless people while also creating an awareness that we should not blame the homeless for their situation. As he explained:

> Some people just lose their jobs, and they don't have the money to pay the rent or whatever. I wonder about me and my mom, if she was to get sick. Would we be homeless, or would my aunt in [another Texas town] be able to help us? Maybe we would have to go live in Mexico with some of my other relatives. I want this class to know that we shouldn't get mad at the homeless. We should try to help them by writing letters to the government and giving food to shelters and stuff like that.

Once he determined his purpose, Abel was able to focus on how to relate his research to the class. He was not finished with his presentation plan, however. Abel had other questions he needed to ask.

Asking Questions and Synthesizing

Who is the audience for this presentation? How much should I assume they already know about the topic? How can I best engage them with the information? What do I know about my own comfort level in presenting information? Questions such as these should become an initial part of presentation planning. This metacognitive awareness about presenting is a process from which all students can benefit.

When students ask themselves these kinds of questions throughout their inquiries, they learn to become more conscious of what they are learning and where the learning is taking them. They also become more aware of the process of learning and thus, begin to realize what information they have and what information they still need or want. Especially when first learning how to inquire and gaining power over their learning, middle level students can become lost in the information they have gathered. Learning to question, often called self-questioning, allows students to have more control over their learning and how best to present it.

Synthesizing is a more complex activity than summarization, which we discussed in chapter 6. "Synthesis is the process of ordering, recalling, retelling, and recreating into a coherent whole the information with which our minds are bombarded every day" (Keene & Zimmerman, 1997, p. 169). Once students have summarized the information from various sources, they need to synthesize—recreate—the information for a particular audience. This transformation includes partial retelling, partial recalling, selective organizing, and adding elements of who they are as inquirers into the coherent whole. This coherent whole can then be organized into a presentation that flows. Once John summarized his research into four cohesive chunks, he then went through and added his thoughts to the information, which created a nice synthesis—and eventually a poster—about gangs.

Determining the Presentation Genre

Once students embrace or begin to "own" the knowledge they have gathered through summarization, synthesis, and graphic organizers, they can think about the presentation format they will use to share that information with their peers. The two most important questions to ask themselves at this time address the purpose of the presentation and the audience to be engaged by the presentation. Similar to deciding how to organize the material for best sharing the understandings they have constructed, students need to determine the type of presentation that would be most beneficial for sharing the information they have gathered from their inquiries. Should the presentation be oral or written? Should it be in a brochure or on a poster? Would dramatizing the presentation be more effective, or perhaps a persuasive essay?

Throughout the inquiry cycle, Ms. Sawyer encouraged her students to keep in mind how they might best present their research. She did not, however, ask her students to make decisions about their presentation formats until well into the inquiry cycle. She did this for a couple of reasons:

> First, I didn't want my students to limit themselves to one idea or another. I used to guide my students at the beginning of a thematic unit toward a couple of ideas, such as dioramas, essays, or book covers. Simple projects that didn't seem to push their thinking or have them really engage the material they were researching. It was as though the formats for presenting directed what information my students would find. Secondly, I felt like they didn't really go deeply into what they were studying because they were just filling in slots to fit their presentation. I want them to get involved, and so I don't talk about presentation formats at the beginning of an inquiry cycle. I let them work at their research a bit, and then I start to think about who they are as individuals. As they get closer to a presentation time, I start to talk to groups or individuals sporadically and then about two weeks before I want them to present, I do a mini-lesson on presentation formats that address questions that deal with their personalities and the way they could best share the information they have collected and journaled about.

Determining the type or genre of the presentation can be especially difficult for middle level students, as they are just learning the multitude of ways they can convert their understandings into mediums that others will appreciate and find useful. Marjorie Siegel (1995) describes that understandings can be expanded through transmediation, which is "the act of translating meaning from one sign system to another. . . . [whereby] learners must invent a connection between the two sign systems as it does not exist a priori" (p. 455). Short, Harste, & Burke (1996) suggest that "the path of the [inquiry] cycle crisscrosses between the alternate sign systems of language, art, music, mathematics, and movement. . . . [which recognizes] that both authoring and learning are multimodal processes. . . . [and that] sign systems have varying potentials to express particular ideas" (p. 29). Thus, middle level students need to become aware of how transforming their knowledge into another format is an application of transmediation as well as communicating across different sign systems. The varying sign systems can also be thought of as genres or types of communications. When Ms. Sawyer discusses presentation formats with her students, she explains how meaning can be expanded by using music, art, and other sign systems. This expanded meaning making allows the presenter to connect with more of the audience since the presenter is addressing other ways of knowing and understanding the information. Ms. Sawyer thus encourages her students to produce multimodal presentations that involve technology, music, art, writing, drama, experiments, and mathematical symbolization. Through this use of multiple sign systems, the students deepen their own understandings of their research while also connecting across different audience types, which we discuss below.

When we think of presentation genres, we find that reviewing and connecting the four general types of "writing" to be helpful as well. These four genres—persuasive, informative, creative, and poetic—include both poetry and prose writing, and will be useful information for middle level students to take with them as they continue their academic journeys. Three aspects of the writing process that can help students understand the differences between the four genres of writing and then help them determine which genre will be most appropriate for their presentations include determining the purpose, determining your most effective message, and determining the type of audience.

Organizational Structures

Advanced Organizers & Structured Overviews

Another way we supported our students in their presentation plans was through the use of an advanced organizer, which is a figure that allows students to see the connections between and among the material or information they have gathered. A graphic representation of concepts, specialized vocabulary, and their relationships, and the general steps to produce a structured overview are shown in Figure 7.2 (Barron, 1969).

Because structured overviews are graphic representations of concepts and their relationships to each other and specialized vocabulary, students have a visual aide from which to work. Questions they may wish to ask as they create or write from this graphic include: "How does this information relate? " "How can I show this relationship to others who may have difficulty understanding this connection?" "What are the specific vocabulary words I should highlight?" "What specific words are necessary for a more informed understanding of the idea or concept?" This last question seems especially relevant to content areas in the middle grades.

1. Select the major ideas/concepts from the information gathered.
2. List and explain the vocabulary necessary to understand each of the ideas/concepts.
3. In a diagram, arrange the ideas according to their relationships and their vocabulary with the particular idea or concept they address. Use graphics to show interrelatedness.
4. Add known words and ideas to diagram so new ideas are connected to what is already known.
5. Analyze and evaluate the diagram. Are the relationships between ideas shown clearly? Are the relationships between ideas and their vocabulary shown clearly?
6. Write essay from diagram, making sure that each idea is clarified and the vocabulary is well defined for peers who may not have the author's knowledge.

Figure 7.2 Structured Overview

We have noticed that when middle level students encounter new and specific vocabulary that addresses a concept with which they are unfamiliar, the students choose to ignore the new word, which can produce less than satisfactory understanding of the concept. Leslie, a vivacious and passionate learner, worked with Leticia on a study of Jane Goodall and chimpanzees. Leslie didn't, however, address the specialized vocabulary that went with primatology. Missing some of the key concepts about the lives of chimpanzees, Leslie found that she wasn't "getting as much out of this inquiry as Leticia." Ms. Sawyer asked her what she thought she was missing:

> I know that some of the things Leticia talks about are important, and I want to know about that stuff, too. But I can't figure out where she's getting the information! I know I skip words I don't know, but I thought I could do that and still figure out what these books are saying. Maybe I need to learn the words Leticia uses. But I hated vocabulary in elementary school. It seemed like such a waste of time. I mean, I never used the words once I passed the test.

Realizing that the vocabulary used by primatologists might be important to her understanding of the world of chimpanzees, Leslie approached Leticia and together they learned how to use the words. Akin to learning a second language, their support of each other helped both girls come to a greater appreciation of primatology as a science. Each content and discipline has its own specialized vocabulary that needs to be addressed and appreciated by students as they learn new information. Teachers can help students with this appreciation by requesting and affirming their use of the discipline's special words and phrases in their presentations.

The use of structured overviews as part of a plan to move students toward presenting also allows students to exhibit their knowledge through formats that use visual evidence to help their audience understand the information they are sharing. They may wish to add colorful photos, other artifacts, or pieces of information to this graphic representation to increase audience interest. For students who have difficulty speaking in front of the class, this overview can serve as an outline for their presentation as well as a prompt for speaking. Leslie, who continued her interest in primates after learning about chimpanzees, created a structured overview of her work about orangutans.

Determining the Purpose of the Presentation

Understanding the purpose of the presentation is perhaps the most crucial question a young person can ask before attempting to engage an audience. This is the time when students should be aware of the four general genres of writing and understand what each involves. Perhaps the best way to bring about this awareness is through a demonstration or mini-lesson that compares informative, persuasive, creative, and poetic writing. Adjusting students' ideas of the writing process and the four genres of writing for formal presentations also includes asking questions such as: What am I attempting to do? Why am I doing this? What do I hope to accomplish with this presentation? Noting the type of information they have gathered throughout the inquiry process will benefit the students as they answer these questions. When asked about what she was going to present, Leslie shared:

> I think I will go ahead and use my structured overview poster on orangutans, but I also want to talk about Jane Goodall and chimpanzees. I am trying to get Leticia to present with me because Ms. Sawyer said we could, but she wants to act something out right now. I like to act, too, but my overview has most of the words I would want to use about orangutans. I really want the audience to learn about both chimpanzees and orangutans, and where they are located in the world, and the vocabulary words like "great apes" and "primates" and "primatologist" along with some other phrases that use geography terms. I am thinking we could pretend to be a news show, or information show like on National Geographic videos, and I could be like the expert on orangutans and Leticia could be Jane Goodall. We could have a discussion comparing the two great apes and then mention gorillas, which is what I want to know about next.

While Leslie seems to know what she wants her audience to learn from her presentation with Leticia, many times students don't understand that there is a purpose for their presentation that goes beyond the idea of school requirements. An approach we have used with middle level students to help them determine the purpose of their presentation is to complete an analysis of information they have synthesized from their notes or learning logs. Reviewing these sources of information may also help add information they had previously missed.

Analysis helps students determine the type of information they have gathered, which in turn will help them choose the most effective purpose, genre, and message for their presentation. Once they have analyzed their notes, syntheses, journaled information, and collected articles, they have more of an idea of whether they should do an "information show" like Leslie's or if they should look toward a more persuasive presentation. By analyzing their information, students also find out what type of reader they are. A reader who is more moved through emotion, one who appreciates "the facts," or someone who attends to a combination of these two elements. The questions in Figure 7.3 can help students with analyzing their research.

Ask the following Questions:

What have I learned?

What information in my learning log supports that learning?

Where in my notes or learning log have I concentrated my efforts in collecting information or relating my understandings?

Is the information in my learning log more fact based, opinion based, or a combination?

How would the notes in my learning log be defined in terms of informative, creative, persuasive, or poetic?

What specific understanding am I attempting to share with others?

What aspect of my inquiry intrigues or interests me the most?

How would the audience I am considering understand this information best?

Figure 7.3   Analysis of Research Information

Determining Your Most Effective Message

Preparing a presentation involves determining the most effective message. By analyzing their learning logs or notes, students can decide where they have concentrated their efforts and interests while they worked through their topic of inquiry. Asking the above questions while thinking about the most intriguing aspect of their research or where they have collected the most information may help students determine what their most effective message will be.

Speaking to Four Audiences

A third important element of any presentation involves determining or understanding the audience. Often, there is no monolithic audience "type" that can be directly identified. Thus, a young presenter may wish to address a multiple of learning styles found within typical audiences. Robert Garmston (1997) suggests "premier presenters target four different audiences in each presentation" (p. 12). These four types of audiences want answers to questions that include "what," "so what," "what if," and "why." Being able to answer these questions or addressing a portion of them should be part of any presenter's introduction and should be considered in the planning stages of an inquiry presentation (see Figure 7.4).

Audience (concern/question)	Necessary Element of Presentation
What? (facts)	• List facts • Share through demonstrations • Give quotations from sources
So What? (story)	• Relate through personal stories • Allow for sharing of audience stories • Discussions
Why? (what questions & where)	• Provide opportunities to discuss information • Ask for audience theories about information
What if? (imagine)	• Explore through Imaginary Stories or Scenarios • "Imagine if . . ." or "Come with me . . ." scenarios

Figure 7.4 The Four Audiences

Engaging part of the audience with facts helps connect with those who want to know the "what" of the topic presented. Attending to feelings will address the "so what" question that some members of the audience wish to know. Involving the audience in formulating ideas speaks to those who are interested in the "why" of the topic, and the "what if" question can be answered by leading the audience through a brief scenario that allows for creative exploration.

Connecting with each of these types of audiences, their learning styles, and their concerns as audience members will help young presenters feel more attuned to their audience and will make the presentation a much more worthwhile experience for both presenter and audience members. Gina, a sixth grader interested in Japanese internment camps, created the following chart to help her with the elements she felt she needed in her presentation.

	Name: Gina
Audience	Necessary Element of Presentation
What?	Describe where the camps were and how they were set up. Tell about how the Japanese Americans got to the camps and how long they stayed.
So What?	Tell the story about going to school in an internment camp, and losing all your friends at home.
Why?	Ask the class why they think the white people did this to the Japanese. Ask them how do they think people would feel about losing all their stuff at home. Ask what they think the government was thinking when they put the Japanese Americans in horse stalls and not even regular houses.
What if?	Imagine if the police just came to your house and said you had to go somewhere else because of the way they looked.

Figure 7.5   Gina's Four Audiences' Planning Chart

Selecting the Appropriate Format

Once the presentation genre, message, purpose, and audience have been determined, middle level students will want to select the appropriate format for their presentation. Mini-lessons on writing formats can help young people choose what Tchudi and Huerta (1983) call the "discourse forms" of content writing, which addresses the elements of either an oral or written presentation (see Figure 7.6). Brainstorming a number of discourse forms ensures that students are "regularly encountering new ways to express their knowledge " (p. 11).

Critical points in selecting the format for the presentation are finding formats that are authentic and best present the ideas for others' consumption. McDermott (1999) suggests that "some topics are best dealt with in discussions; others seem

Journals & Diaries	Biographical Sketches	Letters
Slide Shows & Scripts	Poster Presentations	Reviews
Cartoons & Cartoon strips	Utopian or Practical Proposals	Debates
Collages, Montages, Mobiles	Demonstrations	Brochures
Technical Reports	Dramas or Plays	Interviews
Lab Reports	News Casts	Songs

Adapted from Tchudi & Huerta (1983)

Figure 7.6   Discourse Forms

ready-made for role playing and simulations . . . many lend themselves to projects" (p. 24). Finding the form that suits the presentation is a huge step toward success.

Flow Chart

One way to bring all this information together so that the presentation will be original and effective could involve the creation of a flow chart that addresses each of the elements in turn (see Figure 7.7). Deciding on how to begin the flow chart depends on the presenter and what s/he considers the most important aspect of the preparatory work. Is the message the most important part of this presentation? Or is the overall purpose the strongest part? Is how the presenter decides to connect with the audience the most important element? Or is the genre of the presentation going to be what best connects with the audience?

Strongest Element:
   Message: Students should not be judged by their performance on standardized tests.

Leads to:
   Purpose: Convince others that standardized tests are not the best indicators of

Leads to:
   Genre that will connect Message to Audience: Persuasive piece.

Leads to:
   How best to Persuade Four Types of Audiences: "What if . . ." Dramatization with Character/Audience Interaction after Play. (In the play, give facts about testing and who benefits from testing and who doesn't, touch on characters' feelings about test angst, failure, etc.)
   After play, discuss further facts, feelings, real "what ifs" in connection to them as test-takers.

Figure 7.7   Flow Chart for Presentation

   Beginning with one of these questions, finding the answer and its connection to another question can help young people decide which discourse form might best serve them as individual presenters or as a group of presenters with individual strengths and talents. While we started with what we would consider a strong message, other presenters might consider their strengths before their message. Others might consider the overall purpose. Regardless of where students start, they are attending to all four aspects of preparing a presentation, how this presentation can exhibit what they have learned, and the best way they can present it.

Presentations

Once the format for "going public" has been determined and students have completed their preplanning, they need to consider the presentation itself. Students have already determined their audiences, but gathering or finding those audiences may be another consideration that they had not previously broached. Depending on whether the presentation is a written project or an oral performance, students have a number of decisions to make or elements to consider.

Although teachers will often ask their students to present to a live audience, there will be times and formats that do not have such a direct presenter-audience connection. Such presentation formats include posters, journals and diaries, technical reports, collages or artwork, or work on video or audiotape. With these types of presentations, students may wish to think of ways they can ask for feedback about their work that directly connects to the presentation format, message, and overall message.

If the presentation format is a written work such as a brochure on home and neighborhood safety, a poster on date rape and its prevention, or a cartoon on the misuses of ritalin, students have to consider the best venue for their messages. Deciding on the school newspaper, a community mailing, or postings in community buildings or school hallways is a part of written inquiry presentations that students need to address once they have completed their presentation planning. Making this decision involves the issues of audience engagement and monitoring. Again, asking the right questions can help with this decision. Where can I best engage my selected audience? How can I monitor the response to my project? Asking these two questions guided John toward a decision about finding his selected audience.

John, who had decided to present the diversity of gangs historically in the United States, wanted to share his knowledge with community members who often thought of gangs only as young men of color. He decided that a brochure would be the best way for him to present his information, but he couldn't decide how and where he should distribute his brochures. Eventually, John decided to place the brochures at his local church and supermarket. By noticing how many of his brochures were gone the next month, John had an idea of how many people were interested in his information and how to monitor his distribution of brochures the next month.

For an oral presentation, students will also need to focus on these two major issues—engaging the audience and monitoring the progress of the presentation, which will be more immediate issues in oral deliveries. When John placed his brochures in the supermarket, he did not have to change the pace or the information he was sharing. His project was completed. With an oral presentation, students have the ability to change the information shared based upon the audience's facial and body language, which is immediate feedback. Oral presentations should be practiced so students will have a good idea of how long their presentations take and whether or not they have found ways they believe will keep their audience engaged. Rehearsing in pairs or small groups who serve as practice audiences aids students in revising their presentations before they actually attempt to engage their planned audience.

Engaging the Audience

Presentations include far more than entertainment for an audience; they are a way of sharing "a gift" with them (Garmston, 1997, p. 20). This gift can be a poster, a dramatization, an editorial, a cartoon, or a speech. Depending on whether the information presented is oral or written, there are guidelines that can help middle level students engage their audiences. Garmston (1997) believes there are four elements of an exemplary oral presentation (see Figure 7.8).

Personalize the presentation for a specific audience	Make comments about historic time. (i.e., "At this time in our lives", "On this day in history", etc.) Comment on place. (Reference the school, the classroom, etc.) Address the setting or context. (The room temperature, current news item, something in common with audience.) Use yourself as a point of reference. ("I like to do . . .," which is connected to today's topic . . .) Build in interaction points to create rapport between presenter and the audience.
Create suspense	Create anticipation in opening remarks. ("Later I will . . .") Foreshadow as you go through your presentation.
Add an element of beauty	Make attractive handouts. Make sure everyone in the audience can see you. Include artful phrasing and perhaps a bit of drama. Use clear visual aids. Speak clearly and slowly. Make sure you define specialized vocabulary. Dress appropriately.
Make the information useful	Connect information to the audience's lived worlds. Make suggestions for how this information can be beneficial to the audience's knowledge base. Suggest ways or sources for the audience to continue their inquiries about the information. Create analogies that connect the information to the audience.

Figure 7.8   Four Elements of an Exemplary Oral Presentation

Students also need to remember voice inflection and tone. Being audible to audience members furthest away from them is necessary for any presenter. Ultimately, remembering key points and the genre of presentation will help with voice inflection and audibility. Learning to emphasize particular points by speeding up or slowing down the flow of words, raising or lowering the volume of the words, and using facial expressions and body language all help with voice inflection and its effect on the audience. Practicing voice projection can help overcome the difficulties that often accompany soft-spoken speakers, while the use of microphones also make student voices more audible.

Teachers, through the use of mini-lessons on the key points and how to emphasize them, help their students learn to recognize the main points in their own and other's work. Rehearsed read-aloud activities that allow students to learn how and when to change voice inflection and tone can also ensure that their particular points are heard.

Monitoring Progress Throughout the Presentation

Engaging the audience is probably the most important aspect of the oral presentation. To do this, however, students need to learn how to monitor their progress as they go through their presentations. One way to think about monitoring a presentation is by using a graphic organizer created during the planning stages of an inquiry project. Using this as a way to present the information during the performance allows middle level students to determine time allotments for introducing, discussing, and ending the presentation. Keeping in mind that a good way to keep the audience engaged is to create points of interaction, students need to be mindful of how much time they might wish to allot for these interactions.

An effective outline that builds in time for interaction can help any middle level student stay on track for the duration of their presentation. Using a visual organizer such as the structured overview will also help nervous students remember the information they wish to share while also allowing the audience to follow along. With practice, a structured overview will become more of an aid for the audience than the presenter, but we suggest that middle level students begin with such visual devices to help with organization.

Monitoring the audience, however, is more than following a preset outline and allowing for audience interaction. Presenters also have to maintain momentum, anticipate comprehension breakdown within the audience, and sense when the audience has "left the building." All of these problems can be controlled if the presenter moves back and forth between what Garmston (1997) says is the distance between "the egocentric state of speaking [and] the allocentric perspective of seeing, hearing, and feeling the presentation from the audience's perspective" (p. 85). For example, keeping eye contact with a few particular audience members can minimize the overwhelming feeling of stage fright while also helping the presenter know when the audience may no longer be attentive or clear about what is being shared. When Leticia became Jane Goodall in her news show with Leslie, she often looked at the audience to keep them connected to what she was saying. Between Leslie's structured overview—a visual that captivated the audience, Leticia's eye contact, and pictures of chimpanzees on transparencies, the audience was truly engaged. Ms. Sawyer's mini-lessons on presentation manner were especially evident.

One of the key points of Ms. Sawyer's mini-lessons addressed the reality that sometimes a presentation doesn't seem to be connecting to the audience. Thus, it is necessary for the speaker to make changes. Deciding ahead of time which elements are crucial for audience understanding of the topic and which elements can be left out can help presenters make shifts in their performance. Changing pace in the presentation can also help keep the audience engaged. Students can learn how to make changes if they have practiced on a small audience ahead of time and have asked particular members of their classroom to signal them about their pace, the information shared, or the audience response as they present. When Abel decided to dramatize his research on homelessness, he practiced his monologue with Ms. Sawyer and two close friends after school. Working together in an open and honest forum, the three audience members gave Abel advice on his clothing, his mannerisms, and his language. Abel wanted to be sure that he did not stereotype the homeless through his presentation, but wanted to remain truthful to the typical homeless person in Texas. Ms. Sawyer helped him with his use of language, blending in both English and Spanish so that the rest of the class understood this was not about recent immigrants from Mexico. Abel also decided to use the blackboard in front of the room to write statistical information about homelessness and the populations involved.

Other factors Ms. Sawyer addressed with her class included shifting gears in relation to pace, to information shared, and to interacting with the audience. These elements were not learned overnight; it took many students the whole year with Ms. Sawyer to gain the pacing and the confidence to try oral presentations in front of the class. Her students found that good presentations take practice and that it may take many attempts before they can perfect their own presentation style and repertoire. They also learned to be aware of the complexities in oral presentations and were consistently encouraged to continue their attempts at engaging a real live audience. At the end of the year, many of them presented their inquiry projects to parents and members of the community as part of "Eighth Grade Night," a celebration of their completion of middle school.

While often students can be discouraged by the work involved in presenting, we find that ultimately presentation is one of the strengths of an inquiry curriculum. It provides students with multiple opportunities throughout the year to practice their skills and strategies for going public.

Presentation Issues and Concerns

An inquiry curriculum engages middle level students and enhances their literacy strategies across all content areas. Students should be invited to reconstruct their understandings or apply their knowledge by creating presentations that facilitate the synthesis and organization of knowledge in a way that can be accommodated by their peers and those outside their classroom walls. There are, however, two important issues of concern in relation to inquiry presentations:

- Moving on to another inquiry question or topic before students are finished
- Working with students who feel their presentations were not effective

The Unfinished Inquiry

Although there are no hard and fast "rules" about how long an inquiry cycle should last, there are students for whom no amount of time would be sufficient. This is because they have found an interest that will keep them researching, wondering, and wandering for many weeks or years to come. In cases like these, we find that allowing students to continue their inquiries can be beneficial to their learning and to making connections to new material in a future class inquiry. We suggest, however, that students who wish to continue on a particular inquiry negotiate how they will continue as well as join the rest of the class as it shifts in another direction.

Amanda Bruin, a fourth grade social studies teacher in a small town in west Texas, found that a number of her students wanted to continue their individual inquiries on unique discoveries even after they had presented to their classmates. Amanda, however, needed to move on with the district-mandated curriculum. Discussing her dilemma with the students, they suggested that each student be given an "inquiry" notebook and time on Fridays to work on their individual projects. This way, they could shift with the rest of the class as they headed in a new direction while still having time to work on their own inquiries on Fridays. The students also agreed to one of Amanda's conditions that they present their "new" understandings in an informal manner once every six weeks.

While the class moved on to cover topics of the mandated curriculum, individual students continued their personal inquiries about topics that actually connected to the district curriculum. Students who had chosen not to continue with their inquiry projects found new ideas or questions from the new class focus or chose to spend part of their Fridays reading books of their own choosing. These two lines of study accommodated students' passions and Amanda's needs. The students also believed they were making better connections between what Amanda was teaching about American history and what they found personally intriguing. Sharing this idea with others in the area, Ms. Bruin influenced how Ms. Sawyer worked out a similar plan for her eighth graders.

Ineffective Presentations

We discovered in our own middle level classrooms that most students enjoy presenting to their classmates. They enjoy sharing their new understandings and relish the challenge of finding a great way to present to their classmates. There are times, however, when the best of presentations fall flat. Somewhere the connection wasn't made with the audience, or the bulb on the overhead project went out with no replacement in sight. Other times, classmates just aren't as interested in the topic as the presenter thought. Convincing middle level students that sometimes their preparations just won't bring about the expected response is an aspect of teaching and presentations that teachers must address. Deciding when to address such matters, however, can be a difficult decision. Ms. Sawyer addressed this issue during a mini-lesson on presentation manner. Her students joked about "not making the grade" while discussing this issue, but later a number of students came to her throughout the two weeks they were preparing for oral presentations. Talking with individual students, Ms. Sawyer assured them that school was about learning and not just performing. Her advice to Vanessa, who was to discuss the middle ages while showing the book she had created:

> Take this opportunity to learn two things—how to present orally and to realize that sometimes people aren't going to be engaged because the subject matter does not interest them. This doesn't mean you don't present. It means that you learn to do the best you can, and hold on to those ideas, topics, and questions that inspire *you* to learn.

Vanessa knew that other students weren't as interested in the middle ages as she was, so she decided to do a short "commercial" on "the newest book about middle ages fashions." Keeping her presentation short helped her build confidence, but also incorporated the reality that a longer presentation would have fallen flat. Vanessa knew there were few people in her school who found the middle ages as fascinating as she did.

Because Ms. Sawyer explicitly addressed the reality of presentations and their ability to fall flat with her students, her students were more comfortable with critique. She felt her students needed to understand that critique is an aspect of public endeavors that may not reap the results they planned; but if done well, constructive criticism can benefit them the next time. Her students came to realize that presentation is about learning; and as they learned, they became more at ease in front of each other. This did not mean, however, that all her students were successful. Some of her students attempted oral presentation only once. Ms. Sawyer did encourage each student to try oral presentation once during the year and all complied. As Ms. Sawyer worked with her students throughout the year, she found and has come to see that by inviting students to try, but not forcing them, to orally present gave her students the courage to make steps toward public experiences that in the past they had come to dread.

We have also found that addressing the issues of critique and the negative aspects of public presentations did not give middle level students license to become indifferent to their work, but rather allowed them to see that critique is an aspect of any public venture. McDermott (1999) states "mistakes are to learn from. But make sure the mistakes are identified and discussed. Figure out what is needed to avoid it next time" (p. 28). Taking risks is a part of learning, and middle level students will be better served if they learn that giving and taking honest feedback improves their attempts when going public.

Concluding Remarks

Presentations "force students to take a stance and permit new insights and understandings when ideas are combined . . . to share with an outside audience" (Kaufmann & Yoder, 1990, p. 139). As they engage in presentations—as individuals or as members of groups—middle level learners become more proficient over time. As teachers, the trust we put in our students as learners is manifested in the projects they share with others. These "celebration[s] of authorship" (Kaufmann & Yoder, 1990, p. 139), whether a dramatization on hate crimes, a talk on cleaning up our planet, or a brochure about who to contact in case of emergencies, are some of the most important aspects of authentic teaching and learning.

Strategies Discussed in Constructing and Co-Authoring

- Asking Questions and Synthesizing
- Advanced Organizers and Structured Overviews
- Determining Purpose
- Determining Message
- Speaking to Four Audiences
- Selecting Appropriate Format
- Developing a Flow Chart
- Engaging the Audience
- Monitoring Progress

Eighth Grade Social Studies Inquiry Projects

Vicki Sellers

When my eighth graders have finished researching, they turn to the presentation phase of their inquiry projects. Many times I ask them to follow their creative instincts and present their information in whatever form they prefer. These options often include television talk shows, films, videos, speeches, brochures, posters, magazine layouts, newsletters, essays, and books.

However, after a recent group of students prepared to enter this creative phase, we agreed to consider creating children's picture books. Rather than open the door to the full range of presentation possibilities, we set out to investigate various samples of today's picture books and learned that this type of literature can offer a great deal of high quality information in a concise and appealing way. As we examined the numerous samples, my students' eyes began to dance. Making big plans, my eighth graders excitedly set about doing their best and enjoying their creative freedom.

While some presenters utilize computer graphics and presentation software, others rely on totally original designs by hand. Regardless of their methods, my students' inquiry presentations always amaze me. When they announce that they are done and I begin opening each of their books, it reminds me of the feeling I get when I open a gift. Each book reveals a unique display of accomplishment, understanding, and wonder.

In particular, my last group of students overcame our school's unplanned and unwelcome technology dilemma and produced children's picture books in a wide array of genres and designs. Using Microsoft PowerPoint, some created multiple slides to form alphabet books, counting books, biographies, or multi-genre books detailing the lives and contributions of African American leaders, past and present.

One of my students, Lori, surprised me with her one of a kind multi-genre presentation about Ruby Bridges. Including interview information, a time line, and biographical data, Lori's book went on to share her original fictitious story of a first grader who shares her crayons with the young Bridges. Not understanding the turmoil and prejudice surrounding Bridges' experiences with desegregated education, the fellow first grader finds herself whisked away by her mother to another school, one far away from Ruby Bridges or others like her. Illustrated beautifully and emotionally profound, this picture book surpassed any previous work Lori had submitted in my class. Pride and satisfaction sparkled in her eyes, showing that she knew she had done her best and presented something of great value.

Other students request special materials for producing their books. Although I provide supplies like binding combs, construction paper, markers, colored pencils, wallpaper samples, stencils, yarn, and other textiles, Michael wished for special paper worthy of his topic, Martin Luther King, Jr. Not sure I understood, Michael explained that he wanted to use paper similar to that of the *Declaration of Independence*. When I arrived at school with parchment cardstock, he was overjoyed and busily attacked the pages of his book about the African American civil rights leader.

Designing a book about Faith Ringgold, an African American artist, Rita lagged a bit behind the rest of the class and became overwhelmed with her plans for an alphabet book. She worried that she could not complete the 26 letters of the alphabet, and agreed that reducing the number of letters to those of the artist's name would relieve her stress and allow her to get on to the "fun" part, designing the children's book. Using pinking shears to cut letters from colorful fabrics, Rita glued the letters to her PowerPoint pages of information. The result fulfilled her wishes with an exclusive version of Faith Ringgold and her art. Her book was not so much an expository text of Faith Ringgold and her work as it was Rita's response to learning about this famous artist.

To finalize these projects, students carried their treasures bound with combs to our next-door elementary school. Fifth graders, as well, had just finished writing their own books, either fantasies or autobiographies, and we invited them to participate with us in an Authoring and Book Sharing presentation. Today, I often reflect on the sense of ownership that the book projects caused, and I revel in the sense of accomplishment enjoyed by each of these students.

I have learned that these artifacts of learning, my students' books, contribute immeasurably to my students' appreciation of literature, their valuing of literacy, and their self-respect.

Finally, after presenting their books, most students hurry home with their original works in hand, but some prefer to contribute them to our school and/or classroom libraries, as proof of their efforts and as a legacy to future middle school students. Perhaps, these authors will one day visit and rediscover their books, well worn, oft read, and still alive.

Sixth Grade Language Arts/Social Studies Inquiry Projects

Rebecca Miller

If the whole world is a stage then my classroom at the end of an inquiry unit is a museum. Starting an inquiry project is exciting for my sixth graders as they are ready to dive into researching their topic. After a couple of weeks of discovering new and exciting facts about something, the students are ready to take what they have learned and create a project that shows everyone how far they have journeyed. The final project is the culminating activity in their quest for knowledge and each student delights in choosing a way of expressing herself/himself that is unique to their particular interests.

By far the most popular unit in my class every year is the World War II study. As part of this unit, the students look at the various types of memorials that have been created worldwide to commemorate the events of World War II. The assignment for the final project is intentionally vague so that the students have the most latitude to express themselves. After a field trip to view all the local memorials, the students are instructed to design a memorial for some group involved in World War II. The students then decide what group they want to memorialize and in what manner.

Over the years, I have noticed that the memorials tend to fall into three types. Some students like to build a three-dimensional project while others prefer to design and draw blueprints for a memorial. Then there are students who feel more comfortable expressing themselves through writing and produce a poem, song, or book. These three types of final projects allow the students to be creative in whatever manner they feel most comfortable.

The three dimensional projects are, of course, the most visual. Projects range from simple statues to elaborate landscapes. Several years ago, a group of students decided to commemorate the actions of the early fighter pilots. They built a memorial that included not only a plane, but also a circular wall with bricks engraved with fighter pilots' names. This group decorated their memorial with real grass; each blade glued individually, and placed sidewalks and benches in the appropriate places. Not all the three-dimensional projects are this elaborate. One student built a simple wooden cross and then painted it to look like marble. He included an inscription thanking all the men who gave their lives to guarantee our freedom. It was simple, but effective.

The blueprint projects range from simple black and white sketches to intricately detailed, drawn to scale models. I had a student whose father was an architect, and he helped draw a blueprint of a memorial for Resistance Fighters modeled after the Vietnam Wall memorial. Other students have created blueprints from photographs, magazine pictures, or hand-drawn pictures. Each blueprint includes a written description of the memorial as well as any inscriptions.

The final type of project includes poems, songs, and books. These projects span the spectrum of creative endeavors. Some students choose to write and perform a song in the style of the resistance songs. Many students use the alphabet book style to show what they have learned. By far my favorite was a book of shape poems that a group of students wrote to commemorate the millions of children who lost their lives during the war. Each poem was written by a different student and placed on an illustrated page. All of the poems taken together told the story of the different groups of children who died including children in and out of camps, Jewish children, German children, and Japanese children. The following poem was the first poem in the book and was written by a sixth grader.

> Of all the
> Losses
> That we
> Faced,
> Children
> Were
> The worst.
> Little lives that never ever were lived.
> Little dreams that never were dreamed.
> Great
> Potential
> Never
> Reached
> Because
> One Gov't
> Couldn't
> Control
> One Mad
> Man.

Although my students really enjoy the process of the inquiry projects, they truly blossom during the final stages of the assignment. Because the instructions are rather open-ended, all students are able to participate in a way that is appropriate for them. Taking the knowledge that they have gained through inquiry and presenting it in a suitable manner seems to cement their learning and allows each student to achieve success in demonstrating what she/he has learned.

Chapter 8

Co-Authoring and Confirming: The Importance of Assessment and Self-Reflection

This was a project that I made using information on the Toltecs ancient civilization. That was the Mexican group my project is dealing with. I collected my information using the Internet and informational books. I also collected information using a magazine article. From my project, I leaned that the Toltecs picked the name Toltecs because of their great craftsmanship and artists and poets. [Through the presentations of others . . .] I learned information on the Mayan math system which I learned they use bars, dots, shells, and . . . I also learned information on the Inuit houses and the fact that they use whale blubber for the heat. These are some of the things I learned about mine and other people's inquiry projects.

—Marie, Mr. Hiedeman's seventh grade Geography Class

"Changes in the workplace and society at large suggest people need to be flexible and adaptable and apply as well as acquire knowledge. Assessment in school must be related to what a student knows, applies, and performs" (Stowell & McDaniel, 1997, p. 137). Assessment then should be an integral aspect of learning. Teachers who focus on personal, authentic, and life long learning incorporate assessments that encourage their students to learn even as they are demonstrating their learning.

Within the inquiry framework, the goal is rarely knowledge for knowledge's sake. Rather we want students to apply, analyze, synthesize and critique using the knowledge that they have acquired. Students' learning and their demonstrations of this learning function on a kind of spiral rather than being linear, as they are recursive as well as developmental. In the assessments that fit in with an inquiry, it is easy to recognize the influence of Bloom's taxonomy (see Figure 8.1) and to realize how rarely in a traditional instructional pattern we get to the higher orders. "Ultimately, students need to be prepared in every aspect of their learning environment and their programs to make responsible choices, to find voice to do so, and to take responsibility for those choices" (Liner & Butler, 2000, p. 151).

- Knowledge
- Comprehension
- Application
- Analysis
- Synthesis
- Evaluation

Figure 8.1 Bloom's Taxonomy

In this chapter, using examples from Mr. Hiedeman's seventh grade Geography class, we discuss the importance as well as the procedures for on-going, authentic assessment through:

- Principles of Assessment
- Formative and Summative Assessment
- Assessment Strategies
- Record Keeping

Principles of Assessment

Within a classroom community structured around an inquiry framework, assessment is developmentally responsive so that it both informs the work of the classroom and provides information on student progress and growth. It is understood that learning is never either just high expectations or "coddling" students. Rather, it is both teachers', parents', and students' high expectations for student accomplishments **and** adequate and appropriate support that assures that the students reach these expectations. The continuous development of the four efficacy elements of confidence, independence, metacognition, and stamina are embedded in our students' willingness to meet challenges and take risks.

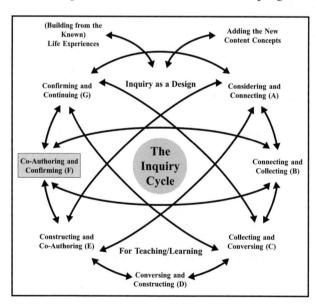

Figure 8.2 The Inquiry Cycle

As educators, we want our students to become consciously aware that learning is a natural part of being human and to see themselves as active, engaged learners.

However, if the challenges become either "a walk in the park" or a "grueling climb to Mt. Everest," what they are learning is that school is not a place where they are apt to learn much. Therefore, assessments that merely generate a number or a letter in order to sort and label students are at best useless and at worst destructive to the learning process.

> The trend today in middle school assessment is toward authentic types of measurement that focus less on recall of information than on processing of information. Product, portfolio, and performance tools, and techniques, for example, reflect the mission of the middle school and its philosophy and components better than do their traditional counterparts of criterion and norm referenced tests. (Lounsbury, 1995, p. 331)

Cooper (1995) talks about eight principles of effective literacy assessment. These principles are important to our discussion of co-authoring and confirming as they reinforce the purpose and intent of assessment as an integral part of the inquiry cycle. As we go through the aspects of assessment and its role in inquiry, literacy, and learning, it is important to keep these principles in mind.

1. Assessment should be an ongoing process.
2. Effective assessment is an integral part of instruction.
3. Assessment must be authentic, reflecting "real" reading and writing.
4. Assessment should be a collaborative, reflective process.
5. Effective assessment is multidimensional.
6. Assessment should be developmentally and culturally appropriate.
7. Effective assessment identifies students' strengths.
8. Assessment must be based on what we know about how student learn to read and write.

Formative and Summative Assessment

In an inquiry framework, assessment strategies vary according to the needs of the learners in the community. Most of the assessment is formative and is accomplished through learner self-evaluations and teacher observation, teacher/student conversation and conferences, and work in progress portfolios. The purpose of formative assessment is to guide instruction and engagement. This kind of assessment is an integral part of the work of the classroom on a daily basis and becomes part of the planning for engagement. As Meghan Luckett states in her Canadian Inquiry vignette (see chapter 2), "Because I know that all my students shine in various areas, it is my job to make my assessments varied."

Summative assessments are more formal and offer cumulative information about student progress. The teacher and students develop rubrics for summative assessment together (Andrade, 2000). "At their best, rubrics are also teaching tools that support student learning and the development of sophisticated thinking skills. When used correctly, they serve purposes of learning as well as of evaluation and accountability" (p. 13). Often these are culminating assessments completed at the conclusion of an inquiry or a particular section of the cycle. Summative assessment includes such strategies as product portfolios, formal presentations and performances, publications, and displays.

While we recognize both high stakes testing and report card grades as a current reality, the goal in an inquiry framework is always to demonstrate learning as evidenced by continuous growth and development (Kohn, 1999; Smith, 1998; Glasser, 1992). Throughout this book, we have shown how the inquiry framework provides for teaching and learning that allows students to develop all of the necessary "skills" and "abilities" to do well on high stakes tests as well as "get good grades." As Brett Seller's (see end of chapter vignette) describes in his discussion of assessment in his eighth grade science classroom, negotiated grades allow all students to evaluate their learning based on actual gains and growth. It allows all students to take credit for the learning that they have gained. It builds the kind of confidence and independence, and demands the kind of metacognition and stamina, that are integral to all students doing their best on standardized tests and other traditional evaluation measures.

Assessments that demand the memorization of narrow fact-based information often demand instruction that is narrow and limited and this keeps students dependent and often dampens their confidence, because their only opportunity for success or failure is dependent on these narrow measures. It discourages metacognition and demands specific behaviors that are thought to assure test success.

A case in point is the Texas Assessment of Knowledge and Skills (TAKS) (Texas Education Agency, 2003), which ranks among the highest achievement scores of all state tests in the country. However, at the same time, Texas students who take the SAT's achieve among the lowest scores of high school students in the country. This to us is an apt example of why assessment and evaluation need to mirror real learning and exemplary teaching.

The International Reading Association's Commission on Adolescent Literacy (see chapter 2 for a complete listing of these principles) includes as the third principle in its position statement (Moore, et al., 1996) that "Adolescents deserve assessment that shows them their strengths as well as their needs and that guides their teachers to design instruction that will best help them grow as readers. In sum, the Commission on Adolescent Literacy believes that adolescents deserve classroom assessments that

- Are regular extensions of instruction;
- Provide usable feedback based on clear, attainable, and worthwhile standards;

- Exemplify quality performance illustrating the standards; and
- Position students as partners with teachers evaluating progress and setting goals. (p. 103)

Assessment Strategies

Observational Assessments

Within the inquiry framework, the teacher becomes an active listener and a "kidwatcher" (Goodman, 1978). Through observation, conversation, and portfolio reviews, she determines with the students what their needs are in terms of content and literacy learning. Kidwatching is a continuous, systematic look at the process of how students learn. Through kidwatching, teachers can take what they know about students and turn that knowledge into effective invitations. Kidwatching can be used to give voice to students who might otherwise be silent by assuring that the teacher gets to know each student in a variety of contexts (see chapter 1 for a detailed definition of "kid watching").

Knowing Students

Getting to know our students is a key to the success of inquiry. It is important for all middle school personnel to know the developmental aspects of this age group (see chapter 1, Figure 1.3). It is equally important to know each student as a unique individual who grapples in unique ways with growing up and becoming a decision-making adult. Knowing our students means talking with them and observing them without prejudgment. One of the best ways to think about what we know about our students and what we need to still find out is to ask "why" questions instead of making concluding statements about them. We discussed this concept briefly in chapter 2, but it deserves reiteration here. For example, saying, "Sarah never does her work. She just won't complete anything" smacks of finality. It is almost as if we are saying that for all time, Sarah simply is someone who will not do work or complete work. We are merely stuck with this "conclusion" about Sarah, which doesn't compel us to any action on her behalf. On the other hand, if we preface our statements with "I wonder why Sarah doesn't do her work?" then we are compelled to think further and to come up with a plan to help Sarah overcome the things that stand in the way of her productivity. It opens avenues for focusing our attention on enabling our students, rather than merely writing them off in ways that either hold them back or push them on, neither of which will lead to their becoming successful academic learners.

It is also important to note here that within inquiry, assessment is not about the teacher being the all knowing Science (social studies, math, language arts, art, music, Spanish, French, Physical Education . . .) teacher who holds up hoops through which they themselves could walk with ease and sort their students by who can also jump through with ease. Rather, it is not necessary that content teachers be absolute experts on the content that we are teaching. In fact, it is important within an inquiry framework, and we would argue within any instructional practice, that we model our learning process as well as our knowing. It is too easy for our students to say to themselves especially when they are struggling, "Yeah, I see you knowing/doing that, I don't see me knowing/doing that." But if we show them the ways in which we approach academic learning, then they can engage in the strategies we demonstrate for them and they can experience the learning more deliberately. When this happens, they do "see themselves knowing/doing" but as a result of a learning process rather than a magical "knowing" ability. This is where metacognition becomes an integral aspect of the inquiry framework. It is through deliberate metacognition that students can become self-reflective. Self-reflection as we will discuss later in more detail becomes a major assessment tool.

Opportunities to Demonstrate Learning

Within the inquiry framework, students show their learning through many authentic uses of both literacy strategies and content knowledge. It is through this demonstration of knowledge, understandings, and applications, that authentic assessment provides the evidence both teachers and students need to determine and to acknowledge academic growth and to plan for continuous development. In Figure 8.3, we have given some examples of engagements that allow students to show their learning through the assessment strategies listed in each box.

Describe: essays, sketch to stretch, literature circles, glossary, pamphlets, posters	**Explain:** logs, journals, notes, literature circles, mini-presentations, reports, essays, conferences	**Predict:** silent readings, uses of context, uses of prior knowledge, quick writes, exit cards, experiments
Infer: logs, intertextual essays, speeches, dramatizations, pictures, concept maps	**Create:** scripts, book-making, pictures, graphic organizers, poems, letters, newscasts, maps, time-lines	**Solve:** journals, interviews, dialogue journals, debates, experiments, uses of analogies and metaphors
Estimate: experiments, problem posing and solving, connecting with prior knowledge/experiences	**Compare:** Literature Circles, Venn diagrams, say something, debates, maps, think-alouds, multi-genre writings	**Discover:** silent reading, browsing, skimming, scanning, viewing, interviewing, experimenting
Synthesize: graphic organizers, essays, using multiple references, sharing across texts.	**Perform:** become the character, say something, read-alouds	**Interpret:** think from multiple perspectives, dialogue journals, paired discussions, debates

Figure 8.3 Assessment Strategies for Student Learning

Relate: similarity and differences charts, this reminds me of…, notes and quick writes, KFN chart	**Inform:** news articles, brochures. books, posters, speeches, maps	**Respond:** logs, journals, say something, pictures, dramatizations, movement
Reason: think critically, give pros and cons, list the whys, use metaphors/analogies	**Communicate:** write, speak, question, debate, agree, disagree, share perspectives, share experiences, present information and ideas	**Invent:** write directions, create machines, solve problems, write scripts, plan events

Figure 8.3 Assessment Strategies for Student Learning *(Continued)*

Student Self-Reflection/Self-Assessment

I liked inquiry learning because this is a good way of collecting information on the Mayan native groups and their way of living. I also liked the inquiry learning because I didn't even know that the Toltecs existed before I did this project. This was a very cool project and I'm glad I did it.

—Sarah, Mr. Hiedeman's seventh grade Geography class

As the above reflection demonstrates, inquiry as a framework for teaching and learning provides the structure and support needed for middle level students to be actively engaged in continuous learning, adding the new to the known. The questions for self-reflection in Figure 8.4 reflect the notion that assessing inquiry work and projects is a matter of finding "value" (Hansen, 1998). We want students first and foremost to recognize their strengths, so that when they pinpoint areas for growth, they can easily develop a plan that builds from their strengths. The questions can be used to assess a day's work or an entire project. It is important that students reflect frequently. A quick way to accomplish this is with an exit card on which students write three plusses and one wish for the day's work—three things they feel went well, one thing they will work on.

1. What criteria are you using to evaluate your work?
2. According to these criteria, list the things you did well.
3. What did you try that was new for you?
4. What was your greatest accomplishment?
5. What would you like to improve? State this as a goal.
6. What will you do to achieve your goal?
7. What support do you need to achieve your goal? Who will you seek out to get this support?
8. What evidence will you use to assess the achievement of your goal?

Figure 8.4 Guidelines for Self-Reflection

Revision of Process and Product

Once students have completed an inquiry cycle and we are in the transition stage, we ask them to revisit their work—both process and product—of the inquiry cycle they just completed. Revisiting at the end of an inquiry cycle allows students to reflect upon their individual contributions to an inquiry as well as the dynamics of the collaboration in the small group work. This revisiting also allows students to contemplate what they would revise in their next inquiry effort.

Revisiting with the purpose of revising encourages students to think about their learning rather than relegating it to the "past and over with" file—a phenomenon that happens frequently at the middle level. We want our students to celebrate their learning while also embedding or connecting it to their prior knowledge as well as being able to call upon it in future projects. To help them with their revisiting and revisions, we created a series of questions they can answer during the inquiry transition (see Appendix 12).

- What did you accomplish during this inquiry?
- What did you do especially well?
- What was the most difficult challenge for you?
- How could the school/librarian/teacher help you during the next inquiry?
- What particular aspect of this inquiry will you take away with you?
- What do you need more work on for your presentation?
- How did you help others learn?
- How did others help you learn?

We allow students to discuss the questions in small groups before they write their answers individually. Through discussion and then quiet reflection, we create an environment that recognizes the importance of our thoughts while also sharing those ideas with others.

Assessing the Inquiry Unit

A third activity that the entire class completes at the end of each inquiry is an assessment of the unit (see Appendix 13). Often students can assess their own participation and their own work, but to ask them to think about the unit and the mini-lessons that we planned and implemented as part of the inquiry is more difficult. We ask our students to complete this assessment so that we can think about how to plan for upcoming inquiry cycles. From our students' comments and suggestions, we are better able to meet their needs as young adolescents as well as learners in our classrooms. The following list of questions are included on our inquiry assessments:

- What was the most interesting part of the inquiry?
- What part of the inquiry did you enjoy most? Least?
- What did you think of the mini-lessons?
- What suggestions would you have for our next inquiry cycle?

When we ask students to assess the inquiry cycle and the lessons we created for them, we list the mini-lessons we taught so students can address those lessons specifically. Our mini-lessons can range from research and data collection strategies to the use of appositives in writing to information on the gestation period of wolves. By listing these on the board, we also invite our students to realize just how much they have been learning through the inquiry.

Record Keeping

The following is a list of the kinds of records it is useful for teachers and students to keep during an inquiry and the kinds of information that can be generated from each. We are rather arbitrarily using the four categories of observational assessments, student self-assessments, working portfolios, and product portfolios. It will be apparent as you read through these that many of the strategies are pertinent in more than one category and that there is a lot of overlap. We have tried to list strategies only once in what we feel is its primary place but, again, this is open to some argument. Therefore, the important thing is not the category into which an assessment is placed, but that it is recorded and the information used to both drive instruction and facilitate student learning.

Observational Assessments

Kidwatching Notes

These include information about interest, engagement, misconceptions, collaboration, communication, strength of efficacy elements, learning, literacy strategies used well, and ones that need strengthening.

Browsing Notes

These make note of students' choices, how they are using skimming and scanning strategies, and how well they are reading pictures.

Informal sharing

Through informal student sharing, teachers can determine interest, enthusiasm, connections, knowledge base, and accuracy of understandings.

Literature Circles

These provide information about students' relationships with peers, accuracy, misconceptions, confusions, intertextual connections, and personal experiences.

Student Self-Assessments

Silent Reading Logs

The students assess the *what, how,* and *why* of the materials they have chosen, the *how* and *why* of the information gathered and organized, how well they have used their time spent, and how they have maintained their focus.

Literature Circles

The students assess their preparation and participation in these discussions focusing on both what they bring and add to the discussion and the ways in which they listen, learn, and facilitate the learning of their peers.

Read Alouds

The students assess their preparation and delivery. They also look at the reading strategies they used in preparing to share the read aloud. They assess also such things as confidence, enthusiasm, and relevancy.

Working Portfolios

Notes

Information on the key ideas and connections they are making. Notes show accuracy, knowledge acquisition, intertextual connections, and use of vocabulary.

Nonverbal artifacts

These include pictures, graphics, maps, and so forth.

Question Asking and Problem Posing

These reflect students' interest and background and indicate levels of questions that are relevant, open-ended, specific, and critical.

Read aloud Preparation

Here the students record the *whys* of their choices, the *how* of their rehearsal, and the connections to the inquiry and to their learning.

Glossary/Vocabulary Use

These records indicate knowledge acquisition; content concepts; critical thinking; and level of confidence with language, accuracy, and relevancy used in multiple contexts.

Use of Various Text Structures in Both Reading and Writing

These records indicate understanding, connection, and integration.

Learning Logs

These reflect students' accuracy, concept understanding, application, and critical thinking.

Reflective Journals

These indicate metacognitive understandings, misconceptions, and confusions.

Graphic Organizers

These indicate information synthesis, integration.

Summaries/Synopses

These indicate depth of knowledge acquisition and critical thinking.

Demonstration and Presentation Preparation

The information that is recorded about demonstrations and presentations reflects the application of the content learned, critical application of this content, and its integration into the unit of study.

Concluding Remarks

We believe that effective assessment, both formative and summative, within a middle level inquiry framework must be multi-perspective, ongoing, learning centered, and it must foster the development of the four efficacy elements. Students need to be "in on" the process and have both a say and a stake in the ways of assessing their academic learning. In order for this to occur, students must have many avenues for demonstrating learning along the way, choices for the ways in which they demonstrate culminating accomplishments, opportunities for self-evaluation and reflection, opportunities for peer feed-back, and opportunities for revision of both process and product.

Strategies Discussed in Co-Authoring and Confirming

Teacher Observation Records

- Kidwatching Notes
- Browsing Notes
- Informal Sharing
- Literature Circles

Student Records

- Silent Reading Logs
- Literature Circles
- Read Alouds

Working Portfolios

- Notes
- Non-Verebal Artifacts
- Questions and Problems Posed
- Read-Aloud Preparation
- Glossary/Vocabulary Used
- Use of Text Structures
- Learning Logs
- Reflective Journals
- Graphic Organizers
- Summary/Synopsis Papers
- Demonstration or Presentation Preparation

Eighth Grade Science

Brett Sellers

Several years ago I had this special student, Jasmine. She was what most people would call the perfect student. She went on to become the valedictorian of her class in a large high school. She did have one small problem. After several attempts at the ACT, she could score no higher than 14. I wondered what I had done to her;

it must have been my fault. It was, because I enabled her not to think. When she asked a question, I answered. When she asked for clarification, I clarified. When she asked about what was expected, I told her. When she acted confused, I helped. I kept her updated on her progress. I gave her extra credit work when she asked. She worked as hard as she could to please me and I worked hard as I could to please her; and she wanted A's. After her time with me, she moved on to the next teacher and did the same. She did the same for 13 years. She graduated with all A's but unable to think on her own.

Matt entered my science class 2 years ago as a seventh grader. I was told that he was brilliant. His past teachers told me this, his student records agreed, and his parents added to his glory. It seemed that they were all right about him, but I soon discovered that he did not like to think.

At the same time, Sally came into my class. She was a little older because of past failures. She was very out going and loved to discuss about any topic as long as she did not have to do anything. The 30 assignments that we were going to do during the marking period were not going to get done.

All the teachers loved Jasmine and Matt but they could not tolerate Sally. I spent a lot of time thinking about these students. Jasmine, I could not help other than advise. Matt and Sally I might be able to help. Sally improved this year by using the negotiation of both the curriculum and grading. She liked having a choice of what she was learning and how she was learning it. She also used her verbal skills in presenting her understanding and in negotiating. School became somewhat interesting again. Matt struggled early in the school year. He wanted to be told exactly what to learn and what answers to give. He had problems making choices. Yet, he was able to grow and develop within this system and to better understand his learning (see Figures 8.5 and 8.6).

SELF REFLECTION SHEET

STUDENT NAME: Matt   DATE: _____

PROJECT/ASSIGNMENT NAME: Storm Chaser

PROJECT/ASSIGNMENT GRADE: (A) (B) C D E

Explain why you selected the grade circled above for this assignment based only on what you have learned or can now do. Describe three if possible.
My assignment did good in some and bad in others. I did get done on time. So I should get at least a B.

Explain how your study skill affected the quality of your learning on this assignment. Describe three ways if possible.
I worked hard, had a little problem in listen to others, and talk some in dissusions.

Explain how your social skills affected the quality of your learning on this assignment. Describe three ways if possible.
I think I have a healthy social status. I think I do well in this class with pairs.

Explain why this assignment is or is not your best ever.
I think I need to improve but I think I am a hard working student

Figure 8.5 Matt's "Storm Chaser" Self-Reflection Sheet

Recently, during conferences a parent asked if her son was slow or odd. She informed me of struggles that she was having with him regarding school. She said that he had made no progress the past 2 years, and she was considering having him repeat eighth grade. I agreed that he was a challenge and did "march to his own drum" but that he had made tremendous progress the past 2 years. I found his seventh grade portfolio, and we compared it to his current portfolio. With tears in her eyes, she realized there was no doubt that he had made a lot of progress. We could also see not only the areas of growth, but the areas where we needed to focus more attention. With extra help and tutoring, he continued to improve and did not repeat eighth grade.

SELF REFLECTION SHEET

STUDENT NAME: Matt _____ DATE: _____

PROJECT/ASSIGNMENT NAME: Tug Tug _____

PROJECT/ASSIGNMENT GRADE: A (B) C D E

Explain why you selected the grade circled above for this assignment based only on what you have learned or can now do.

I have learned what forces are and how they are affected by energy. They affect me in my daily life. I understand that objects move when unbalance forces work on them. I know that energy affects the amount of movement on an object.

What part of this project/assignment are you most proud of?

My representation of the tug of war event and how the forces became unbalanced causing one team to win. I also had a cool drawing.

If possible, how would you improve this project/assignment?

I would expand upon my writen part to explain better what I mean and include so other real life examples.

COMMENTS:

I think I am learning this stuff better.

Figure 8.6 Matt's "Tug Tug" Self-Reflection Sheet

So why was I asked to pen this chapter? I probably drew the shortest straw again. A more likely answer, though, is that after teaching 20 some years as a Middle School utility teacher (the teacher that teaches a different subject or two every year), working many years on curriculum, spending several years mentoring new teachers, being open to new ideas, and not afraid to try new things, I have developed into quite a resource. As a local college professor told me recently, "I tell my classes of future teachers about a dream classroom and they reply that such a classroom can not exist, then I tell them I know where this classroom does exist." I am flattered but like most teachers, I am just trying to improve upon my craft of teaching. I will admit though that I do things in a nontraditional way. So the following is a little about what I do in the area of assessment and evaluation with inquiry.

Like most teachers I sit through a lot of meetings, conferences, and professional development of all types. I hear all sorts of people tell me how I should teach or what I could do to improve my teaching. But, until the last few years I had never asked my students how I should teach. What do students know, especially middle school students, about teaching? Well, they know a lot of stuff about how they learn best. Mix this with some of the latest research on learning and you have a different picture then the one you often get from the meetings you attend. The basic fact is that assessments are powerful tools that are used to craft students' learning, the curriculum of schools, the economics of our country, and our public policy.

I start each school year with a new group of students like most teachers, unless I am looping. The first day of business is the usual stuff, but the students also get to ask me questions. I feel that it is important to be human in the eyes of the students in order to create the best possible learning atmosphere. As the first week begins my focus is to get all of the students to tell me some how what they want to learn. I tell them that there is no set curriculum for me to follow and that they are determining what they are going to learn. In some places this is called negotiating the curriculum, which is a title I like. But what about that set in stone curriculum that I must follow? I follow it! I cannot teach what every student wants to learn, all at the same time. So I develop a sequence that we will follow to create time for the students to learn the answers to their question. Almost all of this can be done within the framework of the curriculum. The small percentage that does not fit into the curriculum is left to the end of the year for special projects. The end result is students have had their questions answered by the time they leave my classroom at the end of the year. If I am looping this gives me even more time and flexibility to meet THEIR interests and needs.

So how do I manage to let students negotiate the curriculum? First, I do cover all the required objectives or benchmarks within the curriculum. (I have an average of 34 benchmarks per year.) I may flex the sequence of content a little but I do get everything covered as expected. I can also show my peers, administrators, parents, and others that all requirements are taken care of. Secondly, I sell this idea to the students and to their parents. Most students don't believe it when I tell them that they have a choice in what they are learning. As we develop community within the class, I constantly sell them the idea that they have the power of choice within my class. I also sell the idea to their parents at open house, conferences, after school events, the grocery store, and anywhere I can. Don't you want your children to be able to make decisions? That is what successful people do. What about the administrators? Remember, you can lead a horse to water but you can't make it drink. Administrators want students to be engaged in learning. If students have no interest in whatever the topic is then they will not drink. Yet, if they believe that they have a choice or see a value to what is being done in the class they will more than likely drink. What administrator would not want this for students?

I also feel that it is important to develop community within the classroom for each class period. In developing community, we are not only developing the guidelines of the class but our identity. It amazes me that some teachers, administrators, and even parents expect each class to be exactly the same. My children are not even the same within my family, how can we expect a bunch of different kids to fit the same mold? As part of this, I spend time helping students identify what quantity and quality are and how it relates to them and others. This is an ongoing process throughout the year, but I focus on it early in the school year and continue to build on it. I also spend time developing a risk free environment where students feel free to express themselves. So it is sometimes several weeks into the year before we begin the actual content of the curriculum. This gives me time to put together the sequence of the curriculum that will guide us through the year. Once that is done and we have a good start at creating a good learning atmosphere, we are ready to begin.

I always start a unit of study by doing some type of pre-assessment piece. As an example, I may have a weather unit to do in a science class. My benchmarks are as follows:

1. Explain patterns of changing weather and how they are measured.

2. Describe the composition and characteristics of the atmosphere.

3. Explain the behavior of water in the atmosphere.

All students have opinions and ideas. I like to have each student express these within the content at the beginning of a unit. I may do this by asking them to respond verbally or in writing to a specific question or questions. As an example, I give each student a picture of a weather map of North America. I tell them that this is a weather map of Monday of this week, they are going to an area amusement park on Saturday of this week, how will they dress. I could also give them some type of activity piece to start their wheels spinning—such as a picture of weather, a cloud drawing activity, or a video clip on weather. Some teachers call this a hook, something that catches their attention. I use hooks to catch their attention and to drive the unit. These same hooks will be used to evaluate the student's progress throughout the unit not just at the end. This way I have embedded the assessment and use it as a way to drive what I do as a teacher and how I prepare the lessons.

Once I have an idea of where my students are, I can develop the unit. I like to use some type of inquiry at this time. I give students some leading questions that allow them to explore for possible solutions. An example is, "What are the causes of weather?" We use a text set of multiple materials with a variety of resource books, picture books, magazines, newspapers, the library, and the Internet. Students will then have the opportunity to share their discoveries with each other and with me. I like to ask a lot of questions at this time as a model but give few answers. Once I have an idea of what the students are thinking I develop what I call mini-lessons to help fill in the missing pieces and to further develop the understanding of content. We continue to hammer away at not only the content but at the specific questions of the students.

As the students in class continue to grow and develop, I continue to assess. I like to use entrance or exit slips. These are questions that students have about what they are studying. I read them to the class where any student is encouraged to comment or answer the question. I may add my understanding of the topic or lead them to question more their ideas or understanding. My purpose is to draw out of them as much as I possibly can. I believe that most students have the ability to think and reason out solutions to problems but are usually not asked to or are not expected to. If I have created a risk free classroom, students will begin to think. The complaint most often uttered by my students is "Why do you make us think?" "That is how you learn," I reply. When students have put a value on what they are learning, they will more likely be internally motivated to learn more and make sense of the world around them.

I also like to survey the class. Often in class I have individual students or small groups of students working on some idea in many different ways. I call this orderly confusion. I have a class record sheet where I can quickly ask students what they are doing, how far along they are, and what their goal is for the class period. I can do this out loud within the class or meet with each student or group individually. I have then collected a piece of data that I can use in different ways, especially to keep track of how the class is progressing.

Eventually I need to know if the students can apply what they have been doing to solve a problem. This past year in my science class we had been investigating weather. My job was to produce students that had a basic understanding of the different types of weather, the causes of weather, the role of water and pressure in weather, and the ability to predict weather. The assessment piece was a 3-day project where students could work individually or with a partner to produce a 30-second weather report, as storm chasers (see Figure 8.7).

You have just been hired as a storm chaser for the Channel 41 Weather Watch Team. Part of your job is not only finding violent storms of every kind and recording them, but also explaining the patterns of changing weather, how they are measured, and the effects of water in the atmosphere.

As part of your job you are given equipment to use to accomplish your task. These include the following:

1. Jeep Cherokee
2. Satellite imaging system, doppler radar
3. Video equipment
4. Thermometer
5. Rain gauge
6. Weather vane
7. Anemometer
8. Cloud charts
9. Barometer
10. Computer
11. Road Maps

Given the last 3 days forecasts, you need to predict where the next storm will occur in the United States, explain how and why, and also create a visual representation to present to the public. You have 3 days to complete your challenge. Good luck.

Figure 8.7 Storm Chaser Assignment Sheet

The problem was to take 3 consecutive days of weather maps, predict the weather on the 4th day, pack the appropriate weather tools and instruments, travel to the site of the predicted weather event, record in journal form what happened, and produce the 30 second weather report about the event you witnessed. Anyone who watched these students' weather reports knew what students knew what about weather. I video taped the presentations and showed some during parent-teacher conferences. This gave parents a good understanding of the progress that their student was making. I also used a variety of weather maps from different times of the year so there would be a variety of weather events including a beautiful sunny day. This gives me a truer picture of student progress.

NAME: ______________________________
HOUR: ________ DATE: ________________

PERFORMANCE RATING:

NO EVIDENCE	1
APPROACHES GOAL	2
MEETS GOAL	3
EXCEEDS GOAL	4
NOT APPLICABLE	5

CRITERIA:

Applies a variety of weather measuring instruments to measure temperature, wind speed and direction, cloud cover, humidity, dew point, amount of rainfall and other weather phenomena.	1 2 3 4 5
Uses weather maps and satellite images to detect and predict weather patterns. Identifies cold fronts, warm fronts, stationary fronts, high pressure, low pressure, and other weather phenomena.	1 2 3 4 5
Utilizes maps, satellite images, and other information to solve weather problem.	1 2 3 4 5
Appropriateness of visual representation.	1 2 3 4 5
Uses creativity in visual representation.	1 2 3 4 5
Neat and well-prepared visual representation.	1 2 3 4 5
Presentation of visual representation clear and accurate.	1 2 3 4 5
Explains presentation of visual representation clear and accurate.	1 2 3 4 5

COMPLETE SOCIAL AND STUDY SKILL RUBRICS ON BACK

Figure 8.8a Storm Chaser Evaluation

I also allow students to grade themselves, a process called negotiated grading. After students have completed an activity or evaluation piece, they complete a rubric of how they feel they did (see Figures 8.8a & b).

I create a rubric for most activities and all evaluations, which the students get at the start. I collect the completed rubrics and materials from each student. I then go through the material the student produces checking for growth and development of skills and knowledge. I then complete the rubric and return it and the materials to the student. I then give the student a grade/refection sheet to complete (see Figure 8.9).

STUDENT: ________________
DATE: ________________

SOCIAL AND STUDY SKILLS

BE—Beyond Expectations
ME—Meets Expectations
PTE—Progressing Towards Expectations
NME—Not Meeting Expectations

SOCIAL	BE	ME	PTE	NME
Assumes responsibility for own actions and words.				
Relates well to others.				
Is courteous and respectful towards others.				
Respects the rights and property of others.				
Listens while others speak.				
Accepts correction.				
Follows school and classroom expectations.				

COMMENTS:

STUDY	BE	ME	PTE	NME
Organizes work and materials.				
Listens carefully.				
Follows directions.				
Works independently.				
Works quietly.				
Makes good use of time.				
Participants in activities and discussions.				
Works cooperatively in group activities.				

COMMENTS:

Figure 8.8b Negotiating Grading Rubric

STUDENT NAME: _____

PROJECT/ASSIGNMENT NAME: _____

PROJECT/ASSIGNMENT GRADE: A   B   C   D   E   S   U
                                      (circle one of these choices)

Explain why you selected the grade circled above for this assignment based only on
what you have learned or can do.

_____

_____

_____

_____

_____

Explain how your study skills affected your grade choice.

_____

_____

_____

Explain how your social behavior affected your grade choice.

_____

_____

_____

STUDENT COMMENTS:

_____

_____

_____

Figure 8.9 Self Reflection Sheet

Students reflect on their learning, study skills, and social skills. They then grade themselves and turn this back into me. I read the reflections and review the rubric. If I agree with the grade choice of the student, that becomes the student's grade, and if I do not, the student and I negotiate the student's grade. Often students will redo or improve their original work.

Assessment Strategies

Quizzes

I feel that the purpose of a quiz is to gain information about knowledge and skills. As a teacher I design a quiz with a specific purpose of checking where my students are at that time. This way I can adjust how I go through the material that needs to be covered. I can also mediate with students who are having difficulty with the material.

The students can also benefit from a quiz. The student can check for their understanding of the content during a quiz. If the student has scored well, they can continue with their progress. If the student does not do well, they can now seek extra help.

As a teacher I do not grade quizzes. I prefer to embed them within the curriculum content as a way to check progress and adjust the curriculum, such as the pace or how I deliver the content. Students are to use quiz results to adjust their progress without the fear of failure. To help them analyze their results, I often have them write a short reflection about their results.

Entrance and Exit Slips

Entrance and exit slips are an idea that I picked up several years ago from a Chicago area teacher. Students put their name and date on a quarter sheet of paper. I then ask a specific question for them to respond to. The question may deal with something that happened the day before (entrance slip) or during class that day (exit slip). I may ask students to respond to a specific idea or to reflect on their learning as an individual or group. This gives the student time to focus on their understanding of an idea or skill. As the teacher, I read these to gain insight on the class and on individual students. Again, the purpose of the slips is to give the teacher and students an idea about their progress, so these should not be graded.

Tests

I hate to give and correct tests. Most tests I see that students take serve little actual purpose. Students who understand the material or guess well do well on tests and those who do not, have problems succeeding. (I used to be the student who understood the material but did not score well on tests.) And then there are the students who do nothing and score well on tests. And if you do not score well on a test, you can just do extra credit to improve your grade. So what is the purpose of a test? Have you ever asked a student?

I sometimes have students design their own test. The "better" students quite often develop tests that require the lowest amount of knowledge and thinking. When asked why, they general reply that they wanted an *A*. The opposite group of students will often develop a test that requires a higher level of thinking. When asked why, they often reply that this is the material that they have been studying, so it should be tested.

I will occasionally test students. The tests I develop are not the true or false or multiple-choice type. I feel that students need the opportunity to display what they can do and know. So a test may ask students for a possible solution to a real-life problem. These are often given as a pre-test and post-test for the content of the curriculum. They allow students to work within their own comfort level and style. I also get a variety of test products to grade instead of the same boring one given to every student.

Portfolios

I have used portfolios for years. What better way to show the growth and development of students then to see it with your eyes. Portfolios can be used for a specific purpose (like writing), for a chapter (like order of operation), a unit (like the study of Asia), or a class (like Science). Artists have used portfolios for years to be able to demonstrate their artistic talents. Students can use them for the same reason. A student portfolio can contain specific items as directed by the teacher. Students can also select specific pieces to be showcased in their portfolio. A mixture of teacher required pieces and student-selected pieces works well. I enjoy having students look at their portfolio and see their development. Parents can also get a good understanding of their student's growth and development with a portfolio.

Observations

I quite often use student observations to assess their growth and development. Over the years, I have put together a quick checklist where I can check any or all students during a class period. These observations most often focus on the study and social skill students need to be successful. I can also check for knowledge during discussions or question and answer activities. To do this, I have a checklist that focuses not only on correct or incorrect responses but also on the types of questions and who generated the questions.

I am quite often asked how I can do this and still be a part of class. Inquiry type lessons give me time to roam the classroom watching and listening to students. I can sit down one-on-one with a student or small group. I can survey them for a variety of items and then move on to others. In a fairly short time, I can get to most of the students if not all of them. This is especially helpful to those students with special needs. I often carry a clipboard with me to record information. I sometimes keep several clipboards around the room so I can record observations on the closest one. I always date information and have a brief description of the lesson and the learning objective(s) being covered. It is nice to be able to sit down with a student, parent, teacher, or administrator and be able to analyze the progress of a student. Observations can be very powerful assessments but do require more organization and record keeping.

Authentic Assessment

Do you want to engage students and assess their understanding and skill level? Authentic assessment is your answer. Instead of meaningless tests, give students the opportunity to demonstrate their growth and development by focusing on real life situations that they can relate to better. It has been a while since I heard a student ask, "Where will I ever use this stuff?" with the use of authentic assessment. Instead of a test on the hydrosphere and pollution, I have actually had students test samples of area water to determine their drinkability. This uses the complete scientific method with writing, spelling, reading, computer, math, geography, and much more, in a 2 to 3 day assessment. This is much richer learning than a test the students memorize and forget by tomorrow.

Projects

Projects are a way of opening the eyes of your learners. Projects can be used as a way of practice or as an evaluation, they can be specific in focus or allow students to be creative, and they can be a way for students to use and to develop multiple skills and knowledge. I frequently use projects as the backbone for the curriculum. These projects are a way of addressing the curriculum in an interesting way that allows students to work towards their strengths as well as to improve areas of weakness without the risk of failure. In fact, the creation of a risk free atmosphere is important in doing projects. Projects must have basic goals for students to work towards, but should not be so controlling as to not give students the opportunity to explore. Figures 8.10 and 8.11 provide examples of projects I have done with my students.

Protecting my lunch!

Student(s) Name: _____   Date: _____

In groups, students will construct an alarm for their given lunch box using materials in class. THE PROBLEM IS TO CONSTRUCT AN ALARM THAT WILL SOUND WHEN THE LUNCH BOX IS OPEN AND SHUT OFF WHEN THE LUNCH BOX IS CLOSED USING ONLY MATERIALS GIVEN IN CLASS. Groups will need to draw a diagram of a pre-plan as to how they will set up their alarm, as well as drawing a post-drawing of the actual set up of their alarm. As a group you will need to hand in one lab report for the whole group, which should include:

Scoring for Assessment SCI.IV.MS.5

Criteria	Apprentice	Basic	Meets	Exceeds
Completeness of previous knowledge	Attempts to present a background of previous knowledge.	Presents background knowledge that is acceptable but not complete.	Presents background knowledge that is detailed.	Presents background knowledge that is detailed and accurate.
Accuracy of diagrams	Completes one diagram of set-up.	Completes a sketch of two diagrams (a pre and a post plan).	Completes three diagrams showing detail (pre, post, and new way to set up alarm).	Display three diagrams that are detailed and concise. Along with a key.
Accuracy of conclusion	Attempts a conclusion.	Provides an acceptable conclusion as to why and how their alarm worked.	Provides a detailed conclusion as to why and how their alarm worked.	Provides a detailed and accurate conclusion as to why and how their alarm worked, which also includes key concepts in explanation.
Completeness of lab report	Presents limited information that is relevant to simple circuits.	Presents information that demonstrates an effort to organize the information.	Presents an accurate, interesting, and well-organized report.	Presents an interesting, well-organized, and accurate report that is clearly focused with explanation of results.

Figure 8.10 "Protecting My Lunch" Project

THIS IS IT

Working individually, students will research and develop a presentation on a topic of their interest. Students will identify a problem, research the problem, develop a hypothesis, do an experiment or data collection through more research, and develop a conclusion. Students will then develop a presentation that must be at least one minute long and include at least one visual aid. Four days of preparation will be allowed, with each student receiving at least 45 minutes to work on a computer for research. Other time should be used to prepare for the presentation. Students should pay special attention to the rubric and their use of class time in their preparation.

CRITERIA	APPRENTICE	BASIC	EXCEEDS
PROBLEM	Identifies the problem	Identifies the problem and interest behind it	Identifies the problem completely and the interest behind it
RESEARCH	Little research	Some research	Complete research
HYPOTHESIS	No hypothesis	Unreasonable hypothesis	Completely reasonable hypothesis
EXPERIMENT/ DATE COLLECTION	No experiment or data	Some data or experiment	Complete data or experiment
CONCLUSION	No real scientific conclusion	A scientific conclusion with some errors	A complete, correct scientific conclusion
PRESENTATION	Unorganized, non-scientific presentation	Organized, scientific presentation	Completely organized scientific presentation
PROMPTNESS	2 days or more late	1 day late	On time

Figure 8.11 "This Is It" Project

Brett Sellers

For seventeen of my twenty-three years with Battle Creek Public Schools, I have been a middle school utility teacher. That means, I have taught almost every subject possible, usually multiple subjects each year. Currently, I am teaching science and math using multiple materials and technology to foster in my students a joy of learning. My classroom is student-centered, active, creative, risk-free and challenges traditional assessments, standardized testing, and traditional homework. I am actively involved in on-going professional development as a learner, a curriculum writer, and a mentor for student teachers as well as new teachers.

Weather: A Sample Text Set of Multiple Materials

Allaby, M. (2002). *The world's weather (How it works)*. Milwaukee, WI: Gareth Stevens Publishing.

Bluestein, H. B. (1999). *Tornado alley: Monster storms of the Great Plains*. New York: Oxford Press.

Claybourne, A., Doherty, G., & Treays, R. (1999). *The Usborne encyclopedia of planet earth*. New York: Scholastic.

Cole, J. (1995). *The magic school bus: Inside a hurricane*. Illus. by Bruce Degen. New York: Scholastic.

Cosgrove, B. (1997). *The world of weather*. New York: Voyageur.

Coster-Longman, C. (2001). *Blow-up! Junior Science: Planet earth*. Illus. by Ivan Stalio. Florence, Italy: McRae Books.

Cox, J. D. (2000). *Weather for dummies*. Hoboken, NY: For Dummies.

DeMauro, L. (1990). *Explorer books: Disasters*. New York: Parachute Press.

Gemmell, K. (1995). *Storms and hurricanes*. Illus. by Gary Bines and Ian Jackson. New York: Scholastic.

Goldstein, M. (1999). *The complete idiot's guide to weather*. Northborough, MA: Alpha Books.

Hiscock, B. (1993). *The big storm*. New York: Atheneum.

Hopping, L. J. (1995). *Hurricanes!* Illus. by Jody Wheeler. New York: Scholastic.

Lauber, P. (1996). *Hurricanes: Earth's mightiest storms*. New York: Scholastic.

Ludlum, D. M. (1991). *National Audubon Society field guide to North American Weather*. New York: Alfred A. Knopf.

Lyons, W. A. (1997). *The handy weather answer book*. Canton, MI: Visible Ink Press.

Maynard, C., & Martin, T. (1996). *Why does lightning strike: Questions children ask about weather*. New York: Scholastic.

Murphy, J. (2000). *Blizzard! The storm that changed America.* New York: Scholastic.

Rose, S. (1999). *El Nino! And La Nina.* New York: Simon Spotlight.

Rose, S. (1999). *Tornadoes!* New York: Scholastic.

Simon, S. (1999). *Tornadoes.* New York: HarperCollins.

Simon, S. (1999). *Lightening.* New York: HarperTrophy.

Simon, S. (1993). *Weather.* New York: Scholastic

Watson, B. A. (1995). *The old farmers almanac: Book of weather & natural disasters.* New York: Random House.

Williams, J. (1997). *The weather book,* 2nd Ed. New York: Vantage Books.

Wyatt, V. (2000). *Weather: Frequently asked questions.* Illus. by Brian Share. Niagara Falls, NY: Kids Can Press.

Chapter 9

Confirming and Continuing: The Importance of Negotiation and Transition

"I'm not finished with my recycling inquiry, Ms. Sawyer."

"Well, what should we do about this?"

"Can't we spend more time asking other questions?"

"Let's see what the class has to say, Angel."

In Ms. Sawyer' eighth grade Language Arts classroom, inquiry is a way of life. Students learn about the inquiry cycle soon after the school year begins, and they launch into various collaborations all year long. Ms. Sawyer incorporates the curricular mandates of the state of Texas into these collaborations and asks her students to help her make many of the curricular decisions. Her students learn that there are times when their inquiries must be placed on hold, other times when inquiries can and should be expanded, and times when a new topic is beckoning.

In an effort to accommodate and integrate her students' interests and prior knowledge with the curricular mandates, Ms. Sawyer together with her students makes a number of decisions about the curriculum and how they will proceed as a community of learners. Because an inquiry curriculum naturally allows students to take ownership of their own learning, students are encouraged to share in this decision making. We find that if students are given responsibility for their learning they will more often than not meet that challenge (Smith & Johnson, 1993). In Ms. Sawyer is language arts class, students are invited to share their ideas and interests with her throughout the year. One group of Ms. Sawyer' eighth graders created a list that included the following:

- Becoming responsible
- How to mark off dialogue in our stories
- Communicating/speaking better
- Hygiene issues
- Democracy and fairness
- Environmental issues and becoming better citizens
- Coherence in our stories and essays

This list includes not only ideas for further as well as intercurricular inquiries but also the language arts that would allow her students to communicate what they are learning in more effective ways. We have found that our trust in middle level students is not unfounded when we ask them what they should be learning. The list of important (and on target curricular) concerns they generate not only helps us to plan what to teach but also guides us toward becoming increasingly responsive and engaging teachers. In this chapter, we use examples from Ms. Sawyer's eighth grade Language Arts classroom and Mr. Hiedeman's seventh grade geography class to discuss:

- Issues to Revisit in Confirming and Continuing
- Using Class Meetings to Negotiate and Transition
- Determining What's Next

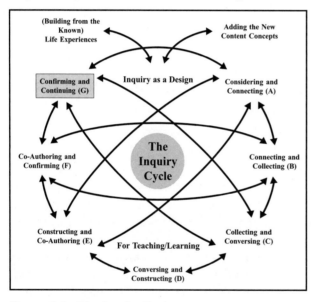

Figure 9.1 The Inquiry Cycle

Issues to Revisit in Confirming and Continuing

As young people and their teachers progress through inquiry, the potential for engaged and long lasting learning increases. An inquiry curriculum encourages students to make connections to each other, to the knowledge they are expected to learn, and to the world in which they live. Inquiry also allows students to reflect upon their learning, how it increases what they already know, and how they can use such knowledge in the future. Inquiry is not an isolated teaching method whereby middle level students can "do it and move on." Inquiry is a living, breathing curricular framework that has the potential to motivate middle level students to learn and to use their learning in a myriad of ways. It is a curricular plan that allows passion and personalities to enter every middle level classroom.

Each inquiry cycle has the potential of increasing not only student learning but also teacher responsibility for assessing and continuing that learning. As students move through an inquiry cycle, we are constantly assessing what they do, what they need help in doing, and what we need to do to assure they are learning what they need to know.

In the confirming and continuing phase there are five major issues to revisit:

- Embedding the curricular mandates

- Engaging all students across an inquiry cycle

- Scaffolding students' self motivation and sense of ownership

- Organizing grouping structures

- Gathering resources

Embedding the Curricular Mandates

We know that our students should not be the ones to carry the burden of curricular mandates, yet we wish to include them in the "work" of being educated in the United States. Thus, we often share our plans and ideas with our middle level students so they have a larger context for their learning and so they can feel more connected to the process of education.

When Ms. Sawyer begins her year, she has already reviewed the requirements for the eighth grade language arts curriculum in Texas. As she plans the first inquiry cycle with her students, she plans activities and classroom practices that address some of those mandates. And with each progressive inquiry, she continues to implement state mandates that have a natural place in her classroom. Depending on the time of the year, she knows whether she can plan shorter or longer inquiry cycles; and she addresses her concerns with her students. Because state testing in Texas is in the spring, Ms. Sawyer and her students engage in inquiry more often and for longer periods of time in the fall semester and late in the spring semester. Then, as the tests loom larger on the horizon, Ms. Sawyer's classroom community engages in more frequent "intensives" to prepare for the test format they must take.

By consulting the mandates of her curriculum throughout the year, and negotiating or planning inquiry cycles and topics that address many of these mandates, Ms. Sawyer does not worry about her students' content knowledge for the state test; she has addressed these topics or what the state has determined as "essential knowledge and skills" in mini-lessons with each inquiry cycle her students have completed. The secret to addressing the state or district mandates is to be aware of them and to find exciting ways to engage middle level students in inquiry topics that include the knowledge and skills they will need for testing situations.

Engaging All Students Across Inquiry Cycles

Although our students are often eager to work in an inquiry curriculum, we also know that each year we are presented with one or two students who do not enjoy or know how to work well in small groups. We also know that there are some students who have difficulty taking more ownership over their own learning. These two issues in student participation require that teachers scaffold learning and engage with the classroom community across time. We have handled these situations through negotiation, choice, and honesty.

To handle the situation where a student has difficulty working in a group, we give the student a choice with the condition, however, that they will gradually work toward small group work as the year progresses. For instance, Ms. Sawyer worked with an eighth grade student who readily admitted that he couldn't work in groups. Upon further discussion after class, the student revealed that he did not feel confident in his ability to work with others or in his ability to learn. The two negotiated how Jorge, the student, could go about learning to participate in small groups. Ms. Sawyer asked him to circle the room when students were in their groups and just listen to what they had to say about democracy, the topic under study. She then wanted him to report to her what he noticed.

Jorge agreed to these conditions; and each day, when students met in small groups, Jorge listened to their comments and watched their interactions. He began to write down what he heard so he could remember it for his discussion after class with Ms. Sawyer. Eventually, Jorge began to talk to the members of specific groups as he became more interested in what they had to say. After three weeks, Jorge was especially interested in one group and hovered over them for most of the class period. Finally, Jorge entered the group, but still did not fully participate in all that the group was doing during that particular inquiry cycle. The next inquiry cycle, however, Jorge agreed to work with one group and to attempt to fully participate. From this example, we see that many of our students wish to participate in their own learning but have difficulty with knowing how. Teaching students to work with others is an essential part of inquiry learning, and one that we frequently forget to address. It was Jorge who taught us that we needed to be more mindful of this phenomenon.

Scaffolding Students Self-Motivation and Sense of Ownership

Often we have individuals in our classes who feel disconnected from the learning process or who have been alienated from it. By working with them individually, we find they do become more willing and engaged participants in our classrooms. Along with this are students who have difficulty taking ownership over their own learning. These students frequently are excited by inquiry and have many ideas, questions, or topics they wish to study. They have difficulty, however, with the freedom that often comes with an inquiry curriculum. They may also have difficulty with organization and may lose the work they have accomplished. With these students, we find that by setting deadlines for completion of particular pieces of work and providing them with closer monitoring and guidance, they are better able to manage their time and their resources.

With knowledge of our middle level students learning strengths and challenges, we are better able to prepare our classrooms, our time, and our teaching to address those conditions. With our help, all our students can participate in and be engaged in their learning.

Organizing Grouping Structures

Another issue encountered during transitioning is group organization. At the beginning of the academic year, with her first inquiry cycle, Ms. Sawyer grouped students according to the interests they expressed in their journals or in an interest inventory. After they had had some experience with inquiry, she generally allowed them to group themselves according to their needs with her input and facilitation.

Although she wanted her students to study and research with those with whom they felt comfortable, she was also concerned about the classroom community as a whole. She didn't want her students to segregate themselves along gender, class, or racial lines, so they discussed these concerns in a class meeting (discussed below). As a class, they negotiated that they should be able to work with anyone in the class at least "once in awhile," and that Ms. Sawyer could guide the decisions about who should go into which group the remainder of the time. Through this arrangement, her students came to understand better each other and the multiple cultural perspectives that were represented in the classroom.

Other times, Ms. Sawyer would also suggest that students group themselves by the strengths they possessed in terms of communication skills. Discussing differing abilities according to speaking, reading, writing, researching, visually representing, and presenting, her students would organize themselves so that the inquiry process went more smoothly. This self grouping was most effective after the winter break when her students began to think about the attributes each could bring to the group rather than the relationships they had outside the group.

Gathering Resources

Finding and using multiple materials that are engaging and useful to our students is always a key issue when ending one inquiry cycle and transitioning to another.

Having our students input on the value of the materials they used during an inquiry is essential in providing them with the best resources we can. Useful sources for text sets of multiple materials include first, the school library with the help of the library media specialist, then community libraries, and bookstores. Other possible resources include community members from local businesses, colleges, and universities. Students also have access to resources. Their connections to people, places, and materials are often varied and useful.

Using Class Meetings to Negotiate and Transition

The class meeting at the end of an inquiry cycle serves two purposes: The first is to evaluate what happened during the latest inquiry cycle, and the second is to decide where and how to proceed. For example, as an inquiry cycle is winding down, and students begin presenting their learning to peers, parents, or community members, Ms. Sawyer is shifting her focus to transitioning from her students' present learning to their future endeavors. Because she shares curricular decisions with her students, Ms. Sawyer is prepared to finish the inquiry cycle with a classroom meeting where class negotiations take place (see Figure 9.2).

Class meetings involve students and teachers communicating issues, problems, or celebrations they wish to share with the class. One benefit includes building a community of learners who respect and work well with one another. Another positive aspect includes the possibilities provided for negotiation (Peterson, 1992). A third benefit is that they allow students to "be reflective about what and how they learn" (Burke & Short, 1991).

The following guidelines can scaffold students when they first experience class meetings:

1. Meetings are open to all members of the learning community.
2. Any type of issue that prevents learning can be discussed.
3. Community members should attempt to be nonjudgmental or blaming.
4. Students need to listen to each other's concerns.
5. Celebrations can be a part of every meeting.
6. Problem posing and solving can be a part of every meeting.
7. Consensus is not necessary, but respect for all opinions is.
8. Community members should attempt to work out their difference.

Figure 9.2 Class Meetings

Throughout class meetings, Ms. Sawyer either takes notes or becomes the class scribe by writing ideas, suggestions, or questions on the board. She also brings her own ideas to the meeting, as well as her concerns. She passes out a "Suggestions for

Inquiry" (see Figure 9.3 and Appendix 14) sheet to her students as they discuss the following three questions they have thought about for the negotiations:

- What is the topic you would like to address next and why?
- What are the connections with what you have just completed?
- Based on what we have brainstormed to learn during this marking period (unit, semester, month, etc.), does this fit into our plan?

Date:

Name:

Last Topic:

New Topic(s):

Observations

Curricular Needs

Ideas/Next Course of Action

Figure 9.3 Suggestions for Inquiry

One Friday Class Meeting—An Example

The students had completed their presentations on Wednesday. On Thursday they wrote up their self-evaluations and worked on the three questions (see above) Ms. Sawyer had given them in anticipation of the Friday class meeting. They had about 45 minutes to get themselves at least partially organized for the next cycle:

"Who would like to start this meeting?" Ms. Sawyer asked.

"I think Roberto should start the meeting since he brought up something just before the meeting about the RAFT (Role, Audience, Format, Topic) strategy we learned." (For information of the RAFT strategy see Meghan Luckett's vignette at the end of chapter 2.)

"Roberto, will you start?"

"Okay. I was just telling some of them that I really liked the RAFT strategy because it gave me directions about how to work on the presentation I wanted to do. So, I think that strategy works good, and I want to use it again."

"Does anyone else have something to add to this?"

"I liked it, too. I want to use it again, too, and not that mapping strategy about organizing my ideas. That doesn't work for me," Claudia explained.

"I think we can do either strategy as long as it works for someone in the class," Ms Sawyer ventured. "The more strategies we have available, the more opportunities we have to find something that will work for everyone. What do you think?" Several heads nodded in agreement. "Is there another issue or idea that we need to discuss about the last inquiry cycle?"

"I had a problem with the time," Michael stated.

"Tell us about it."

"I didn't have the time I needed to get all the information I wanted to find. I didn't have enough time on the computer. How are we supposed to get the information we need if we can only use the computers every three days?"

This was a good question. Ms. Sawyer's students complained about the lack of computers in their classroom and that they were able to use the computer lab only once a week as a whole group. To alleviate some of the anxiety over the lack of time on the computers, Ms. Sawyer usually sent them down to the lab three at a time when they weren't scheduled as a class. Michael was expressing what others in the class had already confronted throughout the last two inquiries.

"Does anyone have an idea of what we can do?" Ms. Sawyer asked.

"Can we go to the media center sometimes, just to work on computers? Maybe then you could send six of us around instead of just three. That would give us more time on the school computers," Patricia suggested.

"We could also see if we could stay after school sometimes!" Sean added.

That idea, while a good one, did not go over too well. Many of the students rode buses to get to school and did not have the opportunity to stay after and work in the lab. For other students, this would work, but none were too keen on staying after school for anything other than participation in sports. Ms. Sawyer was not too surprised. Even Sean didn't need to stay after school since his parents had a computer that he was able to use. The class's decision was to see about more computer lab time, which was possible during certain times of the year, and to ask the library media specialist about students visiting the media center for computer time.

Once this decision was made, the students felt it was time to work on the group's decision about what to do next. Ms. Sawyer had her suggestions for the next inquiry, but wanted the students to discuss the three questions they had worked on the day before:

> *"Please pull out your reflections from yesterday."*
>
> *"I'll start this part," Mitzi volunteered.*

Mitzi was one of my students who did not talk much in class meetings, but they had decided prior to this meeting that each member of the class would have to add something to the dialogue, even if it was just to agree with another idea. Ms. Sawyer facilitated this by using poker chips. Each student was given three poker chips with the directions that they had to use at least one, but couldn't talk once they were out of poker chips. Some of the students got around this "rule" by borrowing chips from their classmates who did not speak as often. The "speaking once" was a hard and fast rule unless, of course, a student was having a particularly bad day.

> "I think we should do things in small groups this time and that we should look at how 'interdependence' works in making the world a better place." Mitzi offered.
>
> "Didn't we do that for the first inquiry cycle?" Jackson asked.
>
> "Not really. We looked at how interdependent we all are," Gillian explained.
>
> "Well, then, I think we could look at that, but can we do stuff like how surfers are interdependent with the waves?" Carlyle asked. We laughed. Carlyle was the "virtual" surfer in class who lived to grow up and "move to Hawaii."
>
> "Hey, surfing makes the world a better place," he argued.
>
> "Does anyone want to work with Carlyle on this topic," Ms. Sawyer asked.

"I don't care about surfing, but couldn't he work with some of us on how sports and physical fitness are interdependent? I mean, a slug can't perform as well on the court as someone who works out and stuff," Jeremiah stated.

Ms. Sawyer saw this as a good time to pass out her suggestions for the next inquiry cycle. She was not adverse to her students studying sports, especially since most of them played a sport either in school or in a community league. She had not, however, placed sports on her suggestion list; and she did want them to at least look at the list before making any decisions.

"Hey, you have stuff on the list that we could do while looking at the positive part of interdependence," Katie observed.

"Yes, I thought we could talk about parts of speech in the next couple of weeks so we could strengthen our writing with more precise language," Ms. Sawyer explained.

"We don't have to do those sentences again, do we? I did that for the last two years!" Keith complained.

"I was hoping to make our discussion of the parts of speech a little more authentic," Ms. Sawyer grinned.

"Okay, so if we decide to do the positive part of 'interdependence,' we can decide what to do, right? As long as we do parts of speech for writing?" Keith asked.

"What do you all say?" Ms. Sawyer asked.

The students agreed to Ms. Sawyer's suggestion about more precise language, and they had made a decision about the general topic of the inquiry cycle. But with the exception of Carlyle, none of the students had decided what they were doing.

"Does anyone have an idea about what they would like to do in terms of the positive aspects of 'interdependence'? Now is the time for brainstorming."

"What about how families work?"

"What about how the government works?"

"Or even the life cycle—you know, wolves eating elk, and how the elk needed to be culled," Tamara suggested.

"What's 'culled'?"

"Tamara will explain later." Ms. Sawyer said.

Their time was coming to a close, so Ms. Sawyer asked her students to think about their ideas over the weekend and each come up with three ideas or questions for the following Monday. She then asked them about the organization. Carlyle had asked about small groups, and they had not made that decision. Ms. Sawyer didn't know if that question could be answered without any real decision having been made about what particular interests her students were going to pursue for the next cycle, but ventured the question anyway.

> "Can we make a decision about grouping at this time or should we wait for Monday?"
>
> "I think we could probably go in groups this time, if the groups can be, like, two to four people," Veronique answered.
>
> "I know what I want to do," Carlyle stated, "Does anyone want to do surfing with me?"
>
> "I think if you move to 'interdependence in sports,' you can look at surfing in particular, as an example, and you might get a couple of folks to join you," Ms. Sawyer suggested.
>
> "If we can do that, I'll be in your group, Carlyle," Jeremiah stated, "I don't care about surfing, but basketball is something else!"
>
> "And I'll do baseball," Michael added.

As they started to pack up for the week, the students started talking with one another about life cycles, sports, animal groupings, and families. They hadn't made firm decisions by the time the bell rang, but Ms. Sawyer could see they were on their way. Monday would be the day they settled into the new ideas, but Ms. Sawyer knew the trip she had planned to her community library would not be made in vain. She had to get books on surfing, basketball, baseball, wolves, the life cycle, and families. She might also pick up some on types of governments while she was there.

Determining What's Next

Transitioning from one inquiry cycle to another involves deciding among three major actions:

- Expanding the inquiry
- Stepping away from inquiry
- Beginning a new inquiry

Deciding on which course of action to take often depends on your students, your curriculum mandates, your community, and your resources. To transition from one inquiry cycle to another or to move away from inquiry altogether is often one of the most difficult decisions a teacher has to make, yet it is an essential element of an inquiry cycle and one that can be made smoothly with careful planning.

Expanding a Current Inquiry

If we find that at the end of one inquiry cycle our students are still interested in the topic, but are beginning to ask bigger questions, then we discuss the option of expanding the current inquiry to broaden the topic to include more connections. For instance, in their study of Racism in America, Mr. Hiedeman found that his seventh grade students wanted to look at Latino/Latina cultures in the United States and the unique forms that racism takes in relation to them. His students also wanted to think about cross-cultural communication and understanding rather than racism per se. They had decided, however, to work individually or in pairs on the next inquiry cycle instead of expanding the inquiry topic. Once they were finished with the individual inquiries, however, they were ready to expand the topic to look at broader issues.

Thus, in a class meeting, they discussed what their new inquiry topic could be that would allow them to expand beyond racism to look at the questions that their racism studies had provoked. Students divided into five small groups, and they began working on a more inclusive and expansive title for their next inquiry project. The students discussed what the more inclusive term or topic could become, and the groups generated these ideas:

- Cross Cultural Relationships
- Social Justice in the United States
- Becoming a Multicultural Nation
- Bridging Cultural Groups in America

It is important to note here that Mr. Hiedeman worked with his students in their small groups to help them articulate their ideas. He circled the room, listened in on their conversations, and then helped them to "name" what the issues were they were discussing. Once the students came together again as a classroom community, he listed the ideas on the white board, and then the entire class negotiated what the next inquiry topic should be. The class eventually settled on "Cross-Cultural Relationships in the United States," blending two of the ideas listed, but arguing that with this umbrella topic, all ideas listed could be included. Mr. Hiedeman agreed and, together with the students, decided how they should be grouped for the next cycle. They decided to work again in small groups.

Although we do not suggest that logistical decisions about proceeding in each inquiry cycle have to be discussed between inquiry cycles, we find that students like to be included in such discussions. We also find that they can be a valuable resource in terms of knowledge or connections to community members who might help as they proceed from one inquiry to another. It is the sharing of decisions that creates a classroom community more willing to learn and to help each member learn.

Stepping Away From Inquiry

As Ms. Sawyer asks her students to join her in a class meeting, she has already reviewed the curriculum mandates and what she may still need to address. She doesn't allow the mandates, however, to determine whether or not her students should launch into a new inquiry or step away from inquiry entirely. She discusses her concerns about the mandates with her students so they will understand how curriculum can be reasonably negotiated among all classroom members. Often, if we use our students as a resource, they will lead us to thinking about our curricular directives in new and exciting ways.

For instance, one of the curricular mandates Ms. Sawyer needed to address involved the parts of speech. We are not sure any middle level student gets excited about pronouns or prepositions; but when Ms. Sawyer discussed the necessity of addressing grammar and parts of speech, her students suggested that they use art as a way of learning some of those requirements. Ms. Sawyer readily admits that this possibility had not entered her mind; but once the class discussed it, she turned it into a mini-inquiry cycle where her students researched artistic media and styles to help them present their learning about pronouns. At the end of the inquiry, students presented their comic strips, bulletin boards, pictures, and book covers to the class.

At other times, however, Ms. Sawyer prefers to teach specific content in a quick manner, and inquiry—because it is so engaging—does not always work for her quick coverage of these topics. She then steps away from inquiry for a few days to a couple of weeks, but returns once her "intensives" are over.

Throughout the year, Ms. Sawyer moves away from inquiry five or six times. Her intensives include parts of speech, test-taking skills, and a short writing project mandated by the district. What she does upon returning to an inquiry curriculum, however, is attempt to build on what her students have accomplished in the last few weeks to help them transition back to a topic of interest.

Creating a New Inquiry

The third possibiity is changing the inquiry focus entirely. Often, the classroom learning community will follow a path through a number of inquiry cycles that starts at the beginning of the year and leads from one curricular concept to the next. Yet, there are times when the curricular demands make it necessary to refocus on an entirely new topic of inquiry. At the end of each inquiry cycle, we revisit our original list to see what questions or interests may connect to what is next and to retain any threads that might help our students make these connections.

To help students transition from one inquiry cycle to another, or to transition back into an inquiry cycle, we find that engaging them in reflective practices about what and how they have learned in the last few weeks is especially beneficial. The following strategy with intertextuality has worked well with middle level students because it involves students revisiting not only their learning process but also their learning products.

Brainstorming Intertextual Connections & Questions

Intertextuality involves the connections students make across texts and other resources including each other during an inquiry cycle. These intertextual connections can be demonstrated visually, orally, in writing, or another sign system such as dance, art, or mathematics. This connecting of content builds, deepens, and strengthens our students' prior knowledge for the next concept they may read about, view, or experience. As part of this strategy (see Figure 9.4 and Appendix 15), students get together and discuss how the current information they have learned connects to information they learned in previous experiences, whether those experiences

---

Name: Date:

Topic:

What connections can be made to your last inquiry?

1.

2.

3.

4.

5.

From the materials you used (books, periodicals, movies, Internet sites), what connections can you make to other materials you have read/viewed?

1.

2.

3.

4.

How does this inquiry connect to what you are learning in other classes?

Figure 9.4 Intertextual Connections

occurred in or out of school. This is related to the use of Intertextual Connections discussed in Chapter Five We also ask students to connect the materials they used to other materials from past experiences.

By asking students to brainstorm their intertextual connections, we are asking them to reinforce their knowledge and understanding of a topic. Yet, with intertextuality we are also deepening connections between content areas. An example of this is when Ms. Sawyer's eighth grade students were studying the circulatory system in their science class. They learned the biology of the heart, but not the affective element of the heart. As Ms. Sawyer asked them to think about vocabulary words that included the word "heart" (such as heartfelt, heartbroken, and heartless), the students discussed why these words would be connected to the part of their anatomy called the heart. Students came to understand how science and language arts do have connections across concepts. But, this is a discussion for another book.

Concluding Remarks

Transitioning from one inquiry cycle to another is a time of closure and a time of expectation. It is a time when students and their teachers regroup, ponder alternatives, and set off toward more knowledge, more adventures, more learning. It is an important stopping place along the way where the wondrous work of reflection is highlighted and where students take time to breathe with both satisfaction and anticipation before moving on again with a new inquiry and Phase A: considering and connecting of the next cycle.

Strategies Discussed in Confirming and Continuing

- Class Meetings
- Intertextual Connections

Eighth Grade Spanish Language Class

Penelope Boyatt

"What are you going to do to teach Culture when you get to the Mexico chapter in the text?" "Oh, maybe we'll do a food unit or a country study, or something about holidays or clothing."

Teaching the textbook sequentially with everyone on the same page has never fit with my understanding of how human beings work. As I thought about how to be true to myself and include the mandated "study of culture," I began asking my-self questions. "What is 'culture' really about? And, off to the dictionary I went. My own knowledge base, ideas and questions began to fill the pages of the "thinking notes" I was scribbling.

I decided to design an in-depth unit around the concept of "culture" and found that the concepts of "life," "learning" and "language" are interrelated within the study of culture. Thus, I clarified to myself that I wanted my students to engage in making these concepts real to themselves and to engage in understanding that all human beings alive are learning and using languages (among other sign systems) to communicate thoughts, ideas, conclusions and feelings. I knew we would have to do the work mostly in English. But, I also knew that working as bilingually as possible, students would be further exposed to the necessity of the use of language to understand culture and vice-versa.

What kinds of engagements would suit my purposes? I decided to use read alouds, videos, literature circles, and reader's theatre as I had had enough experience with these to feel at ease and comfortable. Before we talked about the unit, I introduced the students (a few who had been in my class the previous year had experience) to reader's theatre. They got into groups, worked with short simple scripts in Spanish that I gave them, follow simple guidelines, and enjoyed sharing their efforts with each other.

Because I believe that assessment is part of the learning process, I knew I would use both oral and written student reflections, and "kid-watching" throughout the project. Also, I began to realize after a few sessions into the project that both the students and I would need an efficient way to "keep track" of what we were doing. Thus, what was called "keeping every page safe" developed into "a packet of all pages that would be turned in at the end" to "Your Individual Packet - Life . . . Learning . . . Language . . . Culture" (chronologically ordered). The following is a list of the items in order as they appear in the packet:

1. Una Investigation

2. Getting at some Meanings (part A an part B)

3. Procedure for Readers Theater

4. Quick Write on the Four Concepts

5. Browsing Records: Example here

6. Reading Record(s); La Unidad

7. Vida . . . Aprendizaje . . . Lengua . . . Cultura – PEOPLES (video): Haití, "We live because we hope." The Dominican Republic; El Horario del trabajo; Border Cities: Ayer, Hoy, y Mañana (video)

8. Composing the Content of Your Presentation—a guide for Readers Theatre Possibilities; "¡Viva Chihuahua!"

Phase A—Considering and Connecting

My Name is Jorge On Both Sides of the River, Poems in English and Spanish (Medina, 1999) is the title of the book I chose as a read aloud. We used this book to help us begin to think about life, learning, language, and culture in such a way that the students could make connections. During the reading we did some popcorn sharing, a sketch to stretch, and a student read aloud of some of the poems both in whole group and in pairs.

The river is the Rio Grande. Jorge, his Mom, Dad, and little sister crossed illegally. I asked the students to think about the story as a whole and to sketch one of the events, and next to it on the other half of the page to sketch a connection to their own life.

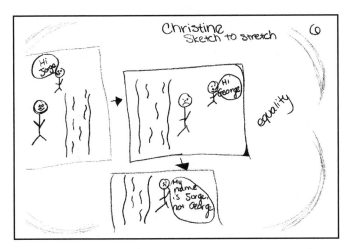

Figure 9.5   Sketch to Stretch Example

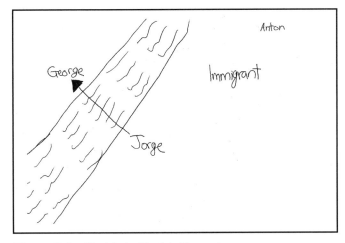

Figure 9.6   Sketch to Stretch Example

The next step was to give the students the "Getting at Some Meanings" sheet with the dictionary definitions I had found. They brainstormed individually, writing down everything that "comes to your mind when you think, "culture." We shared these by making one big web as we commented and asked questions. I then asked them to think about and respond to the following three questions at home and to write down separately one or more adult responses. (a) Is "school" a 'culture'? (b) Is "home" a 'culture'? (c) Is "family" a 'culture'? The sharing of this thinking took the form of small groups each with a facilitator writing on a T square chart, How "school" is / is not . . . a "culture." We shared the other two questions verbally.

A Quick Write followed for which, speaking in Spanish, I asked each student to write down whatever came to mind as they considered each of the four concepts: life, learning, language, culture. Being already comfortable with this strategy, the students began to write at the signal. I stopped and started them anew for each strategy.

Meanwhile, I was gathering all the books I could find in my own library and at school with anything to do with culture. Many of them are in English, some of them in Spanish and some bilingual, some are in the format of one book in English and a second book in Spanish. Now the time was ripe for introducing the books to the students, for them getting into self chosen groups of 4 or 5, and for my demonstrating again, the art of browsing. Before they started I gave out "Browsing record" sheets and we talked through the what's and how's of recording while browsing. They were quickly into the work, commenting spontaneously with group mates, writing down notes, and reflecting in whole group. The challenge for browsing is to skim through several books and other print materials, jotting down a note to yourself about what is or might be of interest to you and where to find it again.

Phase B—Connecting and Collecting

Even though there were five classes sharing the same baskets, the books stayed in their assigned baskets. Each small group had a folder for keeping lists, group notes; and a paper entitled "Responsibilities—reading groups—Mayo, 2003" (see Figure 7.11). Seven job titles—Facilitator, Book Keeper, Recorder, Time Keeper, Creators of Readers Theatre Script, Writer(s), Illustrator(s)—are listed with a space to put the student's name. Each task is explained briefly. Also, each student had a work folder for keeping reading records and any other notes they needed; and I kept a folder for each of the five classes.

The school year was coming to a close and the state testing for 8th grade intertwined with our project as well as various end-of-the-year performance rehearsals. I wanted to arrange the groups so that everyone would feel respected and heard, thus being stimulated to contribute ideas. Even so, in one group of students, the opposite seemed to happen and one of the group members was suspended from school. At first, I was more concerned as the remaining two group members seemingly could not stand one another. But, to my surprise and theirs, they spent their time conversing and exchanging ideas. The following is what they had to say about their dialogue:

> Our group has been talking about the border between America and Mexico for a while. We discussed about how the United States put its

border with Mexico not letting anybody in except for those legal. We also asked each other questions and got into some disagreements like Americans are not legal in a lot of countries and they go there and come back with no problem at all.

Periodo siete – Grupo_____

1. Facilitator_____

   Gets the group together. Keeps everyone going and on task. Facilitates all discussion. Is in charge of group folder.

2. Book Keeper_____

   Takes out and puts away book basket. Is accountable for all the books being in the basket. Reminds group to handle books with loving care.

3. Recorder_____

   Writes down thoughts and ideas during group discussion and during creation of Reader's Theatre script.

4. Time Keeper_____

   Assures that everyone engages in discussion and has a chance to express her/his ideas.

5. Creators of Readers' Theatre Script_____

   Everyone in the group will contribute to the content and wording and form.

6. Writer(s)_____

   Will put the script in final form and assure there are enough copies for each member of the group.

7. Illustrator(s)_____

   Will create a visual (poster, sign, etc.) that enhances the presentation.

Figure 9.7   Responsibilities—Reading Groups—Mayo, 2003

Phase C–Collecting and Conversing

After a couple of sessions with the baskets, I introduced some primary source materials, which I took from the Internet and my files. Each group received a folder (the contents of which differed somewhat from the contents of the other folders) to go along with each basket of books. At this time, I also introduced two videos, one about Haiti and one about the Dominican Republic. We watched the second video just before I asked the students to begin to "pull it all together." Entitled, "The Ties That Bind, Stories Behind the Immigration Controversy," this excellent video presents a clear picture of life along the border between the United States and Mexico. People from both sides of the border as well as from social organizations tell their stories with footage showing crossing the river, hiding from the "Migra" (immigration authorities), and life working in the Maquiladores (factories).

Just as their Browsing Notes were an opportunity to jot down what and where to find what was interesting, after silent reading writing in their Reading Records helped them to pinpoint these and other interests and to go into more depth by becoming aware of any questions and conclusions in their minds. Alternating silent reading with literature circles, the students engaged in talking, discussing and arguing their ideas, questions, and conclusions with the members of their groups, thus adding to their individual and collective thinking and processing. Several examples follow:

> "I don't believe that school, home, and family is a culture. I do believe though that things you do in school, at home, or in your family is."

> "Something can be authentic and different at the same time because you can be true and real, but at the same time you can be different from other people. But you can also be different and non-authentic. Being different is authentic."

> "An American man killed a man who was Hindu just because he looked Arab. This man claims 'he was American' as if that was his excuse."

Some of the activities we engaged in as a whole class gave students even more opportunity to connect with self and with each other. One of the favorites was "popcorn reading." Each student chooses a short passage from the book or article she is reading at the moment and reads it quietly out loud to himself for a minute. Then one student reads aloud to the group and upon finishing another immediately begins to read, and thus they pop in at will. If two begin at the same time, one has to back off. In this way they not only hear each other, but also build and maintain community—a community of learners, a community of respect for each other, a community of *equals* who know they are being heard.

Other strategies we used included "Sketch to Stretch," "Say something," "Do you know or Did you ever ask yourself this question," and "Reflecting." While I did not use a "Word Wall" strategy, I am now thinking what a fine way not only to share but also to keep some of the ideas in mind through seeing them and so an opportunity for extending thought. Just now, as I write, I am realizing that I am *collecting* from my effort to reflect and *conversing* with myself and extending my thinking. Wow!

Phase D—Conversing and Constructing

The individual and group work of literature circles, reading, jotting down thoughts, looking for connections to self, talking to each other, sharing meaning made and meaning making began to slide smoothly into the next task. In order to help them gather up the ideas of each one, I gave them, "Composing the Content of Your Presentation—a guide." I encouraged them to use some kind of graphic organizer and to ask themselves and each other questions to clarify their thinking and to get to the basics of what they wanted to share in their presentations. I ended the guide with as many broad questions as I myself could come up with. This meant that each student would review her notes, records, quickwrite, sketch to stretch, and so forth. Also, each one would have to become more aware of his/her own thinking, feelings, conclusions, doubts and questions.

The Recorder was in charge of taking notes as each one shared what he/she thought important, made an effort to listen to herself/himself and the others and to think about what he/she was hearing. Two examples of this discourse are:

GROUP A:　*"No such thing as acting black. "*
　　　　　　"Yes there is."
　　　　　　"Don't like Eminem cause he's white."
　　　　　　"No one likes him cause he's white."
　　　　　　"He won an award, they thought he was the best."
　　　　　　"How do you know?"
　　　　　　"Eminem has passion."
　　　　　　"Its not real rap."

GROUP C:　*"Stutter . . . people assume you are stupid. Just means they can't hear their brain and have trouble getting ideas out. That's my brother."*
　　　　　　"Boston accent assume you are street smart."
　　　　　　"Southern accent . . . assume you're a red neck."

Simultaneously we revisited the guidelines for Readers' Theatre. At this point I reminded them that their presentations would use the format of Readers' Theatre. As a whole group, we then brainstormed the pluses of this kind of a format:

- The script does not have to be memorized, although that might happen.

- You can have props, or no props, also costumes.

- Even though the original idea is that all the group are in a line, the formation could differ. You could be in a square, for example, always turning to face the audience when your character speaks.

- While you do not look at the other characters you are still required to communicate with them, through voice and feeling, gestures and facial expressions.

- Whatever your content, you can present it effectively as a Readers Theatre piece.

What about the language of the presentation? I told the students it was up to them. We talked about possibilities such as a bilingual presentation, an echo in the back in the other language, only Spanish, only English, script in both and presentation in one, and so forth. They had to decide on content first. Throughout the work both the students and I were discovering connections between and among

Life in Spanish and English, **Learning** in Spanish and English, the **Language**(s) themselves and to us, human beings, i.e. humanitas or **Culture**. I am now wondering if we did use an Inquiry format from the beginning of the school year, would we finish up by being "alive" in Spanish and thus work and presentation would gradually take on the hue of learning in two languages and therefore building an even stronger classroom "culture"?

Phase E—Constructing and Co-Authoring

Once the content and the kind of presentation were decided, each group member chose to work on the script or on the visual. Some worked on both and everyone had suggestions to make them better. When a rough draft of the script was ready, the students played it out, asked classmates for suggestions, made revisions and reissued scripts. Somewhere in this preparation each student assumed a role or roles in the piece. Most everyone in each group engaged with full focus. At this point I realized that in addition to kid watching, my job was to be a "totally objective" critic who watched, listened, asked questions to clarify, and who gave "asked for" suggestions. The classroom bustled, rang with enthusiastic voices, extended to the halls, and looked like chaos had struck unless you knew what you were looking at. There were groups in the hall practicing, and groups in the corners. There were heads bent over elaborate drawings and some folks arguing about last minute details. Amid the mesh of talk, emoting, and laughter, much helping of each other was going on. "Speak louder!" "Keep your face turned this way." "Great voice." "I like your message." "Your face needs to show what you are saying." "That's thoughtful."

Creating "People With Problems," a brief, to the point readers' theatre script, provides a good example of one group's problem solving. Three members of the group seemed to be dealing with their own issues throughout the school year. They were usually engaged in actions that were distracting to others. The fourth member usually engaged quietly in all the work we did. Again I am reminded that even though I am aware of labeling and refuse to listen to other teachers labels for my students, I found that until I really paid attention to the work of these students, I thought they were just goofing off. After recording the following in order to pool their ideas for creating their readers' theatre, they seemed stumped, as if they were finished, but knew they weren't. I read their list (see below) and wrote the following to them on a post it note. "Fine thinking! Fine Recording! Could you turn this into a structured piece by **keeping** what you have, **and** using a question and answer format?" Missy was the one who recorded as everyone pooled his/her ideas. Here is a snap-shot of what she wrote down.

#Every person has two sides
#That everyone is not always nice
#Names can be offences to one person but not to another

#Everyone has their own opinion
#Does everyone have a good side?
#Don't make assumptions
#No one should judge
#What may seem weird to you may be normal to them
#Don't hate people you don't really know

The final draft of Missy's group's script (below) is such a refinement of their discussion above.

Narrator: Welcome to our show People with Problems! And now our host Lauren

Host: Welcome to today's show. Our topic is people judging other people.

Host: Let's welcome Bob, a boy who gets made fun of at school by a girl named Sammie.

Bob: That's right. She judges me on the way I look and the way I play sports.

Host: Well, let's bring out Sammie and talk to her.

Host: Hello Sammie.

Sammie: Hey.

Host: Why are you judging Bob?

Sammie: Cause it is easy and it is fun.

Bob: Just because I ain't popular and a bit different than you are doesn't give you the right to make fun of me.

Sammie: Good point, but I can't help it.

Bob: How would you feel if I made fun of you because you look different and you aren't that popular?

Sammie: Well, that's never has happened to me before, but I'll try to not do it again, but it may take awhile.

Bob: Well I hope you do . . . I hope you know how this feels! It hurts! All I wanted was to be accepted, 'ya know?

Host: I think we all have learned a valuable lesson here.

Narrator: And that concludes our show, people!

When, at last, the moment for presenting came, the room was quiet. Every head was turned to the presenters. We were rewarded. The students showed that they were in touch with each other and with themselves. Shyness, embarrassment, poor diction, half facing the audience, too soft, too loud, minds wondering flew out of existence as together they shared their messages, the conclusion of their thinking. They spoke clearly, varying their voices, using gestures, facial expressions.

For example, Sam played the part of a preacher in his group's readers' theatre. He performed a sermon that Alice had written. Below is an excerpt.

> Does the simple life seem better?
>
> It's a question we all ask.
>
> The world is filled with violence; guns kill millions and millions of innocent people.
>
> Families are growing hungry and scared.
>
> War is not the way to confront your fears and find an answer.
>
> Too many lives are lost, too many tears cried, too many families broken.

One had no doubt that every word came from a deep conviction within Sam in his role as preacher. Sam shone during those moments and his classmates applauded him. A more precious gift he could not have received/given himself at that particularly difficult time in his life.

Figure 9.8   Sam's Group's Poster

Phase F—Co-authoring and Confirming

"I used to think speaking Spanish meant knowing the words and grammar. Now I know what it really means." —6th grade student

Weaving its way in and through the project from beginning to end, assessment (to assess: to sit beside) accomplished its work of continuously increasing our learning. As I reflected daily and, by the minute sometimes, on the overall work, on sticky details that were occurring, on student needs, on how to squeeze more time out of the turnip, and so forth. I sat with my thoughts and conclusions and learned more. As students thought and conversed, read and contemplated, sketched and stretched, related to the known and unknown, questioned, and shared opinions, they sat beside each other and learned more. As we discussed options, shared ways of going about a certain task, decided how to order a presentation and who should do what task, we continually guided each other to greater satisfaction.

Assessment means being aware of where you are and where you want to go and how to get there. It is a community effort as well as an individual task. It includes the input of all the individuals involved and defines the increase of our awareness. For the purpose of assessment in the sense just stated, I designed a seven item reflection opportunity to give each student individually a chance to check in with herself/himself, to clarify still more, to increase whatever meaning she had made during the work, and to nourish the seeds of further wonderings'. To myself I gave the opportunity as I read their responses to "hear" their growth and to reflect on "What comes next?"

---

1. In what ways have your thoughts about the issues, concepts, and topics changed after all this work?

2. What surprised you the most as you were reading and discussing and as you were watching the Border video?

3. What have you found out that you didn't know before?

4. List some connections you made to your own life.

5. Write down two or three questions about things you did not understand and/or about things you were/are wondering about.

6. Describe how working with your group went for you.

7. Evaluate your *participation* in the unit, and evaluate your *contribution* to the presentation.

Figure 9.9   A Final Reflection

What follows is the list of the seven items with a few of the students' responses (with original syntax and spelling) quoted beneath the heading.

A Final Reflection: Life . . . Learning . . . Language . . . Culture

1. In what ways have your thoughts about the issues, concepts, and topics changed after all this work?

> *"...I think the 2 americas should join into an alliance."*
>
> *"Sometimes you really need to think things more than twice to realize."*

"We are very ignorant and we judge people by first look and we shouldn't."

"I have learned to think around problems and see them from the other side."

"It hasn't. At all. Everything I "learned" I know prior to this, a good chunk from ROPES . . . sorry but it's the truth"

2. **What surprised you the most as you were reading and discussing and as you were watching the Border Video?**

". . . the very many varieties of life and how the one concept of life can be different for every person."

"People can be harsh to others who have helped the most."

"How people have so much in common no matter how different they are."

"How poetic all the books I read were."

"That people can read the same thing but have different thoughts."

3. **What have you found out that you didn't know before?**

"It's not really a matter of not knowing, but rather not realizing that the border-guard people were so harsh on the illegal aliens. Is it illegal to dream? To act on those dreams? If it is, lock me up 'cause I've done that before."

"I found out that people are different. Like someoe could be an american and friends w/someone from Cuba, and then there could be another person from American who tells the state theres someone there from Cuba and get them taken away."

"That americans are producing products in Mexico paying low wages and nonsafe factories to save a buck and get away from certain taxes."

"That the message of Islam is to love one another and to have peace between each other.

4. **List some connections you made to your own life.**

". . . my grandparents came here and had trouble assimilating. They came from Europe during WWII, which perhaps was even harder. They were almost turned back at the border."

"I grew up with two different cultures and have learned about both of them."

"I am an immigrant."

"People have said some mean things to me just because I'm Jewish. (Racism)"

"My mom was in a money problem. Sometimes she din't eat becouse she wanted us to eat."

"I made a connection with the workers who can't complain because they might lose a job. I feel I can't complain with my parents because I will get in trouble for it."

5. Write down two or three questions about things you did not understand and/or about things you were/are wondering about.

> "Why people don't protest more against their president?"
>
> "What is our mission in life? Why do we help each other in the world?"
>
> "Why is there a fence? Who desided to put a fence up?"
>
> "Why does the US have a border and many other countries don't?"
>
> "Why do some americans treat immigrants badly?"

6. Describe how working with your group went for you.

> "It was confortable and fun. I learned about others as we worked."
>
> "It went good. I became friendlier with all of them."
>
> "I think it went alright. I like when we presented."
>
> "We had an awesome group. Everyone contributed and listened and was respectful. The group was the best I could ask for."
>
> "It made it alot more easier to converse with your peirs because they are people you see everyday and you are friends with."

7. Evaluate your *participation* in the unit and evaluate your *contribution* to the presentation.

> "It is good to work in a group because everyone even me shared the work evenly instead of dropping the load on one person."
>
> "I did a lot to make the play good and I participated. I was the facilitator, and everyone had to be heard."
>
> "I typed up everything except the poem and I helped us have fun. Good."
>
> "My participation was fair. My contribution to the presentation was for real. And I really mean what I read in my script because it's true about what I was reading."

The following two Reflection pages (reprinted below) are from two young women in the same class. The first was labeled "learning disabled" and was receiving services often during Spanish class. Betsy presented herself as nervous and disinterested and unhappy. Her reluctance to participate slowly waned during the year. Terry carried no labels that I know of. She was involved most of the time, participating with genuine enthusiasm, always a smile, putting forth her best effort with seemingly little effort. What is important here is that out of all my students' (more than 100) responses to this "Final Reflection" these two present the **exact same** honest effort to reach in and to say what came to mind. Both are obviously unedited by them, more a stream of consciousness. Each has indeed "assessed" (sat beside her self in a learning moment) her working self.

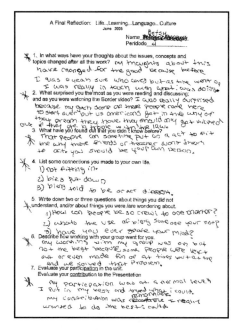 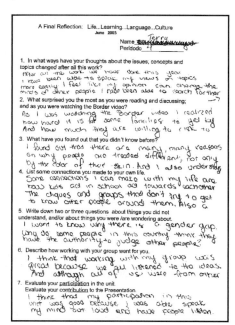

Figure 9.10 Students' Reflection Pages

What are your questions after reading these two reflections? My primary one at this moment is, "Would, *indeed could,* this kind of light have shone from within these individuals if the Unit had not been true to the concept of Inquiry; and, equally important, if the two girls had not believed me, their teacher, when I continuously strived in every way to demonstrate and to communicate with all of my students, "Yes, you have a voice in this classroom" and "Yes! you are as equal and as capable, intelligent, as anyone else."

Phase G—Confirming and Continuing

Imagine how fortunate for all of us that the Chorus Director, for the end of the year concert, chose songs that connected to our "Life . . . Learning . . . Language . . . Culture" Inquiry. I asked the students to reflect in writing about this happening. Here is the response of one of my students who was singing in the 8th grade chorus.

> The music that we were singing and the message it conveys directly connects to the unit in Spanish. As the songs portrayed the importance of love, unity and learning, this is what we are learning in Spanish—except through reading.

My students did not tell me about their Chorus program. I found out when I went to the dress rehearsal. As I think on this now, two questions rise up. The first is, "What if I were to check in with all my students' other teachers, not just chorus, but all the "core" classes and art, physical education, music and shop to find out what they are planning and maybe find a way to interconnect." My second question is, "Why did the students not make a conscious connection between the concert program and the unit? Or, did they and they didn't voice it? If I had begun the unit at the beginning of the year and threaded the prescribed Spanish curriculum through it, would they have become aware, and how soon? Oh my. I now think the unit could have been called, **Inquiry**, Life, Learning, Language, Culture.

Penelope Boyatt

After 17 years as a resident in Mexico City, I returned to the United States and began teaching in public school as an "emergency certified" bilingual teacher of 28 sixth graders who were still part of Elementary. Simultaneously, I enrolled in a Post Baccalaureate program at the University in order to obtain a teaching certificate in Bilingual/ESL. The buzzword then was "cooperative learning". The ideas of community and communication; sharing and taking responsibility clicked with my own thinking and thus motivated I set out to build my "way of guiding" students. Toward the end of that year, the students and I engaged in a Poetry Unit which I created and which actually provided us all with the opportunity to reach into ourselves for content and into our imaginations for how to communicate that content. That Poetry Unit was my first attempt at Inquiry, although I didn't know then to call it that. The LIFE . . . LEARNING . . . LANGUAGE . . . CULTURE project with middle school students is my latest. As I reflect on the growth cycles of my own life, learning, language and culture during those 15 years, I see "INQUIRY " at the core.

Life, Learning, Language, and Culture: A Sample Text Set of Multiple Materials

Altman, L. J. (1993). *Amelia's road.* Illus. by Enrique O. Sanchez. New York: Lee & Lowe.

Anaya, R. (1997). *Maya's children: The story of La Llorona.* Illus. by Maria Baca. New York: Hyperion Books.

Bahti, T. (1989). *Southwestern Indian tribes.* Las Vegas: KC Publications.

Beatty, P. (1981). *Lupita Manana.* New York: William Morrow and Company.

Bruchac, J., & London, J. (1992). *Thirteen moons on turtle's back.* Illus. by Thomas Locker. New York: Trumpet Club.

Cannon, J. (1993). *Stella Luna.* San Diego: Harcourt Brace and Company.

Children of former Yugoslavia. (1994). *I dream of peace—Images of war.* New York: HarperCollins.

Covault, R. M. (1994). *Pablo and Pimienta.* Illus. by Francisca Mora. Flagstaff, AZ: Northland Publishing Company.

Cumpian, C. (1994). *Latino rainbow: Poems about Latino Americans.* Illus. by Richard Leonard. Chicago: Childrens Press Inc.

Dabcovich, L. (1992). *The keys to my kingdom: A poem in three languages.* Translated by Ana M. Cerro. New York: Lothrop, Lee & Shepard.

del Rio, J. (1988). *Eeverybody bakes bread.* Illus. by Peter J. Thornton. Minneapolis: Carolrhoda Books, Inc.

Dooley, N. (1991). *Everybody cooks rice.* Illus. by Peter J. Thornton. New York: Scholastic.

Dorros, A. (1991). *Abuela.* Illus. by Elisa Kleven. New York: Dutton Children's Books.

Durell, A., & Sachs, M. (Eds.) (1990). *The big book for peace.* New York: Dutton Children's Books.

Finch, M. (1999). *La Gallinita roja y la espiga de trigo.* Illus. by Elisabeth Bell. New York: Barefoot Books.

Freedman, R. (1994). *Kids at work: Lewis Hine and the crusade against child labor.* Photographs by Lewis Hine. New York: Scholastic.

Freedman, R. (1983). *Children of the wild west.* New York: Scholastic.

Garay, L. (1997). *Pedrito's day.* New York: Orchard Books.

Garza, C. L. (1999). *Magic windows.* Translated by Francisco X. Alarcon. San Francisco: Children's Book Press.

Griego, M. C., Bucks, B. L., Gilbert, S. S. Kimball, L. H. (translators) (1981). *Tortillas para Mama.* Illus. by Barbara Cooney. New York: Henry Holt.

Grifalconi, A. (1986). *The village of round and square houses.* Boston: Little, Brown.

Grimes, N. (1994). *Meet Denitra Brown.* Illus. by Floyd Cooper. New York: Bantam Doubleday Dell.

Hamilton, V. (1993). *Many thousand gone: African American from slavery to freedom.* Illus. by Leo and Diane Dillon. New York: Alfred A. Knopf.

Hinton, S. E. (1967). *The outsiders.* New York: Bantam Doubleday Dell.

Hirschfelder, A., & Singer, B. R. (Eds.) (1992). *Rising voices: Writings of young Native Americans.* New York: Ivy Books.

Hudson, W. (Ed.) (1993). *Pass it on: African American poetry for children.* Illus. by Floyd Cooper. Orange, NJ: Just Us Books.

Isadora, R. (1991). *At the crossroads.* New York: Greenwillow Books.

Johnson, M. A. (Ed.). (1989). *The many faces of Hull House: The photographs of Wallace Kirkland.* Chicago: University of Illinois Press.

Kendall, R. (1992). *Eskimo boy: Life in an Inupiaq Eskimo village.* New York: Scholastic.

Knight, M. B. (1993). *Who belongs here? An American story.* Illus. by Anne Sibley O'Brien. Gardner, ME: Tilbury House, Publishers.

Krensky, S. (1993). *Los hijos de la tierra y el cielo.* Illus. by James Watling. New York: Scholastic.

Litchfield, A. G. (1989). *Un lugar para el Tio Jose.* Illus. by Gail Owens. Mexico, C.E.L.T.A.: Amaquemecan, A.C.

Little, J. (1986). *Hey, world, here I am.* Illus. by Sue Truesdell. Toronto: Kids Can Press.

Mendez, L. (1987). *La piñata.* Illus. by Felipe Morales. Mexico, D.F.: Editorial Patria, S.A. de C. V.

Medina, J. (1999). *My name is Jorge on both sides of the river: Poems in English and Spanish.* Illus. by Fabricio Vanden Broeck. Honesdale, PA: Boyds Mills Press, Inc.

Mochizuki, K. (1993). *Baseball saved us.* Illus. by Dom Lee. New York: Lee & Low Books.

Mohr, N. (1995). *The magic shell.* Illus. by Rudy Gutierrez. New York: Scholastic.

Mora, P. (1994). *The desert is my mother.* Illus. by Daniel Lechon. Houston: Pinata Books.

Morris, A. (1992). *Houses and homes.* Photographs by Ken Heyman. New York: Lothrop Lee & Shepard Books.

Palacios, A. (1987). *Standing tall: The stories of ten Hispanic Americans.* New York: Scholastic.

Philip, N. (Ed.) (1996). *Earth always endures—Native American poems.* Photographs by Edward S. Curtis. New York: Viking.

Pico, F. (1991). *La peineta colorada.* Illus. by Maria Antonia Ordonez. Puerto Rico: Ediciones Ekare.

Pinkney, A. D. (1997). *Solo girl.* Illus. by Nneka Bennett. New York: Hyperion Books.

Presilla, M. E., & Soto, G. (1996). *Life around the lake.* Illus. by Women of Lake Patzcuaro. New York: Henry Holt.

Ringgold, F. (1991). *Tar beach.* New York: Crowne Publishers.

Scholes, K. (1992). *Tiempos de paz.* Illus. by Robert Ingpen. Translated by Hilda Becerril. Editorial Origen, S.A.

Soto, G. (1997). *Chato y su cena.* Illus. by Susan Guevara. Translated by Alma Flor Ada and F. Isabel Campoy, New York: The Putnam & Grosset Group.

Soto, G. (1992). *Neighborhood odes.* Illus. by David Diaz. San Diego: Harcourt Brace & Company.

Stanley, J. (1994). *I am an American.* New York: Scholastic.

Taylor, M. (1990). *Mississippi bridge.* Illus. by Max Ginsburg. New York: Skylark Books.

Taylor, M. (1988). *The friendship.* Illus. by Max Ginsburg. New York: Puffin Books.

Web Sites:

www.library.arizona.edu
www.clnet.ucr.edu
www.wsu.edu:8080
www.sonic.net
www.ndm.si.edu
www.lsadc.org
www.ufw.org
www.sobrino.net
www.brownpride.com

www.history.acusd.edu
www.bilingualameric.com
www.spanishservices.org
www.cesarechavezfoundation.org
www.azteca.net
www.markguerrero.net
www.americanpatrol.com
www.mexconnect.com

References

Adams, T. L. (2003, May). Reading mathematics: More than words can say. *Reading Teacher 56* (8), 786–795.

Allen, J. (1999). *Words, words, words: Teaching vocabulary in grades 4–12.* Portland, ME: Stenhouse.

Alverman, D., & Phelps, S. (2002). *Content reading and literacy: Succeeding in today's diverse classrooms,* 3rd ed. Boston: Allyn & Bacon.

Alverman, D., Dillon, D., & O'Brien, D. (1987). *Using discussion to promote reading comprehension.* Newark, DE: International Reading Association.

American Association of School Librarians (AASL) and Association for Educational Communicaations and Technology (AECT) (1998a). *Information literacy standards for student learning.* Chicago: American Library Association.

AASL and AECT (1998b). *Information power: Building partnerships for learning.* Chicago: American Library Association.

Anderman, L. H., & Midgley, C. (1997). Motivation and middle school students. In J. Irvin (Ed.), *What current research says to the middle level practioners,* pp. 41–48. Columbus, OH: National Middle School Association.

Anderson, R. C., & Pearson, P. D. (1984). *A schema-theoretic view of basic processes in reading comprehension.* Technical Report No. 306. Champaign, IL: University of Illinois, Center for the Study of Reading.

Andrade, H. G. (2000). Using rubrics to promote thinking and learning. *Educational Leadership,* February, pp. 13–18.

Anneberg/CPB (1997-2003). *The universal language: Math in daily life.* http://www.learner.org/exhibits/dailymath/language.html.

Arnold, J. (1993). Towards a middle level curriculum rich in meaning. In T. Dickinson (Ed.), *Readings in middle school curriculum: A continuing conversation.* Columbus, OH: National Middle School Association.

Atwell, N. (1998). *In the middle: New understandings about writing, reading, and learning,* 2nd ed. Portsmouth, NH: Heinemann.

Barnes, D., & Todd, F. (1995). *Communication and learning revisited.* Portsmouth, NH: Heinemann.

Barron, B. (1969). The use of vocabulary as an advance organizer. In H. Herber & P. Sanders, (Eds.), *Research in reading in the content areas: First year report* (pp. 29–39). Syracuse, NY: Syracuse University.

Beck, I., McKeown, M., Hamilton, R., & Kucan, L. (1997). *Questioning the author: An approach for enhancing student engagement with text.* Newark, DE: International Reading Association.

Belenky, M., Clinchy, B., Goldberger, N., & Tarule, J. (1986). *Women's ways of knowing.* New York: Basic Books.

Berry, J. (Ed.) (bi-monthly). *School Library Journal.* New York: Reed Business Information.

Bowser, J. (1993). Structuring the middle-level classroom for spoken language. *English Journal 82* (1), pp. 38–41.

Bruner, J. (1990). *The acts of meaning.* Cambridge, MA: Harvard University Press.

Bruner, J. (1960). *The process of education.* Boston: Harvard University Press.

Buehl, D. (2001). *Classroom strategies for interactive learning,* 2nd ed. Newark, DE: International Reading Association.

Burke, C., & Short, K. (1991). *Creating classrooms: Teachers and students as a community of learners.* Portsmouth, NH: Heinemann.

Comber, B., & Simpson, A. (2001). *Negotiating critical literacies in classrooms.* Mahway, NJ: Lawrence Erlbaum Associates.

Cooper, J. (1995). The role of narrative and dialogue in constuctivist leadership. In L. Lambert, D. Walker, D. Zimmerman, J. Cooper, M. Lambert, M. Gardner, & P. J. Slack (Eds.). *The constructivist leader,* pp. 121–133. New York: Teacher's College Press.

Daniels, H. (2002). *Literature circles: Voice and choice in book clubs & reading groups.* Portland, ME: Stenhouse.

Dewey, J. (1938). *Experience and education.* New York: Collier Books.

Flippo, R. (1997, May). *Reaching consensus in literacy education: Beginnings of professional and political unity.* Symposium conducted at the International Reading Association Annual Convention, Atlanta, GA.

Freedman, L., Johnson, H., & Thomas, K. F. (2003, November). *The partnership between middle level learners and teachers: The pragmatics of the learning environment/developing confidence, independence, metacognition and stamina.* Poster session presented at the annual meeting of the National Council of Teachers of English, San Francisco, CA.

Gambrell, L. B., Dromsky, A. J., & Mazzoni, S.A. (2000). Motivation matters: Fostering full access to literacy. In K. D. Wood & T. S. Dickinson (Eds.), *Promoting literacy in grades 4–9, A handbook for teachers and administrators,* pp. 128–138. Boston: Allyn & Bacon.

Garmston, R. (1997). *The presenter's fieldbook: A practical guide.* Norwood, MA: Christopher-Gordon.

Glasser, W. (1992). *The quality school: Managing students without coercion.* New York: HarperPerennial.

Goodman, Y. M. (1978). Kidwatching: An alternative to testing. *Journal of national elementary school principals,* 574, 22–27.

Greene, M. (1988). *The dialectic of freedom.* New York: Teachers College Press.

Hancock, M. R. (2000). *A celebration of literature and response: Children, books, and teachering in K–8 classrooms.* Upper Saddle River, NJ: Merrill.

Hansen, J. (1998). *When learners evaluate.* Portsmouth, NH: Heinemann.

Harvey, S. (1998). *Nonfiction matters: Reading, writing, and research in grades 3–8.* York, ME: Stenhouse.

Harvey, S., & Goudvis, A. (2000). *Strategies that work: Teaching comprehension to enhance understanding.* York, ME: Stenhouse.

Herbel-Eisenmann, B. (2002, October). Using student contributions and multiple representations to develop mathematical language. *Mathematics Teaching in the Middle School,* pp. 100–105.

Hoonan, B. (1995). Drawing on the artist's perspective: Ventures into meaning making. In B. C. Hill, N. J. Johnson, & K. L. S. Noe (Eds.), *Literature circles and response,* pp. 153–166). Norwood, MA: Christopher-Gordon.

Hughes-Hassell, S., & Wheelock, A. (Eds.) (2001). *The information-powered school.* Chicago: American Library Association.

INTASC. (1987). Model standards for beginning teacher licensing, assessment, and development: A resource for state dialogue. http://www.ccsso.org/content/pdfs/corestrd.pdf.

IRAINCTE

International Reading Association & National Middle School Association (IRA & NMSA) (2001). *Supporting young adolescents' literacy learning: A joint position statement of the International Reading Association and the National Middle School Association.* Newark, DE: International Reading Association.

Ivey, G. (April/May/June,1999). A multicase study in the middle school: Complexities among young adolescent readers. *Reading Research Quarterly, 34* (2), pp. 172–192).

Johnson, H., & Freedman, L. (2001). Oral and written narratives: Using adolescents' stories to create community at the middle level. *Middle School Journal, 32* (5), 35–44.

Johnson, H., & Freedman, L. (2001). Talking about content knowledge at the middle level: Using informational picture books in content area literature circles. *Language & Literacy Spectrum, 11* (1), pp. 52–62.

Johnston, P. (1992). Coming full circle: As teachers become researchers so goes the curriculum. In N. A. Branscombe, D. Goswami, & J. Schwartz (Eds.), *Students teaching, students learning* (pp. 66–95). Portsmouth, NH: Boynton/Cook-Heinemann.

Just, M., & Carpenter, P. (1987). *The psychology of reading and language comprehension.* Boston: Allyn & Bacon.

Kane, S. (2003). *Literacy and learning in the content areas.* Scottsdale, AZ: Holcomb Hathaway Publishers.

Kaser, S. (1994). Creating a learning environment that invites connections. In S. Steffy & W. J. Hood (Eds.), *If this is social studies, why isn't it boring?* Portland, ME: Stenhouse Publishers.

Kaufmann, G., & Yoder, K. (1990). Celebrating authorship: A process of collaborating and creating meaning. In K. G. Short & K. M. Pierce (Eds.), *Talking about books: Creating literate communities,* (pp. 135–153). Portsmouth, NH: Heinemann.

Keene, E. O., & Zimmerman, S. (1997). *Mosaic of thought: Teaching comprehension in a reader's workshop.* Portsmouth, NH: Heinemann.

Kintch, W., & Van Kijk, T. (1978). Toward a model of text comprehension and production. *Psychological Review, 85* (5), 363–394.

Kohn, A. (1999). *The schools our children deserve: Moving beyond traditional classrooms and "tougher standards."* Boston: Houghton Mifflin

Lindfors, J. W. (1999). *Children's inquiry: Using language to make sense of the world.* New York: Teachers College Press.

Liner, T., & Butler, D. (2000). "You want to read what?": Giving students a voice in their literacy and in the literacy program. In K. D. Wood & T. S. Dickinson (Eds.), *Promoting literacy in grades 4–9: A handbook for teachers and administrators,* pp. 139–154. Boston: Allyn & Bacon.

Lounsbury, J. (Ed). (1995). *Teaching at the middle level: A professional's handbook.* Lexington, MA: D. C. Heath.

Manzo, A. (1975). Guided reading procedure. *Journal of Reading, 18* (4), 287–291.

McDermott, J. C., (1999). *Beyond the silence: Listening for democracy.* Portsmouth, NH: Heinemann.

Mee, C. S. (1997). *2,000 voices: Young adolescents' perceptions and curriculum implications.* Columbus, OH: National Middle School Association.

Michigan Curriculum Framework. (2001–2003). http://www.michigan.gov/mde.

Moore, D. W., Bean, T. W., Birdyshaw, D., & Rycik, J. A. (1999). Adolescent literacy: A position statement. *Journal of Adolescent and Adult Literacy, 43* (1), 97–112.

Mooney, M. E. (2001). *Text forms and features: A resource for intentional teaching.* Katonah, NY: Richard C. Owens.

National Middle School Association (NMSA). (1995). *This we believe: Developmentally responsive middle level schools.* Columbus, OH: NMSA.

Nisbet, J., & Shucksmith, J. (1986). *Learning strategies.* New York: Routledge.

Opitz, M. F., & Rasinski, T. V. (1998). *Good-bye round robin: 25 effective oral reading strategies.* Portsmouth, NH: Heinemann.

Peterson, R. (1992). *Life in a crowded place.* Portsmouth, NH: Heinemann.

Peterson, R., & Eeds, M. (1990). *Grand conversations: Literature groups in action.* Ontario, Canada: Scholastic.

Public Education Network (2003). http://www.publiceducation.org.

Raphael, T. E. (1982). Teaching children question answering strategies. *The Reading Teacher, 36,* 186–191.

Robertson, J. F., & Rane-Szostak, D. (1996). Using dialogue to develop critical thinking skills: A practical approach. *Journal of Adolescent and Adult Litearcy, 39* (7), 521–556.

Rosenblatt, L. M. (1938, 1995). *Literature as exploration,* 5th ed. New York: The Modern Language Association.

Rosenblatt, L. M. (1978). *The reader, the text, the poem: The transactional theory of the literary work.* Carbondale, IL: Southern Illinois University Press.

Ruiz, R. (1991). The empowerment of language-minority students. In C. Sleeter (Ed.), *Empowerment through multicultural education,* pp. 217–227. Albany, NY: State University of New York Press.

Scott, J. (1994). Literature circles in middle school classrooms: Developing reading, responding, and responsibility. *Middle School Journal, 26* (2), 37–41.

Siegel, M. (1995). More than words: The generative power of transmediation for learning. *Canadian Journal of Education, 20* (4), 455–475.

Short, K. G., Harste, J. C., & Burke, C. (1996). *Creating classrooms for authors and inquirers,* 2nd ed. Portsmouth, NH: Heinemann.

Smith, F. (1998). *The book of learning and forgetting.* New York: Teachers College Press. ⚹

Smith, J. L., & Johnson, H. (1993). Sharing responsibility: Making room for student voices. *Social Education, 57* (7), 362–364.

Stowell, L. P., & McDaniel, J. E. (1997). Assessment. In J. L. Irvin (Ed.), *What current research says to the middle level practitioner.* Columbus, OH: National Middle School Association.

Texas Education Agency (2003). Stgudent assessment division: TAKS information booklet. http://www.tea.state.tx.us/.

Tchudi, S., & Huerta, M. (1983). *Teaching writing in the content areas.* Washington, DC: National Education Association.

Trelease, J. (2001). *The read aloud handbook,* 5th ed. NY: Penguin Books.

Vacca, R., & Vacca, J. (1999). *Content area reading: Literacy and learning across the curriculum,* 6th ed. Boston: Addison-Wesley.

Venezky, R. L. (1995). Literacy. In T. L. Harris & R. R. Hodges (Eds.). *The literacy dictionary: The vocabulary of reading and writing.* Newark, DE: International Reading Association.

Vygotsky, L. (1978). *Mind in society: The development of higher psychological processes* (M. Cole, V. John-Steiner, S. Scribner, & E. Souberman, Eds.) Cambridge, MA: Harvard University Press.

Wertsch, J. (1981). *The concept of activity in Soviet psychology.* Armonk, NY: M. E. Sharpe.

Wilhelm, J., Baker, T.N., & Dube, J. (2001). *Strategic reading: Guiding students to lifelong literacy 6–12.* Portsmouth, NH: Heinemann.

Wood, K., & Dickinson, T. (Eds.). (2000). *Promoting literacy in grades 4–9: Handbook for teachers and administrators.* Boston: Allyn & Bacon.

Zemelman, S., Daniels, H., & Hyde, A. (1998). *Best practice: New standards for teaching and learning in America's schools,* 2nd ed. Portsmouth, NH: Heinemann.

Wells ? 1986 ? Ref. p. 13, Source not cited.

Trade Books Cited

Adler, D. (1994). *A picture book of Sojourner Truth.* New York: Holiday House.

Allen, T. (2001). *Remember Pearl Harbor: American and Japanese survivors tell their stories.* Washington, DC: National Geographic Society.

Anaya, R. (2000). *Elegy on the death of Cesar Chavez.* El Paso, TX: Cinco Puntas Press.

Atkins, S. B. (1993). *Voices from the field: Children of migrant farmworkers tell their stories.* Boston, MA: Little, Brown.

Bial, R. (2002). *Tenement: Immigrant life on the lower east side.* Boston: Houghton Mifflin.

Bridges, R. (2001). *Through my eyes.* New York: Scholastic.

Burns, M. (1995). *The greedy triangle.* Illus. by Gordon Silveria. New York: Scholastic.

Burns, M. (1975). *The I hate mathematics! book.* Illus by Martha Weston. New York: Scholastic.

Carbone, E. (2001). *Storm warriors.* New York: Alfred A. Knopf.

Coleman, E. (1998). *The riches of Oseola McCarty.* Morton Grove, IL: Albert Whitman & Co.

Fritz, J. (1991). *Bully for you, Teddy Roosevelt!* New York: Scholastic.

George, Jean (1972). *Julie of the Wolves.* New York: HarperCollins.

Haskins, J., & Benson, K. (2001). *Building a new land: African Americans in colonial American.* New York: HarperCollins.

Hesse, K. (1997). *Out of the dust.* New York: Scholastic.

Ishigo, E. (1972). Lone heart mountain. In *Japanese-American internment* (pp. 142–148). Evanston, IL: Nextext.

Johnson, A. (1996). *Humming whispers.* New York: Scholastic.

King, C., & Osborne, L. (1997). *Oh, Freedom!* New York: Alfred A. Knopf.

Krensky, S. (1989). *Witch hunt: It happened in Salem village.* New York: Random House.

Kudlinski, K. (2003). *Sojourner Truth: Voice of freedom.* New York: Aladdin.

Lewis, J. P. (2000). *Freedom like sunlight: Praisesongs for Black Americans.* Mankato, MN: Creative Editions.

Madden, D. (1993). *The Wartville wizard.* New York: Aladdin Books.

McKissack, P., & McKissack, F. (1999). *Black hands, white sails: The story of African American whalers.* New York: Scholastic.

Montgomery, S. (1992). *Walking with the great apes: Jane Goodall, Dian Fossey, and Birute Galdikas.* New York: Mariner Books.

Morris, M. (1993). *Katherine and the garbage dump.* Toronto: Second Story Press.

Murphy, S. J. (1998). *Circus Shapes.* Illus. by Edward Miller. New York: HarperCollins.

Myers, W. D. (2001). *The greatest: Muhammad Ali.* New York: Scholastic.

Myers, W. D. (2000). *Malcolm X: A fire burning brightly.* New York: HarperCollins.

Nelson, M. (2001). *Carver: A life in poems.* Asheville, NC: Front Street.

Neuschwander, C. (1997-2003). *Sir Cumference* series. Illustrated by Wayne Geehan. Watertown, MA: Charlesbridge.

Okubo, M. (1946). Citizen 13660. In *Japanese-American internment* (pp. 134–141). Evanston, IL: Nextext.

Park, F., & Park, G. (1998). *My freedom trip: A child's escape from North Korea.* Honesdale, PA: Boyds Mills Press.

Perl, L. (1987). *Mummies, tombs, and treasure: Secrets of ancient Egypt.* New York: Scholastic.

Samson, J. (1990). *Nefretiti and Cleopatra: Queen monarchs of ancient Egypt.* Oakville, CT: David Brown Book, Co.

Shore, N., & Horner, M. S. (1989). *Amelia Earhart.* Minneapolis, MN: Sagebrush Education Resources.

Sone, M. (1953). Nisei daughter. In *Japanese-American internment* (pp. 124–133). Evanston, IL: Nextext.

Stanley, D. (1994). *Cleopatra.* NY: William Morrow.

Stanley, J. (1994). *I am an American: A true story of Japanese internment.* New York: Crown.

Tanaka, S. (2001). *Attack on Pearl Harbor: The true story of the day American entered World War II.* New York: Hyperion Books.

Tunnell, M., & Chilcoat, G. (1996). *The children of Topaz: The story of a Japanese-American Internment Camp.* New York: Holiday House.

Waldman, N. (2001). *They came from the Bronx.* Honesdale, PA: Boyds Mills Press.

Warren, A. (2001). *We rode the orphan trains.* New York: Houghton Mifflin.

Woodson, J. (2001). *The other side.* New York: G. P. Putnam's Sons.

Yolen, J. (1996). *Encounter.* New York: Voyager Books.

Appendices

Book Review Form

Bibliographic Information (Author or Editor, Date of Publication, Title, Illustrator, Place of Publication, Publisher, number of pages, ISBN number):

Brief Summary or Key Ideas:

Authenticity:

Accuracy:

Content Area Use: Exploratories   Science   Social Studies

                     Math   Language Arts   Other

Concept Load:

Vocabulary:

Appendix 1: Book Review Form

Style:

Cautions:

Support Material:

     Graphics (maps, graphs, charts, photographs, Illustrations, etc.):

     Glossary:

     Index:

     List of sources used:

     List of references:

     Appendix material:

     Other:

Appendix 1:   Book Review Form *(Continued)*

Browsing Sheet

Name: Date:

Title of Book:

Author:

Pages browsed:

1.   Item of interest:

        Information:

        Response/questions:

2.   Item of interest:

        Information:

        Response/questions:

Appendix 2: Browsing Sheet Form

Power Notes	
Name:	Date:
Topic:	
Reference: (include page numbers)	
Notes:	
Concept Map of Information:	

Appendix 3: Power Notes Form

Reflection Journal
Name: Date:
Topic:
Brief Summary of Topic:
How This Topic Affects Me, My Community, the World:
Negative and Positives About Topic and Process:

Appendix 4: Reflection Journal Form

Record Keeping Journal	
Name:	Date:
Topic:	

Information:	Response:

What I Read:

What Else I Want to Know:

Appendix 5a: Record Keeping Journal Form

Check List for Record Keeping		
Name:		
Inquiry Topic:		
Question or Information Sought	Y/N	Journal Date Where Information is Recorded

Appendix 5b: Check List for Record Keeping Form

Dialogue Journal Entry

Date:

Discussion Topic:

Discussion Partner:

Key Points of the Discussion:

Appendix 6: Dialogue Journal Entry Form

<table>
<tr><td colspan="1">

Individual or Text Quote

Name:

Topic:

Bibliographic Information:

</td></tr>
</table>

Quotes Taken From Text:

1.

2.

3.

4.

5.

6.

Generalization: _____ is/was the type of person/thing
who/that_____.

Other traits/aspects of this person/thing include(d)_____
_____
_____
_____.

Appendix 7: Individual or Text Quote Form

Summary and Response

Name:

Topic:

Points of Interest:	Response:
1.	
2.	
3.	
4.	

Ideas From Others:

Appendix 8:   Summary and Response Form

Making Intertextual Connections	
Name:	
Topic:	
Materials Read before Discussion:	Connections Made to Other Ideas:
	1.
	2.
	3.
Titles of Materials From Discussion:	

Appendix 9: Making Intertextual Connections Form

Proposition & Support Outline
Names:
Topic:
<u>Proposition Statement</u>:
Facts: 1. 2. 3.
Statistics: 1. 2.
Examples: 1. 2.
Expert Authority: 1. 2.
Logic & Reasoning: 1. 2.

(Buehl, 2001, p. 101)

Appendix 10:   Proposition & Support Outline Form

QAR	
Name:	
Text:	
<u>Questions</u>:	<u>QAR</u>:
1.	1.
2.	2.
3.	3.
4.	4.
<u>Inferences</u>:	

Appendix 11:   QAR Form

Revisit to Revise

Name: Date:

Topic:

Questions to Ponder:

- What did you accomplish during this inquiry?
- What did you do especially well?
- What was the most difficult challenge for you?
- How could the school/library/teacher help you during the next inquiry?
- What particular aspect of this inquiry will you take away with you?
- What do you need more work on for your presentation?
- How did you help others learn?
- How did others help you learn?

Write a Brief Reflection Addressing the Questions:

Appendix 12: Revisit to Revise Form

Inquiry Assessment

Name: Date:

Topic:

Discuss the most interesting part of the inquiry and the least:

Discuss the mini-lessons and which you enjoyed the most and least:

What suggestions would you have for our next inquiry cycle?

Appendix 13:   Inquiry Assessment Form

Suggestions for Inquiry

Date:

Last Topic:

Last Group Organization:

Observations

Curricular Needs

Ideas/Next Course of Action

Appendix 14:   Suggestions for Inquiry Form

Intertextual Connections

Name: Date:

Topic:

What connections can be made to your last inquiry?

1.

2.

3.

4.

5.

From the materials you used (books, periodicals, movies, Internet sites), what
connections can you make to other materials you have read/viewed?

1.

2.

3.

4.

How does this inquiry connect to what you are learning in other classes?

Appendix 15: Intertextual Connections Form

About the Authors

Lauren Freedman is currently an Associate Professor in the Department of Teaching, Learning, and Leadership at Western Michigan University. Her current research interests include inquiry and the use of multiple materials across the curriculum; integrated curriculum at the middle level; teacher preparation in literacy education with an emphasis on middle level and secondary; and issues of diversity and multiculturalism in teacher preparation. She received her Ph. D. in Language, Reading, and Culture from University of Arizona, Tucson.

Holly Johnson is currently an Associate Professor in the Language Literacy Education Program at Texas Tech University. Her areas of interest include teacher preparation in middle level literacy education; adolescent and children's literature; middle school language arts/literacy education; and multicultural education and literature. She received her Ph. D. in Language, Reading, and Culture from University of Arizona, Tucson.

Index

Book of
learning + forgetting

1230 wichita
12 45 parked car
(pulled into airport!
120/125 called Macie

a ran ma
water mellon

2 40 took off

Settling Scores: German
Music, De Nozification
the Americans
1945-1953
David Monod

Celia Applegate
Music & German
National Identity

C¹

↓

C16